T0327947

SEMIOTEXT(E) FOREIGN AGENTS SERIES

Originally published as Psychanalyse et transversalité © Paris: François Maspero, 1972, and republished by La Découverte, 2003.
© This edition 2015 by Semiotext(e).

Published by Semiotext(e)
PO BOX 629. South Pasadena, CA 91031
www.semiotexte.com

Special thanks to John Ebert and Robert Dewhurst.

Cover photography by Claude La Borde
Back Cover Photography by Tahara Keiichi
Design by Hedi El Kholti

ISBN: 978-1-58435-127-6
Distributed by The MIT Press, Cambridge, Mass. and London, England
Printed in the United States of America
10 9 8 7 6 5 4 3 2

PSYCHOANALYSIS
AND TRANSVERSALITY

TEXTS AND INTERVIEWS 1955–1971

Félix Guattari

Introduction by Gilles Deleuze

Translated by Ames Hodges

Contents

Gilles Deleuze

Preface: Three Group-Related Problems

A militant political activist and a psychoanalyst just so happen to meet in the same person,[1] and instead of each minding his own business, they ceaselessly communicate, interfere with one another, and get mixed up—each mistaking himself for the other. An uncommon occurrence at least since Reich. Pierre-Félix Guattari does not let problems of the unity of the Self preoccupy him. The self is rather one more thing we ought to dissolve, under the combined assault of political and analytical forces. Guattari's formula, "we are all groupuscles," indeed heralds the search for a new subjectivity, a group subjectivity, which does not allow itself to be enclosed in a whole bent on reconstituting a self (or even worse, a superego), but which spreads itself out over several groups at once. These groups are divisible, manifold, permeable, and always optional. A good group does not take itself to be unique, immortal, and significant, unlike a defense ministry or homeland office of security, unlike war veterans, but instead plugs into an outside that confronts the group with its own possibilities of non-sense, death, and dispersal "precisely as a result of its opening up to other groups." In turn, the individual is also a group. In the most natural way imaginable, Guattari embodies two aspects of an anti-Self: on the one hand, he is like a catatonic stone, a blind and hard body invaded by death as soon as he takes off his glasses; on the other hand, he lights up and seethes with multiple lives the moment he looks, acts, laughs, thinks or attacks. Thus he is named Pierre and Félix: schizophrenic powers.

In this meeting of the militant and the psychoanalyst, there are at least three different problems that emerge: 1) In what form does one introduce politics into psychoanalytic theory and practice (it being understood that, in any case, politics is already in the unconscious)? 2) Is there a reason, and if so how, to introduce psychoanalysis into militant revolutionary groups? 3) How does one conceive and form specific therapeutic groups whose influence would impact political groups, as well as psychiatric and psychoanalytic groups? The series of articles from 1955 to 1970 which Guattari presents here, addresses these three different problems and exhibits a particular evolution, whose two major focal points are the hopes-and-despair after the Liberation, and the hopes-and-despair following May '68—while in-between the double-agent is hard at work preparing for May.

As for the first problem, Guattari early on had the intuition that the unconscious is directly related to a whole social field, both economic and political, rather than the mythical and familial grid traditionally deployed by psychoanalysis. It is indeed a question of libido as such, as the essence of desire and sexuality: but now it invests and disinvests flows of every kind as they trickle through the social field, and it effects cuts in these flows, stoppages, leaks, and retentions. To be sure, it does not operate in a manifest way, as do the objective interests of consciousness or the chains of historical causality. It deploys a latent desire coextensive with the social field, entailing ruptures in causality and the emergence of singularities, sticking points as well as leaks. The year 1936 is not only an event in historical consciousness, it is also a complex of the unconscious. Our love affairs, our sexual choices, are less the by-products of a mythical Mommy-Daddy, than the excesses of a social-reality, the interferences and effects of flows invested by the libido. What do we not make love with, including death? Guattari is thus able to reproach psychoanalysis for the way in which it systematically crushes the socio-political contents of the unconcious, though they in reality determine the objects of desire. Psychoanalysis, says Guattari, starts from a kind of absolute narcissism (*das Ding*) and aims at an ideal social adaptation which it calls a cure; this procedure, however, always obscures a singular social constellation which in fact must be brought to light, rather than sacrificed to the invention of an abstract, symbolic unconscious. *Das Ding* [The Thing] is not some recurrent horizon that constitutes an individual person in an illusory way, but a social body serving as a basis for latent potentialities (why are these people lunatics, and those people revolutionaries?). Far more important than mommy, daddy, and grandma are all the personnages haunting the fundamental questions of society, such as the class conflict of our day. More important than recalling how, one fine day, Oedipus "totally changed" Greek society, is the enormous *Spaltung* [division, rift, fissure] traversing the communist party today. How does one overlook the role the State plays in all the dead-ends where the libido is caught, and reduced to investing in the intimist images of the family? Are we to believe that the castration complex will find a satisfactory solution as long as society assigns it the unconscious role of social repression and regulation? In a word, the social relation never constitutes something beyond or something added after the fact, where individual or familial problems occur. What is remarkable is how manifest the economic and political social contents of the libido become, the more one confronts the most desocialized aspects of certain syndromes, as in psychosis. "Beyond the Self, the subject explodes in fragments throughout the universe, the madman begins speaking foreign languages, rewriting history as hallucination, and using war and class conflict as instruments of personal expression […] the distinction between private life and the various levels of social life no longer holds." (Compare this with Freud, who derives from war only an undetermined death-drive, and a non-qualified shock or excess of excitation caused by a big boom). Restoring to the unconscious its historical perspectives, against a backdrop of disquiet and the

unknown, implies a reversal of psychoanalysis and certainly a rediscovery of psychosis underneath the cheap trappings of neurosis.
Psychoanalysis has indeed joined forces with the most traditional
psychiatry to stifle the voices of the insane constantly talking politics,
economics, order, and revolution. In a recent article, Marcel Jaeger
shows how "the discourse produced by the insane contains not only
the depth of their individual psychic disorders: the discourse of madness also connects with the discourse of political, social, and religious
history that speaks in each of us. [...] In certain cases, the use of
political concepts provokes a state of crisis in the patient, as though
these concepts brought to light the very contradictions in which the
patient has become entangled. [...] No place is free, not even the
asylum, from the historical inscription of the workers' movement."[2]
These formulations express the same orientation that Guattari's work
displays in his first articles, the same effort to reevaluate psychosis.

We see the difference here with Reich: there is no libidinal
economy to impart, by other means, a subjective prolongation to
political economy; there is no sexual repression to internalize economic exploitation and political subjection. Instead, desire as libido
is everywhere already present, sexuality runs through the entire social
field and embraces it, coinciding with the flows that pass under the
objects, persons and symbols of a group, and it is on desire as libido
that these same objects, persons and symbols depend for their distribution and very constitution. What we witness here, precisely, is the
latent character of the sexuality of desire, which becomes manifest
only with the choice of sexual objects and their symbols (if it need be
said that symbols are consciously sexual). Consequently, this is political economy as such, an economy of flows, which is unconsciously
libidinal: there is only one economy, not two; and desire or libido is
just the subjectivity of political economy. "In the end, the economic
is the motor of subjectivity." Now we see the meaning of the notion
of *institution*, defined as a subjectivity of flows and their interruption

in the objective forms of a group. The dualities of the objective and the subjective, of infrastructure and superstructure, of production and ideology, vanish and give way to the strict complementarity of the desiring subject of the institution, and the institutional object. (Guattari's institutional analyses should be compared with those Cardan did around the same time in *Socialisme ou Barbarie*, both assimilated in the same bitter critique of the Trotskyites.)[3]

The second problem—is there a reason to introduce psychoanalysis into political groups, and if so how?—excludes, to be sure, all "application" of psychoanalysis to historical and social phenomena. Psychoanalysis has accumulated many such ridiculous applications, Oedipus being foremost among them. Rather, the problem is this: the situation which has made capitalism the thing to be overcome by revolution is the same situation which has made the Russian revolution, as well as the history immediately following it, not to mention the organization of the communist party, and national unions—all just so many authorities incapable of effecting the destruction of capitalism. In this regard, the proper character of capitalism, which is presented as a contradiction between the development of productive forces and the relations of production, is essentially the reproduction process of capital. This process, however, on which the productive forces of captial depend in the system, is in fact an international phenomenon implying a worldwide division of labor; nevertheless, capitalism cannot shatter the national frameworks within which it develops its relations of production, nor can it smash the State as the instrument of the valuation of capital.[4] The internationalism of capital is thus accomplished by national and state structures that curb capital even as they make it work; these "archaic" structures have genuine functions. State monopoly capitalism, far from being an ultimate given, is the result of a compromise. In this "expropriation of the capitalists at the heart of capital," the bourgeoisie maintains its stranglehold on the State apparatus through its increasing efforts to institutionalize and integrate the working class, in such a way that class conflict is decentered with respect to the real places and deciding factors that go beyond States and point to the international capitalist economy. It is by virtue of the same principle that "a narrow sphere of production is alone inserted in the worldwide reproduction process of capital," while in third-world States, the rest remains subjected to precapitalist relations (genuine archaisms of a second kind).

Given this situation, we see the complicity of national communist parties militating for the integration of the proletariat into the State, such that "the bourgeoisie's national sense of identity results in large measure from the proletariat's own national sense of identity; so, too, does the internal division of the bourgeoisie result from the division of the proletariat." Moreover, even when the necessity of revolutionary struggle in the third world is affirmed, these struggles mostly serve as bargaining chips in a negotiation, indicating the same renunciation of an international strategy and the development of class conflict in capitalist countries. It comes down to this imperative: *the working class must defend national productive forces*, struggle against monopolies, and appropriate a State apparatus.

This situation originates in what Guatarri calls "the great Leninist rupture" in 1917, which determined for better or worse the major attitudes, the principal discourse, initiatives, stereotypes, phantasms, and interpretations of the revolutionary movement. This rupture was presented as the possibility of effecting a real rupture in historical causality by "interpreting" the military, economic, political and social disarray as a victory of the masses. The possibility of a socialist revolution suddenly appeared in place of any necessity for a left-center sacred union. But this possibility was accepted only as a consequence of setting up the party, which only yesterday was a modest clandestine formation, but now must become an embryonic State apparatus able to direct everything, to fulfil a messianic vocation and substitute itself for the masses. Two more or less long-term consequences came of this. In as much as the new State confronted captialist States, it entered into relations of force with them, and the ideal of such relations was a kind of status quo: what had been the Leninist tactic at the creation of the NEP was converted into an ideology of peaceful coexistence and economic competition with the West. This idea of competition spelled the ruin of the revolutionary movement. And in as much as the new State assumed responsibility for the proletariat the world over, it could develop a socialist economy only in accordance with the realities of the global market and according to objectives similar to those of international capital. The new State all the more readily accepted the integration of local communist parties into the relations of capitalist production since it was in the name of the working class defending the national forces of production. In short, there is no reason to agree with the technocrats when they say that two kinds of regimes and States converged as they evolved; nor with Trotsky, when he supposes that bureaucracy corrupted a healthy proletarian State, whose cure would consist in a simple political revolution. The outcome was already decided or betrayed in the way in which the State-party *responded* to the city-States of capitalism, even in their relations of mutual hostility and annoyance. The clearest evidence of this is that weak institutions were created in every sector in Russia as soon as the Soviets liquidated everything early on (for example, when they imported pre-assembled automobile factories, they unwittingly imported certain types of human relations, technological functions, separations between intellectual and manual work, and modes of consumption deeply foreign to socialism).

What gives this analysis its force is the distinction Guatarri proposes between *subjugated groups* and *group-subjects*. Groups are subjugated no less by the leaders they assign themselves, or accept, than by the masses. The hierarchy, the vertical or pyramidal organization, which characterizes subjugated groups is meant to ward off any possible inscription of non-sense, death or dispersal, to discourage the development of creative ruptures, and to ensure the self-preservation mechanisms rooted in the exclusion of other groups. Their centralization works through structure, totalization, unification, replacing the conditions of a genuine collective "enunciation" with an assemblage of stereotypical utterances cut off both from the real and from subjectivity (this is when imaginary phenomena such as Oedipalization, superegofication, and group-castration take place). Group-subjects, on the other hand, are defined by coefficients of *transversality* that ward off totalities and hierarchies. They are agents of enunciation, environments of desire, elements of institutional creation. Through their very practice, they ceaselessly conform to the limit of their own non-sense, their own death or rupture. Still, it is less a question of two groups than two sides of the institution, since a group-subject is always in danger of allowing itself to be subjugated, in a paranoid contraction where at any cost the group wants to perpetuate itself and live forever as a subject. Conversely, "a party that was once revolutionary and now more or less subjugated to the dominant order can still occupy, in the eyes of the masses, the place which the subject of history has left empty, can still become in spite of itself the mouthpiece of a discourse not its own, even if it means betraying that discourse when the evolution of the relations of force causes a return to normalcy: the group nonetheless preserves, almost involuntarily, a potentiality of subjective rupture which a transformation of context will reveal." (To take an extreme example: the way in which the worst archaisms can become revolutionary, i.e. the Basques, the Irish Republican Army, etc.)

It is certainly true that if the problem of the group's functioning is not posed to begin with, it will be too late afterwards. Too many groupuscles that as yet inspire only phantom masses already possess a structure of subjugation, complete with leadership, a mechanism of transmission, and a core membership, aimlessly reproducing the errors and perversions they are trying to oppose. Guattari's own experience begins with Trotskyism and proceeds through Entryism, the Leftist Opposition (*la Voie communiste*), and the March 22nd Movement. Throughout this trajectory, the problem remains one of desire or unconscious subjectivity: how does a group carry its own desire, connect it to the desires of other groups and to the desires of the masses, produce the appropriate utterances thereto and constitute the conditions not of unification, but of multiplication conducive to utterances in revolt? The misreading and repression of phenomena of desire inspire structures of subjugation and bureaucratization: the militant style composed of hateful love determining a limited number of exclusive dominant utterances. The constancy with which revolutionary groups have betrayed their task is well known. These groups operate through detachment, levy, and residual selection: they detach a supposedly expert avant-garde; they levy a disciplined, organized, hierarchized proletariat; they select a residual under-proletariat to be excluded or reeducated. But this tripartite division reproduces precisely the divisions which the bourgeoisie introduced into the proletariat, and on which it has based its power within the framework of capitalist relations of production. Attempting to turn these divisions against the bourgeoisie is a lost cause. The revolutionary task is the suppression of the proletariat itself, that is to say, the immediate suppression of the distinctions between avant-garde and proletariat, between proletariat and under-proletariat—the effective struggle against all mechanisms of detachment, levy, and residual selection—such that subjective and singular positions capable of transversal communication may emerge instead (cf. Guattari's text, "L'étudiant, le fou et le Katangais").

Guattari's strength consists in showing that the problem is not at all about choosing between spontaneity and centralism. Nor between guerilla and generalized warfare. It serves no purpose to recognize in one breath the right to spontaneity during a first stage, if it means in the next breath demanding the necessity of centralization for a second stage: the theory of stages is the ruin of every revolutionary movement. From the start we have to be more centralist than the centralists. Clearly, a revolutionary machine cannot remain satisfied with local and occasional struggles: it has to be at the same time super-centralized and super-desiring. The problem, therefore, concerns the nature of unification, which must function in a transversal way, through multiplicity, and not in a vertical way, so apt to crush the multiplicity proper to desire. In the first place, this means that any unification must be *the unification of a war-machine and not a State apparatus* (a red Army stops being a war-machine to the extent that it becomes a more or less important cog in a State apparatus). In the second place, this means that unification must occur through *analysis*, that it must play *the role of an analyzer* with respect to the desire of the group and the masses, and not the role of a synthesizer operating through rationalization, totalization, exclusion, etc. What exactly a war-machine is (as compared to a State-apparatus), and what exactly an analysis or an analyzer of desire is (as opposed to pseudo-rational and scientific synthesis), are the two major lines of thought that Guattari's book pursues, signaling in his view the theoretical task to be undertaken at the present time.

This pursuit, however, is not about "applying" psychoanalysis to group phenomena. Nor is it about a therapeutic group that would somehow "treat" the masses. It's about constituting in the group the conditions of an analysis of desire, on oneself and on the others; it's about pursuing the flows that constitute myriad lines of flight in capitalist society, and bringing about ruptures, and imposing interruptions at the very heart of social determinism and historical causality; it's about allowing collective agents of enunciation to emerge, capable of formulating new utterances of desire; it's about constituting not an avant-garde, but groups adjacent to social processes, whose only employment is to advance the cause of truth in fields where the truth is not usually a priority—in a word, it's about constituting a revolutionary subjectivity about which there is no more reason to ask whether libidinal, economic, or political determinations should come first, since this subjectivity traverses traditionally separate orders; it's about grasping that point of *rupture* where, precisely, political economy and libidinal economy are *one and the same*. The unconscious is nothing else than the order of group subjectivity which introduces explosive machines into so-called signifying structures as well as causal chains, forcing them to open and liberate their hidden potentialities as a realizable future still influenced by the rupture. The March 22nd Movement is exemplary in this respect, because while it was insufficient as a war-machine, it nonetheless functioned exceedingly well as an analytic and desiring group which not only held a discourse on the mode of truly free association, but which was able also "to constitute itself as an analyzer of a considerable mass of students and workers," without any claims to hegemony or avant-garde status; it was simply an environment allowing for the transfer and the removal of inhibitions. Analysis and desire finally on the same side, with desire taking the lead: such an actualization of analysis indeed characterizes group-subjects, whereas subjugated groups continue to exist under the laws of a simple "application" of psychoanalysis in a closed environment (the family as a continuation of the State by other means). The political and economic content of libido as such, the libidinal and sexual content of the politico-economic field—this whole *turn of history*—become manifest only in an open environment and in group-subjects, wherever a truth shows up. Because "truth is not theory, and not organization." It's not structure, and not the signifier; it's the war-machine and its non-sense. "When the truth shows itself, theory and organization will just have to deal with it; it's not desire's role to perform self-criticism, theory and organization have to do it."

The transformation of psychoanalysis into schizo-analysis implies an evaluation of the specificity of madness. This is just one of the points

Guattari insists on, joining forces with Foucault, who says that madness will not be replaced by the positivist determination, treatment, and neutralization of mental illness, but that mental illness will be replaced by something we have not yet understood in madness.[5] Because the real problems have to do with psychosis (not the neuroses of application). It is always a pleasure to elicit the mockery of positivists: Guattari never tires of proclaiming the legitimacy of a metaphysical or transcendental point of view, which consists in purging madness of mental illness, and not mental illness of madness: "Will there come a day when we will finally study President Schreber's or Antonin Artaud's definitions of God with the same seriousness and rigor as those of Descartes or Malebranche? For how long will we perpetuate the split between the inner workings of pure theoretical critique and the concrete analytical activity of the human sciences?" (It should be understood that mad definitions are more serious and more rigorous than the unhealthy-rational definitions by means of which subjugated groups relate to God in the form of reason.) More precisely, Guattari's institutional analysis criticizes anti-psychiatry not only for refusing to acknowledge any pharmacological function, not only for denying the institution any revolutionary possibility, but especially for confusing mental alienation with social alienation and thereby suppressing the specificity of madness. "With the best intentions, both moral and political, they managed to refuse the insane their right to be insane, the *it's-all-society's-fault* can mask a way of suppressing deviance. The negation of the institution would then be the denial of the singular fact of mental alienation." Not that some general theory of madness must be posited, nor must a mystical identity of the revolutionary and lunatic be invoked. (Certainly, it is useless to attempt to forestall such a criticism, which will be made in any event.) Rather, it's not madness which must be reduced to the order of the general, but the modern world in general or the entire social field which must *also* be interpreted in terms of the singularity of the lunatic, in its very own subjective position. Militant revolutionaries cannot not be concerned with delinquence, deviance, and madness—not as educators or reformers, but as those who can read the face of their proper difference only in such mirrors. Take for example this bit of dialogue with Jean Oury, at the start of this collection: "Something specific to a group of militants in the psychiatric domain is being commited to social struggle, but also being insane enough to entertain the possibility of *being with* the insane; but there are definitely people in politics who are incapable of belonging to such a group…"

Guattari's proper contribution to institutional psychotherapy resides in a certain number of notions (whose formation we can actually trace in this collection): the distinction between two kinds of groups, the opposition between group phantasms and individual phantasms, and the conception of transversality. And these notions have a precise practical orientation: introducing a militant political function into the institution, constituting a kind of "monster" which is neither psychoanalysis, nor hospital practice, even less group dynamics, and which is everywhere applicable, in the hospital, at school, in a militant group—a machine to produce and give voice to desire. This is why Guattari claimed the name of institutional analysis for his work rather than institutional psychotherapy. In the institutional movement led by Tosquelles and Jean Oury there indeed begins a third age of psychiatry: the institution as model, beyond the contract and the law. If it is true that the old asylum was governed by repressive law, insofar as the insane were judged "incapable" and therefore excluded from the contractual relations that unite so-called reasonable beings, Freud's stroke of genius was to show that bourgeois families and the frontiers of the asylum contained a large group of people ("neurotics") who could be brought under a particular contract, in order to lead them, using original means, back to the norms of traditonal medicine (the psychoanalytic contract as a particular case of the liberal-medical contractual relation). The abandonment of hypnosis was an important step in this development. It seems to me that no one has yet analyzed the role and effects of this contractual model in which psychoanalysis lodged itself; one of the principal consequences of this was that psychosis remained on the horizon of psychoanalysis, as a genuine source of clinical material, and yet was excluded as beyond the contractual field. It will come as no surprise, as several texts in this collection demonstate, that institutional psychotherapy entails in its principal propositions a critique of repressive law as well as the so-called liberal contract, for which it hoped to substitute the model of the institution. This critique was meant to be extended in several directions at once, in as much as the pyramidal organization of groups, their subjugation and hierarchical division of labor are based on contractual relations no less than legalist structures. In the collection's first text, dealing with doctor-nurse relationships, Oury interjects: "There is a rationalism in society that is nothing more than a rationalization of bad faith and rotten behavior. The view from the inside is the relationship one has with the insane on a day-to-day basis, *provided a certain 'contract' with the traditional has been voided*. So, in a sense, we can say that knowing what it is to be in contact with the insane is at the same time being a progressive. [...] Clearly, the very terms doctor-nurse belong to the contract we said we had to void." There is in institutional psychotherapy a kind of psychiatric inspiration à la Saint-Just, in the sense that Saint-Just defines the republican regime by many institutions and few laws (few contractual relations also). Institutional psychotherapy threads a difficult passage between anti-psychiatry, which tends to fall back into desperate contractual forms (cf. a recent interview with Laing), and psychiatry today, with its tight police controls, its planned triangulation, which will very likely cause us to regret the closed asylums of old, ah the good old days, the good old style.

What comes into play here are Guattari's problems concerning the nature of cured-curing groups capable of forming group-subjects, that is to say, capable of making the institution the object of a genuine creation where madness and revolution send back and forth, without being confused, the face of their difference in the singular positions of a desiring subjectivity. For example, in the article entitled "Where does group psychotherapy begin?," there is the analysis of BTUs (basic therapeutic unities) at La Borde. How does one ward off subjugation from already subjugated groups, with which traditional psychoanalysis is in competition? And psychoanalytic associations: on what side of the institution, in what group, do they fall? A great portion of Guattari's work prior to May '68 was dedicated to "patients taking charge of their own illness, with the support of the entire student movement." A particular dream of non-sense and *empty chatter*, instituted as such, against law or the contract of saturated speech, and legitimized *schizo-flow* have ceaselessly inspired Guattari in his endeavor to break down the divisions and hierarchical or pseudo-functional compartimentalizations—educator, psychiatrist, analyst, militant… Every text in this collection is an article written for a specific occasion. And they have a twofold goal: the one is connected to their origin at a certain juncture of institutional psychotherapy, a certain moment of militant political life, a certain aspect of the Freudian school and Lacan's teaching; the other looks to their function, their possible functioning in other circumstances. This book must be taken in bits and pieces, like a montage or installation of the cogs and wheels of a machine. Sometimes the cogs are small, miniscule, but disorderly, and thus all the more indispensable. This book is a machine of desire, in other words, a war-machine, an analyser. So, I would like to single out two texts in particular that seem especially important in this collection: a theoretical text, where the very principle of a machine is distinguished from the hypothesis of structure and detached from structural ties ("Machine and Structure"), and a schizo-text where the notions of "sign-point" and "sign-blot" are freed from the obstacle of the signifier.

1

On Nurse-Doctor Relationships

Oury: We can start by defining, on one hand, the social status of doctors, nurses and, of course, the patients that they both interact with; and, on the other, by saying that nurses are "stuck" between patients and doctors, and in fact that everything is "stuck" in the system of hospitals and social status. It's well known, but it is worth mentioning. We should begin by defining the relationships that exist between doctors and nurses, with all of their mystical implications.

Félix: It seems to me that, before discussing these relationships in more detail, it is always important to begin by situating them, not in a general way but as a whole. Even if it has already been done, we can understand exactly what is happening from there. If, for example, I am looking at the relationships between the owner and employees of a factory, I have to start with the fundamental information: What is a factory? What is an owner? What is an exploited person? In the same way, we should start here by asking: What is a doctor? What is an illness?

Oury: True, it is very important. There is a mystified relationship between doctors and nurses, in the sense that doctors embody a caste more than a class. Even if doctors and nurses are on the same side of the boundary, inside the boundary, there is a caste, the caste of doctors and then the world of nurses, which is often healthier.

Félix: We could go even further. Doctors—even if they are conned by other bureaucratic or capitalist directors—bolster and are responsible for the mystification, and as such, they reflect their class ideology. The mystification does involve a certain relationship, based on a certain conception of the world, humanity and patients. I think that the problem must not be too distinct from class relationships, but completely fundamental. While there are apparent divergences between doctors and the administration, it seems that the relationships of the same type as those between the police and the justice system, between charitable work and prisons; but in fact, it must be the same support, the same type of relationships, the same definition, the same image of the problem. Are we going to talk about psychological cons or charitable cons or ask the question in full, which seems to involve both a singular division of labor and an "anomality" of normality?

Oury: It is obvious that the role of the doctor is to be a defender of state institutions. He or she is empowered by the state to ensure that hospital rules are followed without intervening in its economic-social structure. The role necessarily implies that he or she be respected so that patients are presented with the perfect image of respect and dignity. There is some typical clowning around, since it is a reflection of the society in which nurses work. It nonetheless remains a fact, especially in psychiatric hospitals, that doctors are sanctioned by the state but the state is jerking them around at the same time. If a doctor realizes it, he or she ends up in a very difficult situation: scorned by the state and hated by nurses. The doctor has several possible solutions: the solution of not giving a damn; the dictatorial solution, a stupid choice; or the paternalist solution. All of these solutions respect the structure in which he or she lives with the nurses.

Félix: The most important aspect of the doctor-nurse relationship is above all its implications for the doctor-patient relationship. There is a schism in the way nurses are presented to patients. On the one hand, there are the medical imagos, types that can be seen from time to time, whose actions seem almost like magic, and on the other, there is the nursing staff. The characteristic of both of these imagos is a certain inhumanity, a fixed way of being on one side or the other, with doctors taking the spiritual side and nurses taking discipline and things like that. We could speak of the doctor-nurse relationship as if it were a résumé of society's attitude to transcendence, the way it reacts, the way it divides labor, the way it avoids or distorts the problem so that it does not have to contemplate the phenomena of madness and singularity.

Oury: The relationships between *what we call* madness, madmen and society must be situated on a historical level and a transcendental level at the same time. It would take too long to retrace the history of ways that society has represented madmen. We should just limit ourselves to what is happening now: people have been delegated by society to live with madmen, making them into a kind of rampart of people, a wall of heads, arms and legs to protect society from madmen. Let them do what they want as long as society remains peaceful. And all of society's struggles are inevitably reproduced in this wall, which is part of society.

Félix: And this wall definitely conditions the patterns of illness.

Oury: Which is why I said what we call madmen, in the sense that an illness exists because there is a certain wall surrounding it. In the end, nosologies are only frameworks for imprisoning madmen. They are put in books, like a butterfly collection. A psychiatry book is the same thing: what the butterflies are like, in what room; to *preserve* them you drop them in formaldehyde, to *observe* them you put them in rooms with portholes. It doesn't stop there: now they have to be *occupied*, you have to put them on machines, give them tools, but it is all the same thing. There is a type of dialectic between people who fill the roles of madmen and those who have the role of guarding the madmen, all inside a closed society.

Félix: I think that the phenomenon of madness can be seen as a contemporary phenomenon. We can see that madness now acts as a social phenomenon and has a growing role in culture; it is increasingly integrated in society, a more universal concern, an anthropological role. What we are experiencing as administrative difficulties and the reason that we raise the question here is a legacy of the 19th century, bureaucratic inertia, the old style of the bourgeoisie for interning madmen. Why would we want to do anything else? Because we are now realizing that madness is an essential phenomenon in contemporary society and we need to revise our old categories of thinking, the old doctor-nurse relationships, to respond to modern society's need for a better understanding of the phenomenon of madness. This is precisely what could be called a progressive perspective: understanding madmen, abandoning racism, colonialism, with different methods of education, etc.

Oury: It is not very clear. In this supervision of madmen, you could say that there is the "view from the outside," the "view from the inside" and the "madmen's view." The traditional view from the outside, for example, is the idea that the more education you receive, the longer you go to school, the more you can understand madmen: you have to be a doctor. While those at the bottom of the nurses' ladder, uneducated in principle, cannot understand anything. There is a rationalism in society that is more of a rationalization of bad faith, of nastiness. The view from the inside is the relationship with madmen on a daily basis, on the condition of breaking a certain "contract" with tradition. You could say, in a sense, that knowing what being in contact with madmen is like is also being progressive.

Félix: We could even say that awareness of this "contract with tradition" and the decision to break with it are the conditions for a phenomenological approach to madness.

Oury: Yes, exactly, because this notion of a contract shows how quick people are to confuse social alienation and mental alienation. They are not the same thing, and wanting to combine them is a new confusion that will lead to others. It is the same thing as saying: "They are not madmen, they are patients." Which is pure bullshit. They're madmen.

Félix: We have to distinguish between different modes of alienation in the hospital system. There is a very complicated interaction between modes of alienation. Generally, we deal more specifically with the mode of the patient alienated from society. It seems fundamental that illness as such is alienating and, at the same time, patients are alienated from society because they are interned. Yet it is also very interesting to consider the phenomenon of alienation of nurses from the hospital establishment and its working conditions; and that of the doctor, very poorly situated, from the administration; and finally the alienation of the corporation, the moral person of the hospital as a whole from the state. These conjugated modes of alienation all have obvious repercussions on the alienation of madness and we should be able to look at all aspects of the problem from this angle.

Oury: It is interesting to situate this problem as a period problem. Instead of replacing the rational relationships from object to subject and subject to object, we can study anthropological relationships. What we are saying here, for example, would have no meaning for people who lived one hundred years ago or even now in a traditional context. There is a leap, like the broken contract earlier: replacing rational administrative relationships from subject to object with existential relationships from person to person. The notion of alienation only makes sense on an anthropological level. It seems to me that Marxist alienation is primarily anthropological; it would be ridiculous if it was object alienation. What interests us is the basal notion of person to person relationships. A nurse-doctor relationship is not exactly a nurse framework-doctor framework relationship, it is something more difficult. I mean the relationship between roles as different from the personal relationship; precisely by playing these roles, of the madman or the doctor, they hide the personal relationships. And it has a necessary effect on nosology: the schizophrenic, in his or her "role," still has personal relationships. Everyone agrees on this, but no one knows exactly how and where to grasp these relationships that no longer exist in a given framework. If they exist, it is by infiltration, a crack or split in the traditional framework, something that is particular, personal existence.

Félix: The main perspective is therefore the disappearance of a certain number of roles and stereotypes: playing the madman just like playing the doctor or nurse in order to promote human relationships that do not automatically lead to roles or stereotypes but to fundamental relationships, metaphysical relationships that make the most radical and fundamental alienations *appear* in madness or neurosis. I think that this is the perspective from which we should consider all of the technical specifications, the workshop and sociotherapy proposals and situate them firmly in this anthropological perspective that we could call the "Modern Times" perspective.

Then we could clearly see what not to do, the dangers of workshops, whether they are focused on performance or rehabilitation, or on social relations, whether they are working for science, psychology or to treat a patient. We cannot lose sight of the idea of a constitutive person, constituted at the root of a language and who, instead of losing him or herself in social relationships and stereotypical medical relationships, has to reconstitute him or herself in a world with a minimum of normality in terms of language and behavior. Then the inherent abnormality of the subject or, if you will, of his or her troubles will appear most distinctly. That is how I interpret what you said earlier: "They're really madmen!"

Oury: We have to be able to say that the problem of doctor-nurse relationships is a false problem. There is not *one* doctor or *one* nurse; there are people who are with madmen, people who are there without being there, mystified in their myth. And the only real relationships that they have between each other should be technical relationships involving particular skills for treating madmen, madmen for whom they are responsible and constituent.

Félix: We could take a paradoxical position and ask which ones have fundamental relationships with madmen: nurses. Yet nurses are, for the most part, alienated and not suited to the affective work of approaching and understanding madmen. There is a modernist tradition that wants to turn nurses into little doctors, whereas it would be more a question of transforming doctors, so that they can at least reach the level of nurses in terms of contact with patients. Nurses should not only have access to your P.Psy.F.,[1] but there should be a bias in favor of admitting them, something like the trial period before entering the Bolshevik party, which, if I remember correctly, was six months for workers and employees and much longer for intellectuals.

Oury: It is obvious that these terms "doctor" and "nurse" are part of the contract that we are saying should be broken. I still felt resistance, from some of the best members of the aforementioned P.Psy.F., when I asked them if people who were not doctors could join. It is still deeply rooted, even among the best. They say, "What will happen? It will go downhill," etc. That is the problem: there have to be doctors, because they have the most to learn from it. What needs to be studied is a manifesto for this whole group of schmucks who are doctors by chance, nurses by chance, psychologists by chance, by chance in contact with madmen.

Félix: Yes, there is a question in fact: being "I, you" in a strange situation, honestly or without vocation…

Oury: Who cares if they have the vocation; it's just important to be there. If you are honest, you analyze why we are there, what we are doing, etc. or you don't join. But to come back to our topic, it would be interesting to have observations of the behavior of each hospital, like images in a text. We can't do it because we don't have enough experience.

Félix: I think that we still could, if we wanted an example, use the example of Saint-Alban, or even mention the total transformation of nurses here. We call them monitors and do not differentiate them. How do you recognize nurses at La Borde?

Oury: Here, you could say that if you have a diploma in nursing you are almost chased off, it is strange. The same for doctors; it is enough to say "I am a psychologist, a doctor" to be blacklisted. You could say that we have a technical team that is maturing all of the time, each one specializing in his or her own domain; and not only in his or her domain but in the group itself, on a level of "syntality."

The "syntality" relationships of a group are important. People are there, growing like grass in a pot, and other people pass by who are patients. We joke around saying that we are the chronic cases and the patients are the ones passing through, no matter how long they stay. In saying that, we reverse the values: before, the madmen were the "ones who stayed." This reversal is connected to an overall movement in psychiatry, with the discovery of shock treatments, because the pure shock, the absolute shock is the boot to the ass that kicks a guy somewhere other than where he was. Seriously, they have to pass through and let it be used for something else. Who cares if it is strange for the alienating alienists…

Félix: In summary, we have to expose the concrete possibilities of breaking up the fixed roles between doctors and nurses in a team, where there is different work but where they work together towards a certain unity of the work climate, where each person is differentiated, not in function of his or her status, the money in his or her pocket or his or her prestige but in terms of sharing labor on a strictly technical or practical basis to create an atmosphere of treatment, of socialization of patients.

Oury: We have to distinguish two problems: the way to reach this situation, which requires a global revision of the administration and, on the other hand, what has already been done in a traditional framework. Everything that we have been talking about here is only an introduction. Maybe we should ask the fundamental question: what is it for? What is treatment for? What does the P.Psy.F do? Is it just shooting the shit, a bunch of wise guys hanging out? The gentlemen with experience already think of us psychiatrists that way: a bunch of wise guys, how nice! They encourage us, like they encourage everyone, starting with the boy scouts, but…

Félix: Others already see us as a special group, but that is not the whole story. The P.Psy.F. also has to have an original position in terms of psychiatric policy. There is now political psychiatry; the need for it came from the fact that Stalinist psychiatrists did not have a policy, they followed tradition instead of searching for what a progressive psychiatry might be. If the P.Psy.F. shocks anyone, it won't be as wise guys but because it has to develop a theory and practice that will attract young psychiatrists, from a Marxist-existentialist-something-or-other perspective.

Oury: It's tricky to say things like that. The fact that the Stalinist psychiatrists don't have a policy, etc. puts me to sleep. It's not true. There are excellent Stalinist psychiatrists who have a very serious policy, even if it does not agree with us, but it is very serious in terms of the contemporary renewal and foundation of psychiatry. Naturally, it is hard to admit psychiatrists who are affiliated with a party; it's a problem, in the sense of a betrayal, an escape.

Félix: We can compare it with the Freinet movement, where there were some Stalinists who applied the best current methods from a pedagogical point of view, but who had to withdraw at the request of the Party. It seems obvious that if the Freinet movement had been well put together, it would have taken clearer political positions, which would have allowed the communists in the movement to avoid being obliged to leave. All of the communist school teachers would have been concerned. It's the same for the communist psychiatrists: the good ones are in the minority, and someone like Le Guillant himself is far from being able to do and say what he wants. Not only because of the current state of the administration, but also because of the attitude of the Stalinist psychiatrists. Each person doing what they can is one thing, but a real policy is something else, it means having a coherent perspective. I doubt that a lot of psychiatrists have one, not only a Marxist one but one that is complete in terms of the domain in which they work. The work that we are doing is precisely what left-wing and communist groups are lacking, from a psychiatric perspective. This is the only true meaning of the P.Psy.F., which otherwise would just be a masonic group in the hospitals. It is a policy that will only take on its true meaning when it starts situating psychiatric problems on a platform that does not yet exist. There is no fundamental difference between bourgeois psychiatry and the psychiatry of contemporary movements on the Left. Stalinist psychiatry, in its fundamental concepts, is exactly aligned with bourgeois psychiatry. We can't confuse Marxist alienation and the alienation of madness like the Stalinists do; we have to reclaim all of what both Marx and Freud have provided. A deep understanding of Marxism and Freudianism cannot allow this confusion.

Oury: To study nurse-doctor relationships or therapeutic group-madmen relationships, we have to study the relationship of the group with society before anything else. That is why we have to introduce what has been called the transcendental dimension of the madman from the start.

Félix: There are different positions to be established: a metaphysical pole; a political pole, in the sense of a strategy against the adminis-tration, against constituted social groups; and a pole of theoretical development starting with the major authors—on the one hand, the Lacan pole if you like, and on the other, the Tosquelles pole, which is already more political.

Oury: It is hard to put names on it. It is a question of distinguishing an order, which is difficult, because it seems to exclude some political positions radically; it is a negative encircling of the group's position (group is a better word than party). We exclude someone because he or she is not part of "religiousness B," because he or she doesn't share a universal vision inspired by Lacan or the political presuppositions of the Tosquelles side… But I don't think we can define the group as Trotskyist or anarchist, or whatever. We said earlier that we had to be progressive, in other words breaking contracts with traditional frameworks that are now meaningless. Our language will become completely incomprehensible to those who stay in those frameworks and to those who pretend to understand us, but who add kindly that we should still start wearing a tie and try to speak proper French. It is an aspect of originality, you can't be afraid of it, you have to say: "That's the way it is and I don't have to change…"

Félix: Being engaged in social struggle but also being crazy enough to have the possibility of being with the madmen should be specific to a group of militants in the psychiatric domain. There are people who are on the right path politically but who are incapable of being part of that group. There is also the Kierkegaardian aspect of "religiousness B."

Oury: That aspect is essential, in the sense that you first have to pass through madness, digest it. You have to assume the madman, be madder than the madmen. This notion of transcendental madness is absolutely denied by some political groups: "It is ridiculous thingism, a deviation from Marx's thinking," etc.

Félix: When you start to account for this metaphysical dimension, the main danger that you face is to be placed in the ranks of the idealists and the class that traditionally defends idealism. The "Modern Times" current has the same problem: they have all kinds of problems keeping a minimum of the metaphysical dimension while remaining a progressive movement that is traditionally materialist.

Oury: In the end, we are just beating around the bush to avoid talking about nurse-doctor relationships. Madmen must be defined first, to the extent that nurse-doctor relationships are only defined if there are madmen. We therefore have to make some madmen, because madmen are made. How do you make madmen? You could relate it to the theory of images, that an image is the reflection of a diminished object. There are interminable treatises on images only to find out that it is all bunk. Psychiatrists are like image collectors or butterfly collectors; they collect fake butterflies that they call madmen and that they don't even want to call mad anymore but "mentally ill."

Félix: You would have to redefine the object of psychiatry in the way that Politzer tried to redefine the object of psychology, of concrete psychology.

Oury: We could call it the group of concrete psychiatry.

Félix: We would also have to take a position on the giant farce of social psychology, microsociology. Moreno and all of the others who fall into the same mystified circuit of the little group. Our questioning of the hospital and its social status should differentiate itself, in ideological terms, from several positions.

Oury: Questioning the hospital must define a group that is interested in the problem of its nature in its relationships with society. We have to use this group as a tool, not as a research device. There will be necessary effects on research, but it should first be presented as a tool.

2

Monograph on R.A.

After various, vain attempts to integrate R.A. directly into the clinic's ergo-social-therapy system, Dr. Oury and I came to the conclusion that it was necessary to rely on a special psychotherapy technique to allow this patient to regain contact with reality. It was a recent attempt and we cannot yet clearly appreciate its scope. We started it just after R.A. had run away, an escape that now seems to me to have "replayed" the time that he ran away when he was 15 and that can be considered the starting point for the psychotic aggravation of his illness.

Until then, I had a good relationship with R.A., but not one that was noticeably different from the relationship that a staff member is supposed to have with every patient. In truth, R.A.'s general attitude was one where he was somewhat "cut off" from everyone else: systematic opposition to everything going on at the clinic (going down to the dining room, participating in activities, meetings, evening events, etc.); stereotypical responses that were always more or less aggressive (such as: "what?," "hunh?," "I can't hear anything," "I don't feel anything," "I don't want to," "I'm dead," "This place made me like this," etc.) and that regularly interrupted anything anyone said to him as soon as the first words were spoken. Most of the time, he laid down on his bed and froze completely when someone came to see him. We could only sometimes get him to do something by pushing him and forcing him. My relationship with him was somewhat different due to the fact that when I started to look after him, it happened to be a vacation period and there were several young, emotionally disturbed patients in the clinic who "adopted" him and brought him along for different activities that we had been unable to get him to accept before. We saw him playing volleyball, ping-pong, checkers, chess; he went swimming, drew, typed, participated in an amateur film, worked with a puppetry troop and even acted in a more or less improvised play, in which they could only find him the role of the fake mute.

During this period, the episode that I mentioned and the relapse that followed it showed us the unstable and somewhat artificial side of this training, at least for him. Having followed him closely during all of these activities, having been lucky enough to find him in the woods and bring him back after he ran away and also because we got along, it was relatively easy for me to get him to accept the idea of a dialog. It was very important from the start for us to avoid creating a "transfer" type of relationship. First, because some psychotherapy sessions had been interrupted three years earlier for external reasons and had left him with an unfortunate failure, and then because of the structure of the clinic which makes it necessary for each staff member to be present alternatively as "caregiver," "authority," "friend," etc. A psychoanalytic transfer would have difficulty standing up to the fact that the analyst, at the end of the session, would take on an entirely different attitude with the subject.

With Dr. Oury, we decided that my conversations with R.A. would take place in the presence of a tape recorder. Ostensibly, I started the recording when the dialog entered what I considered to be an impasse, or when something "bothered" me. It was then as if a third person had appeared in the room. *Two bodies psychology*[1] and the associated perspectives of the imagination disappeared; an objectivation of the situation took place that had the effect, most often, of deviating, if not blocking the dialog. It was only a few months later and with an entirely different method that R.A. accepted to speak with someone other than myself, and to write a text that "anyone could read." We did not dwell on its contents. We never did, even though the temptation was sometimes great. Before us, at arm's length, so to speak, we had oedipal situations forming and unraveling in a few days' time, multiple transfers occurring with those around him ("this guy is my brother," "that guy is my father," "this girl is my sister," etc.) that opened, it seemed, onto deeper regressions, especially during a dream where the central image was a poisoned breast from which R.A. could not determine whether he had suckled.

We have focused our attention on the "symbolic restructuring" of R.A. Here, in summary, are its stages:

Recognition of the voice and "body map"

During the first sessions, when we listened to the tape (which we erased together the next day), R.A. lost his temper. The opposition that he had turned against the world, the "what?," "hunh?," etc., he now turned against himself. The recorded voice, the drawling tone, the hesitations, the breaks, the constant incoherence revolted him, and he took me as a witness that he must have truly fallen "lower than everything" to end up speaking like that. From there, it was easy for me to have him recognize that it was absurd to persist in claiming that the cause of his illness was Dr. Oury, electroshocks, etc. and that in fact he was confusing everything. Let us note in passing the apperception that he had of his behavioral unity when the amateur film was shown, in which he could be seen participating in various activities and where, despite a certain slowness, he remained generally brilliant. After a short period of surprise, he gathered himself, declared that we could see from the film how he

had become a "schmuck" and he took up his refrain: "it's the electroshocks," "this place made me like this," "you have to x-ray my
brain," etc.

Only a few weeks later, he passed through a type of "mirror
stage" in which, facing the mirror, touching his face, he rediscovered
the jubilant comprehension of himself described by Lacan in "The
Mirror Stage."[2] It occurred at the same time as, to bring him out of
himself and have him abandon his apparent insensitivity, I pinched
him so hard that he cried like a child. Yet this assumption of his
body map remained tentative and was always more or less called
into question. (Let us note in this regard two self-castrating
attempts: a deep cigarette burn and a cut to his hand.)

Recognition of language

I noticed that he practically hadn't written or read anything for
years. As with other registers, it seemed to be due to a lack of self-
control, a loss of the "ego" and correlatively of organized behaviors
in reality. A third term needed to be found: a control that, temporarily, would be outside him. I first tried to have him read out
loud, but it was materially impractical, and difficult to have him
avoid interrupting his reading to say "he doesn't understand anything," that "this is where he fell ill," etc. I then proposed that he
copy a book, telling him that it was not important whether he
understood it or not but only that he make a copy. There was a ruse
there that he did not discover until later. The book was not selected
by chance. It was *The Castle* by Kafka. Dr. Oury and I had noticed
the similarities between R.A. and Kafka, from psychopathological
and religious points of view as much as his external appearance, at
least to the extent that we could judge from a photograph. Nevertheless, he was "hooked" by the book and now he has almost
finished copying it.

Recognition of his own situation

I undertook to teach him to "speak" about his illness in a more coherent way. After a certain time, the tape recorder had conditioned the situation of our dialog to the point that I almost did not need to turn it on. I abandoned it and in its place, I wrote down the things he said that I found interesting in a notebook. I left the notebook at his disposal and we quickly reached the point where he did the writing in my place. In other words, during our conversations, I would interrupt him to say, "you could write that down," and I would repeat what he had said word for word (he was usually unable to remember it himself). I took on the role of the tape recorder (or the mirror), but in a more human way, the "disautomatization" of the machine was correlated to the fact that he was now the machine recording the words circulating between us.

Recognition of others

Until then, we had remained reciprocally parasitical in the dialog. The circuit between us was closed by this more or less unreadable and incommunicable notebook. A first attempt to break up this bell jar structure quickly ended in failure. R.A. fell in love with one of the employees. He experienced it as a kind of opposition to me, and of course the "harsh reality" was revealed to him in the bitter awareness of the inanity of his own situation. Just as his running away, it seems, replayed the episode that triggered his illness, this imaginary episode replayed a failure in love from around the same time. All of the order in his behavior, which had developed little by little, collapsed. He stayed frozen on his bed for a few days, without eating or saying a word.

I started from zero. After a few days, however, the situation became "normal" again: he returned to the dining room, started working on typing again, etc. What we had done before had retained a certain consistency, there was a certain resistance of what we called his symbolic restructuring. This episode had a positive result: on this occasion, he started to write on his own, almost *against* me. Once our relationship had improved again, he continued this initiative. For example, he wrote a few letters to his parents. As his "technical" acquisitions allowed him to do it, I undertook to have him systematically recopy and type the thick notebook that we had been using. He reworked, corrected, trimmed and sorted it, made comments and changed the order of what we had developed together. It became *his* text.

Now he continues to write each day and he brings me his texts typed directly (sometimes, he is willing to type my correspondence). I have also changed my attitude, and I have tried to get him to begin a real recognition of others. I have the doctors and friends who visit us read his texts. He discusses the texts with them. Until now, he had declined to act when faced with others, saying that "he didn't exist," "he was dead," "he was like his father," "he had nothing to do," etc. For example, hardly a month ago, I suggested that he go light the fire in my fireplace; he was finally able to do so, and not without a certain satisfaction. Later, someone asked if he was the one who did it; he found enough bad faith to deny it.

Today, the situation is different. He is entirely in his text and he is the one who put himself there. He has now acquired a kind of symbolic personality, one to which he is attached, and that changes the meaning of his illness, which is no longer experienced through the feeling of his almost magical membership in his family, where, according to him, "everyone is sick." He is no longer exactly "like his father," the obsession that he was constantly struggling with, in vain. In reading his text, it seems that he has gained a much more phenomenological understanding of the "essence" of his illness, and that this is a good way to help him find ways out of it.

3

Collapse of a Life Not Lived. Loss of the "I"

(Extracts from the Journal of R.A.)

September 27

What bothers me the most is the lack of all the feelings that I still had the possibility of experiencing. In short, they all left at the same time as my natural senses. In short, they are even dead. I say "in short" as if I were a steam machine, both living and dead, that sometimes makes a small sound of steam being released, somewhat regularly, as if it were woken up a little bit by a sound in its dreams of clouds. It does not move but jumps while releasing the words "in short" in one sentence, then two, then… All of my subsequent "in shorts" serve the same cause (remember this when you read them). A young girl just entered the office.

—It doesn't bother you if I stay here a few seconds, she says.

—No, I replied, not understanding a word of what she said to me.

—You would rather be alone, she told me.

I replied with a sort of sign that hurt me, in other words, I could not respond to her like… absolute LACK of contact, of both physical and moral contact.

Seeing the sign, she says to me: "You don't care. Okay, I will leave you alone." Then she left.

This afternoon, I played volleyball. I say that to try to return to reality, but I cannot do it. Can a cloud with no color play? Anything that comes out of me, now, precisely does not come from the heart. Félix just told me: "Trust me." I cannot. Parasite. These are physical "things" if I remember the present way that I remember, in other words, things that touched me at the time, things that, unconsciously, I say because… it is related to the state that I am in.

September 28

Would have liked to remember all of the ideas that I had on insulin. I open my eyes, I see M. before me… I raise my thing… I look at the position I am in, I had my leg a little bent like that. It was especially my arm because the nurse had given me a shot. I put the cotton back; I thought it wasn't over yet.

And then, when I lifted up the sheet, I saw that it wasn't my chest. All of the bottom, only the penis, had a little bit of feeling. It bothered me because it's animal. Before being in this state, I was too sexual. I attach some importance to sexuality (masturbation) because I am ill and withdrawn. I should have noticed it when I slapped Mrs. A. This "mobile state" is not conscious. But the "immobile state" would need to be described better. I tell myself something, and then later it does it… it is complete abandon, worse when I was a kid. It was more stationary. It was boiling, but I felt more than I do now. The top is gone, the bottom is still there, but…

Kafka, December 6, 1910

"I will never leave this journal. Here I must be resolute, because I can only be like that here."

When I was a baby is an origin.

I am a bastard, I would have liked to write on smooth paper with no folds. I just went to the bathroom, it is worse than rot. I am worse than dead. I no longer have any natural senses. I am never hungry, never thirsty, never want anything, be it physical or moral, and I am more attached to the physical because I have lost all of my organic functions (breathing, digestion, sight, hearing, etc.) like I did before, a little. As I write this, I have no awareness of what I am writing, but a kind of silent word (I think of Félix when saying that); it makes me have attitudes, that is all. And I cannot believe that I will get out of it. What I am afraid of is sucking my thumb and walking like when I was little.

September 30

Don't want to write. My organism is still not working. No impressions. No feeling. No sensations. I am an idiot, a rusted steam engine. No contact with others. Too content and so-called proud of what I write as I am writing. Dimly heard the disk on which my voice was sleepy and like a schmuck. Not yet writing of myself. It reminds me of when I was little and I swung back and forth saying "Mom, my meal." I said it mechanically. Have not yet understood what Félix just said to me about… I don't remember.

October 11

When I force myself to understand with my head… Félix just explained to me that I am a baby. As I write that, I feel (so to speak) withdrawn in myself. He just told me that since we have been talking together there have been different stages. First, there was silence (when I said: "What?," it was as if I was saying: "Mom, my meal"), then words, and then, if you will, language. As for me, the language will be true from the moment when I will be able to start feeling what I hear being said by a person in front of me and be able to try to understand what this person is saying to me (physical and moral contact at the same time… for me).

I remember when I ran away at age fifteen. Before running away, the same day, I was talking to a guy on a bicycle (it happened in the Seine-et-Marne at Mitry-le-Neuf). Once I finished speaking, so to speak, with him, I went back on my bike to... (I don't remember very well). "In short," I set out on the road in the evening, at sunset; I was walking like I wanted to be a Hun (clicking my steps). Then there were people returning from work; I may have been afraid when seeing them, but I watched them, without seeing them, trying to scare them, glaring at them. (At that moment, my so-called brutality came, of which I will have to explain all of the origins.) "In short," I walked all night; at six in the morning, I saw a pile of sand; I ate some... not much. Then I kept walking; I arrived in a town. I entered a house. I asked the lady from the café... I don't remember what... in a complete fog. I am writing all of this like a baby, without being aware of it and without wanting to write it (not a parasite). These are not even words, not even letters... if only I still wrote like a baby!

October 12

Was a little upset when we started to speak. Told him it was the electroshocks that made me the way I am. Let me continue saying a few words. (When I write, I still have the pride which is basically stupid, but I will explain more later.) When I write, I am a little bit like a baby who wants to speak, to babble, as if I was the only one who understood what I was saying (explanation of silent speech). In truth, I have always been like that, alone in the world... I don't remember very well. Then Félix asked me to go get a pack of cigarettes and matches. When I entered the little office, I expected to see Félix by himself. But a surprise, a little blow to the heart so to speak, Mrs. A. was sitting on the windowsill. I do not like her, and during the day, several times, I wondered how the doctor could like her. It is foolish to worry about it because I don't understand anything about it and I do not exist.

Am I becoming hysterical? Because I tried to attach myself physically to someone to whom I could not attach myself because I do not have "arms and legs" to do it. I no longer think, I can no longer think. I would like to be able to live corporally. MOM-MY-MEAL. My hysteria is a little like papa.

October 13

Still have a jumble of words in (so to speak) my head. Spoke with Félix. Told him, saw Dr. Oury leaving his room, when I was going down for lunch. Dr. asked me (this ballpoint pen reminds me of when I was at the Maimonides School, when I was copying a paper, when I wrote my name in the margin; in the end, my paper was never any good, never had any meaning for me; I never noticed it; (I) did not "do" it):

—You haven't gone down yet?

—No, I responded.

—You know, now, you look better, he said to me.

I looked at him making a strange face. He told me with a laugh:

—You are not happy about that. You don't like people to say that. Seemed like another.

Feel terribly alone this evening. Just put away my notebook and turned off the light that scared me, and the white machine that is next to the table, because it is a thing with wires (confusion), "in short" I don't know. I am afraid of anything now. I am afraid of electricity. I feel myself becoming all alone like before we talk. Am in my pride; it is the only thing that makes me move a little. But what there is: I am introverted because I no longer have anything physically. Morally, I do not know what it is. I am a piece of wood, not a big, solid log but a tiny, little twig that will disappear before it has even appeared. It may be your departure that made me like this, but I don't think so, because I have almost always been like I just described above.

Dr. Z. just came back right at the moment that I was putting away my notebook and "the" ballpoint pen; he came up to me. The dead twig that I am had the impression that he would ask what I was doing there, as if I was being taken for a thief.

You see, Félix, if I use the imperfect tense to describe my so-called impression that I didn't feel, it is not only because I do not have a notion of time, but simply and terribly for me that the dead twig was scared, moved without doing it when Z. entered; and since it didn't see Z., since it couldn't see him, since he frightened it, it used the imperfect to make Z. more distant, from a presence of which it was not aware… then the distancing, the change in tense (from the present to the imperfect), and then especially that the twig saw a big, strong, hard, solid log that "seemed vaguely" to be Z. That is what frightened it (to be analyzed). I am imagining this, because in the end, I cannot be in reality. Can a dead twig cry out? "My heart is not clear." I am still afraid, Félix, that you will ask me why I marked that last sentence. (Afraid of the feelings that I don't have and that come from the "mom my meal" period, when mom and dad laughed when I sang it while cradling me like a foundling. But, in the end, I know that if mom always answered my call, so fragile in truth, if she came close to me and spoke at least a word instead of putting the food directly in my mouth, an almost little "I" would have been formed. Dad never said anything to me. In truth, I don't feel like I had parents, only silent clouds.) It is true that two years ago, I would not have talked about any of this. I was fragile, but not as fragile as now. The "I" existed a little bit, or at least I thought it existed. I have no more control over myself. Personally, I think that my excessive masturbation caused me to have the physical state that I have now.

October 14

It is seven o'clock at night. Just saw the movie *Forbidden Games*. Made me think of a lot of things. I am lost. My state will never change. (I) cannot want. When M.C. died, I also thought that I was having a stroke, otherwise I would be aware of what I (see) or don't even understand. I am going to eat now. Did not understand the film at all. But it almost made me cry. When would I have a life, contact, light, an awakening? It is true, I am a real shit now. My cloudy pride has not gone away. But when everything comes back? I don't think it will come back. I am unable to catch on to you, Félix, but you are the only one who can do it for me here, for you see it is a cloudy affectation that I try to give to "myself," but I can't.

You tell me that the two of us are only there to chat, but I can't say that it is a chat, because if I accepted to listen to your words, I would not hear them…, you hear them for me. I am like someone paralyzed. Tell me how I can be healed. I have never loved anyone. I am like a paralyzed person. Tell me… I am still a dead twig. I am nothing, not even a pile of shit. When will I see the world? When will I live in the world, with others, experience joy, love a girl, have a friend, and all the rest that I asked or told you? You told me very correctly that I have to see myself and that I have to be happy to see myself…

Dr. Oury just entered the little office to see how a patient lying down was doing. I did not even realize it. There is nothing living in me. BEFORE relapsing, I felt that I had a head, and then a body; but it was only debris; now…

I am very weak at present. You tell me that I am trying to hold on to something, but I cannot. It is true that before, when I was in school, the nothing thought it could believe it was something among the other classmates. But he did not have any schoolmates, they came to him; he did not go to them to speak with them. No me, no I. Still somewhat nastily attached to the air bubbles that my parents represented for me. I have lost everything physically.

October 15

Copy of the (awakening) of insulin:

The way I turned the page, I should be on the other side of the page (for me, it is the other side). We are in the awakening of insulin. I was just given a shot two or three minutes ago. (Awake) now like with the electroshocks: when the shot woke me, I was dead, I felt dead.

October 19

Dream on insulin of the poisoned breast. I don't know if I suckled it. Associated with Bernadette, whom I saw without seeing her. My brother knows how to deal with girls; it is the same thing for me as the poisoned breast of my mother. In the end, I am too much with my mother whom I never had (cloud). I did not have a father. At the henhouse committee, I had an unpleasant impression: "It is as if they were talking about me when they said that hens lay eggs" (to analyze well, I think). Complete immobility (nervous, corporal and sensitive). Everything, according to me, comes from the poisoned breast of my mother, and I am certain not to heal from it one day.

October 24

Félix spoke to me of the maternal transfer on Evelyne. In place of my father, I would have wanted my dead brother. He was sixteen and a half, Marcel. He was good at drawing. He did industrial drawing. There was no union in our family. Dad and mom argued about little things in Yiddish.

I stayed with Evelyne. She told me that I was nice. I took her in my little baby arms. She kissed my cheek. Then she left. I called for mom like an abandoned child (imaginary "mom my meal"). Marcel drew "himself" well by looking in a mirror (false mirror stage).

October 28

I do not feel infantile any more. I feel dead, unborn. I have no contact. Everything is mercurial. I am inert. Continuous. I think I will not get over it. I was good at spelling when I was little. I am making myself like this… maybe.

October 29

I am with Evelyne in the office. I can't see anything. I don't have a brain. I can't walk. I can't feel anything physically. I am not breathing. Crush on Hélène at fifteen, at the Maimonides School. I have to get my body analyzed, especially the brain. I am lost. No physical "thing" (I repeat it on the imaginary rhythm of "mom my meal" when I was little). I can't any longer. Have no glands that function. No organism. Analyze me. This is where I became dead. I am a little like my father.

Saw Evelyne earlier with J. I am a little bit jealous. Especially since I cannot do anything (like a wasp stuck in honey that has stopped fighting).

November 4

Didn't eat. (AM) still in this black hole. Have no contact. I like Evelyne a lot. Have you seen Arthur? Vive la France. I am afraid of you. I did three lines of printing. I can't see anything. Dr. Oury told me to wait. Don't understand. I finished.

Still have fear that they see it when I talk about sex. Because of the family, father, brother. A.[1] Sex glands. It is imaginary. No contact with Félix. For the Jews… What happens? What it is, is that I am more attached to Félix like before he left recently. Just went to the big living room. I cannot see Catholics now. It is my father's fault. Feeling (as they say) of oppression. Just kissed Evelyne. Am like at home… Like my mother… Immobile and drowsy. Never had contact. It is both funny and awful. I do not like J., and yet I do not see him at all… pretending "almost" to see him.

November 5

In PARIS, dad (gave) me a gunshot. I was with my brother Maurice. It happened in the evening. I had just come home. I had sold my newspapers all day long. DAD was yelling at me. I was afraid, but I didn't move. My little brother told me to leave. I did not see the revolver. I saw it without seeing it. It only lasted a few seconds. I still went to my sister Rachel and my brother-in-law's house. But I was sure when I was facing my father that he did not want to shoot. He was doing it like a moron.

November 14

"The 'IN SHORT' of my mother."

When my sister came to see me, it had no effect on me. Jeanette came to find me in my room. Surely when I was little, I don't know, I… My father did not train me. Now, I cannot. He was not the father that I needed. Why? Because I am not able to control myself. He never raised me. Always give something to eat. Masturbation also did a lot… starting at fifteen. I love myself too much because I am still running after the "two" times imaginary breast of my (mother). (She) did not teach me to see things in this world as would have been necessary to overcome my weakness, like normal parents. NO. Always giving something to eat. She was a real baby, my mother (mom my meal). I often felt queasy. My father worked, but he never told me anything…

November 19

Have no more sexual desire. It wasn't because he was a seducer that my brother was successful with women, it was because he was, more or less… normal. When I went to the psychoanalyst one day, I was like that, it bothered me. He said: "Sit down." He thought that I wanted to cry. I let out some tears but I didn't really feel like crying. "Don't hold back, it will help." No, it completely emptied me.

I fight it, but I can't. I don't accept this suffering because it is awful, and especially because I cannot accept it.

November 20

My mother never taught me how to speak. Don't remember at all what I learned in school and high school. I have no body, no head, no heart, nothing. My parents did not love me as they should have. I am always abandoned, I would like to want to be able to want that someone take care of me. Maybe because Evelyne likes me? Or maybe because I think like an idiot that she pities me. My brother Jacques is not at all like me. When I said: "Mom, my meal," I was lagging behind. Other babies call for life. Not me.

Just danced with Jeanette who pulled my arm. Am like a piece of wood. The ladies have to invite me to dance, it's awful. No contact. Am like my father, like my mother. It bothers me, this imaginary physical pleasure… of dancing. No more control of myself.

December 2

The main thing is words. I never had them when I was little. That is why I always see things written and I love myself (to be analyzed). When I said: "Mom, my meal," no one responded. Debated them, it was to try to free myself of my parents? I always return to (my) air bubbles and I cannot even do it… air current. In the end, if my father had wanted to shoot me, he would have wanted to shoot himself. We are too much alike.

When I punched my brother? It was automatic, not even automatic, it was to reach my brother, to have contact with him. My fist went through the tile, it was a wall for me, but not a physical wall or a moral wall but the type of wall that meant that I was always drowsy, always soft.

I want to say something to Félix? But… presence of Evelyne, of my real mother, of the rotten breast, of the mother that I cannot grasp on to because she did not give me real maternal love, because if I am always abandoned, it is because of that, and especially because Evelyne is coming towards me and I cannot accept it. When I write all of this, it is foolish things that I try to feel. "In short," it is simply Evelyne's return that interrupted my wanting to talk about me. I have always been afraid of women because I have always been afraid of my real mother who quickly, when I was a baby, became imaginary for me because of the lack of confidence in life that my mother never gave me. That is the first wall that meant that I was always enclosed without truly being enclosed. It is always as if I am falling to sleep.

The sound of Félix's footsteps disturbs me. (It surely comes from the bomb… that I didn't even hear? But that shook me during the war.) I am folded in on myself. I am able to write all of this because the pseudo-presence of Evelyne and Félix makes me write it.

December 3

My mother never instilled me with any confidence. It was always physical. Right now, I am not, and to try to be... What I am saying is spontaneous. My parents think I am a bag of dirty laundry. In place of me I put imaginary mom and dad because I never saw the real ones (rhythm of "mom my meal"). I am like my father. When he made me with my mother, I think that he did not do it because of his feelings, but because of a certain sexual weakness.

It is like when I left my house one evening, I was sick like now, less physically?, like when I went with a whore. I could not even see the room. I didn't know what to do. I rushed in. I wanted to kiss her... *I* did not want to.

December 19

If I was well, I would think the girl was nice. It is like with my other friends. Maybe I am more extroverted now? But when she told me to go to the piano, I didn't hear... I am a little bit like my father. When she comes up to me, I can't talk, it is only physical, I only smell perfume and I am ashamed, because I don't feel it deep down. Why isn't it ever the voice? Probably because no one ever talked to me at home. When you said to me: "Go sit at the table and write," it was a break, because my imaginary father never spoke to me... like that... "In short"... am in a dream.

Each time that you talk to me about family, that you attack my family, it touches me, it makes me think, it upsets me, because deep down I am not thinking... and I never had a family. It is because I am too sensitive to silly things that I can never have. It is like the bomb, it is like my father.

In your writing, I think that you are a little bit like me, Félix. For me, writing is death (silent word). I remember that my father, one night when we were at the table, said to my mother, in Yiddish: "Like a wasp in the honey." He was laughing as he said it. I asked him what it meant. He answered that you couldn't say it in French. Félix says that in this scene my father is a little like Mr. Klamm, *who you can never talk to.*

December 22

What broke me was the arrival of M. and the little girl (M.'s sister), and then… her mother. The kid, I can tell that she came out of her mother's belly. And she is already a big girl. It was the same for me as the slap I gave Mrs. A. The main thing is the thing with the mirror. Why wasn't I happy to recognize myself? Because I have never seen myself. Why is it that I am never hungry? It feels to me like I never sucked on this bottle. While the other kids, why is it that I am not like the other kids? Not even like my brothers and sisters. When I just said "like my brothers and sisters," I felt something bad, bubbling?… something in the stomach (I imagine myself when writing this because I feel "nothing at all," I am not even breathing); that is what I can't explain. It's strange. One day I fell like my father. Masturbation… Plop, I collapse (Félix's parenthesis).

Je suis tout en cire,	I am made of wax,
C'est pourtant pas l'âge;	Yet it is not the time;
Que puis-je te dire,	What can I tell you,
Je suis dans le cire âge.	I am waxed out.

It is like when I copied a giraffe this morning. I wasn't the one copying it: the giraffe was copying itself slowly and with difficulty.

4

Ladies and Gentlemen, the SCAJ

Throughout La Borde, over time, this phrase, having become the fulcrum of the giant socio-therapeutic verbal machine, tends to evoke either a carnival pitch: "Come inside, come inside, and you will see…," or a religious ritual with its procession of priests and droning liturgy. What is it? The skit, the course? No, the SCAJ.[1]

Usually, newcomers do not take it any further. Like us chronic cases, they quickly forget to ask questions about the nature of this sub-committee on who knows what, so much so that its gender has gone from feminine to masculine.[2] From the proliferation of institutions in the summer of 1955, retrospectively troublesome to systematize, most have disappeared or degenerated as expected, leaving behind institutional compost that has only served to enrich the SCAJ. In fact, it almost automatically began to fill in the gaps left by the committees—bar, henhouse, radio, menu, cleaning, etc.—the secretariat, the activity commission and the general assembly. Is it because it met daily? It is not clear that doing something seven times a week is easier than doing it once. Is it a routine? How then do you explain that it is one of the activities that attracts the most patients? My idea, in 1955, was that it would be useful to have four or five people organize, each day, a precise program of activities that was outlined each week in a much larger "activity commission." The doors of this meeting were then forced open by a growing number of participants, to the extent that it would now be surprising if less than half of the total number of patients showed up.

At the same time, the SCAJ took on multiple tasks in terms of information, discussion, organization, even the exchange of ideas and as a tribunal; it sometimes has the euphoric atmosphere of a nightclub where anyone can speak. This mirage-like ambiance often reminds me of the broadcasts of Radio-Luxembourg: there is no obligation and you only come if you like. In reality, there is all the more obligation when you are not paying attention, and just like toothpaste brands spinning around your head, here the public will have their gaping laziness and boredom filled in by the temptation to go where "people say" something is happening, and bring others along, like a long chain of Panurge's sheep, where each one has an image of the other in front of it, seen from behind.

This imaginary factor, in its pure state in the SCAJ is—it seems to me—a constant that we can find in all of the other activities: meetings, workshops, games, but where it is less apparent due to their greater "utilitarianism." For me, it is undoubtedly behind the "local resocialization" of patients. In order to understand how we should bring patients to be taken in by the words of psychiatric therapy, let us first attempt to grasp the tricks of normal life when we become the puppet of another person's words.

A salesperson knows that the game is half won when he or she is able to engage in conversation on any subject other than his or her wares. The seducer, in order to "make" an acquaintance, must first find a harmless expression, with no relationship to what he or she has in mind. However, unless one "is mad," one will not be "taken in" by these empty words and formalities of decorum. Then one moves on to the serious matter at hand, the financial transactions or the establishment of a more or less contractual relationship which, if not always on the same level of social jurisdiction as marriage, nevertheless establishes a structure of permanence in the relationship, with the difference residing in the character of the witnessing third party. That is how one becomes a friend, lover, employee, hourly rental and even enemy, since it is true that aggression is always structured in societies, even the most primitive ones; one must only look at the rites of vendetta or "mob law."

Madmen are people who have slipped outside of these relationships of socially normalized exchanges. They can no longer find their way in them and are therefore faced with only one type of person delegated by society for this purpose: the psychiatrist. The only contract they have with society is the *assessment* by the psychiatrist that in fact "they are no longer there," that they are outside contractual relationships with their family, work, etc.

Ejected from the social, the patient is brought into the society of the psychiatrist, surrounded by his or her "henchmen" and "officials responsible for small tasks and diverse treatments." The "mastery" of the psychiatrist transforms him or her, in a traditional structure, into a "slave" of his or her role as chief warden or as "grand sorcerer" of medicinal magic.

More often than not, madmen are not mad enough not to know that they are not well in their being, and deal with this situation as best as possible, albeit more often poorly than well.

The "voice" of the SCAJ and artifices of the same type can change how rigid this edifice is. It is not a magic wand, nor does it change anything essentially. The contractual exchange is not reestablished, because nothing that is done there is really serious. Nevertheless, as if by mistake, the "agents" of society and symbolic coherence known as nurses are transformed into interlocutors. The dialog that was broken on the harshness of reality begins again around trifles adjusted to the fragility and destructuration of the patient. Instead of "prison guards," nurses are in a position to become psychotherapists. The task of the doctor returns to healing, in other words to integrating biological treatments into the actions of the groups, sub-groups and individuals that he or she must "control" in the psychoanalytic sense.

Seen from this angle, the networks of verbal exchanges that make up institutions should not be considered to be like those of the normal world. Nothing is exchanged there. No one speaks "against" anything. The patient's participation is not in exchange for "healing," for example. It is nothing. It is because he or she "wants to do it." Very often, we insist that a patient participate in a workshop. But it is the same problem. You have to say that it is not "for his or her own good," that's the way it is! The arbitrariness of exchange is necessary to help patients escape themselves, according to their own rhythm, according to an inaccessible dialectic, outside of the hole they are in due to their inability to make themselves understood and recognized.

The ruse consists of making it so that it is *truly* always the patient who makes the first step, even if we have prepared everything in advance, even by forcing the patient's hand by bringing him or her in front of a sheet of paper and paint.

This daily meeting is like a skimmer picking up everything relatively well integrated that floats up in the entire discussion, like a barometric control of the dissociation of local society. It is determined according to obscure relationships of force, between those who come and those who do not, those who speak and those who remain silent, those who organize and take themselves seriously, and those who are less rigid and better integrated and who are more flexible in their behavior, understanding more or less what is going on, with monitors and semi-monitors no longer included in this type of resocialization organism.

In summary, I would define the SCAJ as a machine of empty words, essentially a place for unequal, heterogeneous, temporary exchanges between *imaginary behaviors*: turning inwards, bearing, aggressive opposition, recrimination, non-recognition of the desire of others, etc., and a *symbolic integration*: verbal expression of disagreement, exchange of ideas, awareness of common activities, community service, etc.

5

Introduction to Institutional Psychotherapy

(Excerpts from presentations made to the GTPSI)

Introduction

The origin of the current of thought that led to the present propositions on institutional psychotherapy can be situated, somewhat arbitrarily, in the period before the Liberation of France. One could certainly trace it back further, after the First World War with the development, in various psychiatric hospitals in Westphalia, of Hermann Simon's "active therapy," or even further, to England, with the "no restraint" and "open door" methods, etc. Many things had already been tried to "humanize the fate of the poor mentally ill," yet the systematic enterprise of revolutionizing psychiatry on both a theoretical and practical level did not truly start until the psychiatric hospital of Saint-Alban in Lozère and the work of the successive teams formed around François Tosquelles.

After the prison camps and concentration camps, a few nurses and psychiatrists started to look at the problems of psychiatric hospitals from an entirely new angle. Incapable of supporting concentration camp institutions, they undertook to transform services from top to bottom, knocking down fences, organizing the fight against famine, etc. The strongly militant spirit of the activities at Saint-Alban also came from its history as a former base of Resistance fighters. Surrealist intellectuals, doctors strongly influenced by Freudianism, and Marxist militants all mingled. In this crucible, new instruments of disalienation were forged, with, for example, the first intra-hospital therapeutic club[1] (le club Paul Balvet).

A new attitude and a new militant method of mental illness were born, ones that would shake up the usual stereotypes and confront the reactionary circles of the administration as well as those "on the left." The order word proposed was that before attempting any individual treatment you had to "take care of the neighborhood!" The development of "intra-hospital therapeutic club" techniques was aimed at sweeping away received ideas about agitation, chronicity, etc. and even traditional semiology was called into question by establishing new relationships between patients and caregivers, nurses and doctors,[2] doctors and families, etc. Step by step, the entire framework of psychiatry was undone, so that a real connection between hospital practices and psychoanalysis could begin, allowing an old wound—the break between Jung, Bleuler and others from Zurich with Freud—a wound that had long divided psychoanalysis and psychiatry, to be healed. From there came the perspective of an "institutional psychotherapy" that showed, by means of a somewhat paradoxical shortcut, that one could not consider psychotherapeutic treatment for the seriously ill without taking the analysis of institutions into account. Reciprocally, the conception of individual treatment came to be revised, bringing greater attention to the institutional context. In 1960, a few of us gathered to form a working group, the GTPSI (Working Group on Institutional Psychology and Sociology). In 1965, we formed a larger association: the SPI (Institutional Psychotherapy Society).

1. Starting point

All of these attempts imply a methodological reassessment of research in the human sciences: direct access to the individual is not possible, or it is misleading; we may *think* we are talking to the child or the neurotic, we may think he or she hears us, but this may be a false impression. Effects of suggestion appear despite the best intentions of the observer. A psychology of adaptation could achieve results, but in fact it can never really reach the level of the subject. Access to the most fundamental desires implies certain detours, a certain amount of mediation. This is where we introduce the notion of "institutionalization," the problem of the production of institutions: who produces the institution and articulates its subgroups? Is there a way to modify this production? The general proliferation of institutions in contemporary society leads only to reinforcing the alienation of the individual: is it possible to operate a transfer of responsibility, of replacing bureaucracy with *institutional creativity*? Under what conditions? Are there particular techniques that allow the object we want to study to speak? In fact, if we—implicitly or not—reify the object of study, if we do not give it the means to express itself, even and especially when it does not have adequate means of communication (the means could be dreams, fantasies, myths, pictorial or praxical expressions, etc.), then we are taken in by a mirage effect, by relationships of projection on the object considered. In the end, it is a calling into question of the old, poorly expurgated categories of universalizing and abstracting psychology.

There are several ways to define the psychiatrist: in strict social determination, relationship to the state, situation into which he or she must be integrated leaving only the results of the objective possibilities of the institution as the margin of intervention, personal self-determination, energy, age, problems, ability to cope, etc. From there, we could establish a local definition of psychiatric roles and functions; however they take on another meaning if considered from another angle, when defining madness as something that escapes social determination. If we say that the psychiatrist is the one who deals with madness, we find ourselves with a definition that does not easily agree with the first, with a type of schism between the vocation of catching the responses of madness and the fact of being an agent who inserts this madness into a structure of social alienation. One could then ask the question: what more do you want? A raise or philosophy?

In terms of the psychiatrist's social determination, we are faced with Tosquelles' political turn: the articulation of a social group with global society. However, if we approach it from the angle of the existential development of a particular relationship with madness, we are faced with the keenest aspect of cultural and anthropological research: Freudianism, and all of the forms of exploration of human praxis, be it cinema, or the study of primitive societies, etc. A certain number of conceptual problems will have to be addressed, problems that cannot be seriously elaborated in a group. A response can come in function of dimensions that are so personal that it is very rare if we can reconstitute a basic culture simply by gathering together and sharing monographs, etc. Some of the concepts we will discuss may have started out as personal concepts, but they must be reworked, become concepts of the GTPSI, turned into "order word" concepts of the group, operational concepts. This is how we are able to transform concepts from different sources: psychoanalytic, philosophical, etc. It may be the case that this updating, in particular for those concepts that conserve the articulation of analysis with the political field, will allow a truth to emerge from situations that tended to establish opaque ideology. It is therefore not a humanist perspective. It is a question of knowing how to get out of a particular place when stuck. With support from a minimum number of avant-garde groups, the problem of analytical, political and ethical control will be posed starting with the need to find a common approach to a total strategy more than actions alone…

2. What is a group?

The object that we are aiming for must be distinguished methodologically when we talk about groups. If we think of historical groups, for example during the formation of the first states in ancient Egypt, when the association of sedentary agricultural tribes into larger territorial units drew greater benefits from draining and irrigating the Nile, there is the impression that the emergence of a unifying law with political and religious characteristics came about almost mechanically. The elementary particles seem to have combined according to objective laws, and the political and ideological superstructures were put into place almost despite themselves. Whether true or false, I only suggest this image to illustrate what I mean by *subjugated groups*: groups that receive their law from the outside, unlike other groups that claim to be based on the assumption of an internal law. The latter would be groups that found themselves; their model can be found in religious or militant societies and their totalization depends on their ability to incarnate this law.

How do we recognize these symptom-groups? How do we recognize the fact that a society, at a given moment, carries a mutation? How do we recognize that the objective development of a social upheaval comes from a social demand? There is no mechanism here. The appearance, at a certain period, of a demand for social transformation in French feudal society does not automatically imply the start of a revolution, only the desire for something else, a passion for upheaval perceptible in thousands of symptoms.

When a subject wants to assert itself on the group level, it must first recognize that there is no place for it in the current state of social mechanics. It is then forced to intrude on, to cause violence to the existing system. It is precisely the extent to which it succeeds in this assertion that it will play the role of a subjective cut in society, a role that it may, under other circumstances, pass on as a heritage to a wider segment of the socius. To the extent that the GTPSI, for example, finds itself incapable of asserting and maintaining its autonomy as a cultural group, it may very well be recuperated as the phallus of progressive French psychiatry, and it would therefore be literally caught, with all the risks this entails of being structured serially.

How does it happen? We must examine the mode in which the effect of subjectivity moves. If it is true that the constitutive law of the group becomes intentional and explicit, it has repercussions on fields outside itself in relationship to which this group is posited as a potential unconscious subject. We are now the unconscious subject of the psychology of tomorrow, the unconscious of those who will do their psychiatry tomorrow, but only to the extent that this group continues in the direction of the truth. If not, we are nothing. This is where I say: take it or leave it! There is the possibility of reaching significant existence on this level; otherwise, it goes without saying that we will only be just another school and we will remain a part of pre-established circuits.

In order to understand this play of seriality and the alternatives of the subject—a conscious subject in the law that it gives itself, but unconscious in the determination that others take from it—we must not lose sight of the fact that it is something that develops from words and the field of language, words that are taken in a given circuit but that will also bring a certain amount of information into its open totalization, that capitalizes on a certain expression, that is woven in the totality of the language put into circulation in the society in the state of a code. We use notions (institution, psychiatry) which are already manipulated externally, and we give them a private, determined use. We thereby tend to constitute a *subjective unity of the group* by diverting the meaning of habitually used concepts. Recognition of the *subjective consistency* of this dialog between social persons depends on this unity. We are intruding on the existing societies of psychoanalysis, the Marxist, Christian and existentialist currents and the intrusion is all the more radical in that they ignored us completely at first and could not, at least for a certain time, determine our strategic choices. Isn't the most unsettling form of intrusion to enter a field where one is not only not invited but not even imaginable, like the camel driver in *Hellzapoppin* who "got the wrong gang"!

Our problem is to be able to find a structure of social utterance. If you keep notions like Ego Ideal and the Ideal Ego, you are considering a subject who is not attempting to integrate him or herself in a particular social field but only, through the function of speech, in the field of the Other. You start with an initial situation marked by absolute contingency, by *absolute narcissism* (*das Ding*) and end up with a hypothetical opening onto society in general, a "treatment" that implies, indeterminately, many different problems of integration into subjugated groups (school, sports clubs, barracks, union, party, etc.). In fact, you start with a singular unconscious social constellation and move towards uncovering of the abstract Unconscious.

For us, however, there is also the opposite direction that leads to exploring this unconscious social structure. In this sense, words proffered in the group no longer have the repressive function attributed to them as soon as it is a question of revealing instances related to a personal *das Ding*. The *das Ding* is only a stage in uncovering signifying potentialities, and we could ask: what kind of society is this with madmen on one side and revolutionaries on the other? A society where there is no group-subject to refocus these elements? The *das Ding* stops being a recurring horizon—*Nachträglich*—the illusory foundation of an individual person.

The problem of the destructive unconscious of the group is something that responds to the need for it to introduce itself in the form of a cut into a socio-historical world that did not ask for it. The structure is bothered by nothing! A simple question in this blind world: "Why take part in one group instead of another?" The group's *death instinct* introduces a dimension of violence into the initiatory aspect that it has for the participants. Being in the world in an ordinary mode, being obliged to marry, enlist, attend church, sacrifice for all sorts of rituals, is something suffered in function of this society. Whereas, in a revolutionary mode, you make yourself a victim of society; you postulate and institute ritual meetings; you reveal elements of additional code in the violating group that equate to social transgression. (The first time that I was given duties in a meeting, I wanted to leave immediately.) In this way, social violence is repeated, reiterated and accepted. Phenomenologically speaking, a process is started that immediately implies that these groups accept the principle of their finiteness and their dissolution insofar as they introduce a new characteristic of castration that is no longer the castration of repressive initiation in a dominant social structure. Militant initiation means accepting the finitude of the entire human enterprise, the absence of any transcendental guarantee, the death of God and not the guilt-ridden death of the father and his castrating sanction in oedipal initiation.

By the group's death instinct, I mean the drive that is the opposite of the drive to gather together. It is vital to locate this reversal, which comes at the same time as the positive figure, to understand the level of aggression and violence implied in the life of a group. If we analyze closely the demands of the young people who come to us, we can see that they are asking for the satisfaction of a drive that is deadly in its object and that, like any drive, tends to seek short-cuts to satisfy it and avoid the detours of sublimation in its dominant models: "give me the good word...," and I could do without being integrated in this culture and its repressive demands, or at least come to a compromise. This is why there is a complexual structure in this demand drive syncretizing terms opposed to the emergence of a subject-group: a refusal to submit to the demands of subjugated groups and a possible access to desire, while the risk of alienation remains, even at this level. It is to the extent that there is a rearticulation with a totality that draws its law from elsewhere that there can be a release of deadly fantasies and an opening to reality. The group's death instinct is thus expressed and averted by ritual elements, empty words, meetings that give a feeling of security, and all of the other elements of group mechanics. This aspect is undoubtedly unavoidable in constituting a group; without it, it would only be a temporary gathering around some phallus. Necessary conquests, specific to this dimension of the group, structures expressing this unconscious drive always threaten to shift into a system of alienation and anti-culture.

3. Institutions

What is a patient? A citizen, first, then an individual, and one might ask what relationship it might have with the fact of being a speaking subject.

Relationships of citizenship are important because they are used to determine the filter of official normality. A mentally ill individual may or may not accept a certain number of pathways to the most rational significations. This plane can refer us to other planes, but not automatically. From this point of view, it is interesting to understand the word transfer in the sense of transport,[3] in the particular meaning of transport as it was understood in the 18th century in the notion of amorous transport. A certain number of signifiers in a given society are transferred or blocked as significations, such that a singular individual cannot express him or herself in it, under particular historical conditions and in a certain context, save through an encounter with an institution such as, for example, a doctor. The problem of the individual may be to know how to arrive at being a subject under these conditions. What does he or she have to do to continue being a speaking subject and to speak effectively? A subject is not necessarily the individual or even *one* individual. It has to be unearthed at the heart of its alienation, reopening the potentiality of its history in the opaqueness of its situation. A mentally ill subject who comes to find us may be there, body and soul in front of you, but he or she may have remained the prisoner of a sheet in the supervisor's bag at the factory, or maybe we will find him or her by letting him or her wait at the bar of the club where other patients will welcome him or her much better than we could…

What does the unconscious subject reveal at that moment? A speech act, the manifestation, albeit minimal, of an event that will cause him or her to come to his or her senses. Under these conditions, the meetings, medicines, electroshocks, newspapers, Chinese Revolution, and jingles can all produce effects of meaning that are capable of decisive intervention as interpretations, in the broadest sense, in an institutional situation with a psychotherapeutic vocation. "If the psychic energies of the average mass of people watching a football game or a musical comedy could be diverted into the rational channels of a freedom movement, they would be invincible. This is the standpoint which guides the sex-economic investigation."[4] While psychoanalysts content themselves with a pitiful range of interpretations, the institution has the characteristic of being a potential analysand-subject that does not correspond to an individual. It does not become one automatically, however: more often than not, it remains a blind structure, active essentially on the level of alienation, with the subject only sent back to itself and the individual left in an impasse, the status quo.

Why institutional psychotherapy? It means that we want to get rid of doctors as the individuals, colleagues, citizens who offer to "speak for…," to be the "spokesperson" of the subject that the institution could be. This is not necessarily done knowingly. Aren't they the unconscious prisoners of this process just as much as its agent, with married life, culture, opinions, etc.? The question is whether they can become an element that is articulated in a relationship of truth with healthcare personnel and with all of those who engage with what is spoken there. This is the only way we can hope to restructure the different authorities, the different levels of psychoanalytic treatment, or institutional psychotherapy treatment. It is the precondition for the possibility of writing real institutional monographs.

If we do not start with the definition of the subject as an unconscious subject, or rather as a collective agent of utterance, we risk making the institution a thing, in the form of a *structure*, along with society as a whole. From there, we risk ending up with a false dichotomy between the institution as a sublimatory factor or a factor of alienation. This misconception of the function of the subject corresponds to a functioning in reverse, no matter the modernist intentions of a project for all of the articulations of the system and a paralysis of all of its utterances. Unavoidably, we would then have the *same roles*, maybe with more flexibility: doctor, nurse, patient, all of the internal hierarchies and other fantasy systems would be reinstated and codified in the same way. The same is true of traditional mythologies: a society with some stability always finds representatives of its Church to reinterpret the religion and reformulate it in terms of the new situation.

However, from the moment when we can shift and disrupt the totalizing character of an institution (of the state or a party), instead of turning in on itself like a structure, it can acquire subjective consistency and start making all sorts of changes and challenges. This was my intention in highlighting, and perhaps exaggerating, the differences between groups that are only something passive for themselves, subjugated groups, and those that propose to interpret their own position: group-subjects. Religious groups, political groups, or—why not?—institutions that would be psychiatric, analytical and political at the same time. But to avoid any confusion with a psychological or boy scout type conception, let me insist on the idea that a group cannot have analytical virtues in itself! Except for periods of religious fervor, there is on the contrary an entire, particular practice, a chemistry of the group and the institution which is necessary for producing "analytical effects." Do we need to repeat that this praxis could only be the result of a collective agent—the group itself—in its project to be a subject, not only for itself but for history!

4. A new direction for psychoanalysis

The way that psychiatrists reproduce what is understood as a symptom shows us how psychiatrists of an analytical culture always tend to seek references in personal history, and rearticulate this history in the form of imaginary historicity where each individual myth is connected to a larger reference myth. This larger myth finds its cohesion in a totalized and totalizing system. It is a reference to the great Other. All of the imaginary references that are made with individual histories, the various personal complexes and hitches are related to this fundamental mythical authority.

It is similar to the way in which a primitive society tries to explain everything that is happening in reference to a central myth, even if it means modifying it to take better charge of the totality of the manifestations to be interpreted. It corresponds to the simple desire that everything fit together, in particular in a given territorial area, in a given language and in function of a process of collective encoding that does not dispose of the same means as writing. Analytical interpretation, however, implies an exacerbation of this procedure, a sort of deranged Hegelianism: everything must enter into the idealist and reactionary framework of a closed society that does not think that social movement means that classes were made to disappear or be, detotalized, that ideologies were made to abolish each other or that there will never be an inherent guarantee of a moral order. It is unfortunate that Freudian ideology relied increasingly during its development on the most famous and most beautiful classical myths. Since contemporary myths were pitiful and degenerate, it was seen as necessary to bring back the myths of ancient society. It is not by chance that Greek myths had a leading role. No one can reproach Freud for it, because otherwise he would have had to invent others, which he did in *Totem and Taboo*. He took what was handy! In any case, no matter what, homogenous references had to be found that were convincing, reassuring and made people want to hold on to them.

It raises a fundamental philosophical problem: should the plane of reference of language be considered to be entirely articulated with the plane of being itself? Is there a biunivocal correspondence between being and language, such that the guarantee of stability of references is founded on being itself, such that one advances in analysis towards the anchoring points of an absolute being? It leads to Heidegger's philosophy, which turns elucidation towards a series of articulations that are called fundamental, like so many "cutting blows" to the possibilities of expression themselves. This regressive analysis of the so-called anchor points of language may be of some literary interest, but it remains saturated with a character of permanence, an eternity of reference and being. After all, this passion for poetic etymology does not have a limited clientele. In truth, original Freudian analysis never went in this direction. For Freud, the interpretation of a slip, for example, was not etymological. And it is hard to see why God Himself should be the prisoner of a passion for etymology!

The consequences of this attitude are that psychoanalysis, especially by the epigones, has the imperative of a double selection:

repressive and limiting in its myths, and corresponding to what it can handle, in other words, a certain category of neurotic patients and then only certain aspects of these neuroses, a limited number of mental illnesses and also precise social categories, a very limited cultural milieu. One can imagine that as psychoanalysis evolves, psychoanalysts will no longer be able to treat patients, only bureaucrats… One can also imagine that psychoanalysis will only be performed to psychoanalyze psychoanalysts; it would become an initiatory system, a society whose only function would be to produce another identical society, or a religious society enclosed on itself, a simple social delegation allowing people to meditate, as much as possible in complete silence and comfort. The comparison with the anchorites reaches its limits here. Grabbing psychoanalysts by the collar and putting them in an asylum is like putting a medieval priest in a factory, or a pool! They would both try to escape by exorcisms and excommunications. In some cases, it would work, it would draw attention, and then…

Practice remains; it pushes us to find something no matter what: what should one do when stuck in any situation? A factory, an asylum, or a patient, they stink… You have to look for something. The first item on the agenda is to open up to the complete alterity of the situation. If you claim to know where it leads in advance, you would be doing the same thing as the psychiatrists who doze in their chairs and are definitively disconnected…

A fundamental problem remains: what is the reference? When the unconscious is said to be "structured like a language," does that mean that belonging to this structure implies an aspect of impermeability, or permanence, that it is a tunic that tends to remain identical to itself or in permanent codependency with the other structures to which it is connected? All research, be it ethnological or living psychiatry, shows that representations, myths, everything that feeds the second scene, all of these characters are not necessarily the father, the mother, the grandmother, or the sacred monsters of the secondary era; they are also characters inhabiting the fundamental questions of society, in other words, the class struggle of our period. If there is a philosophical foundation of psychoanalysis, it implies that psychoanalysis is also the elucidation of the cultural and social stalemates in which we hold our debates. Supposing that we are still debating!

It is clear that certain neurotic impasses cannot be removed face to face with an analyst, if the latter does not understand elements that are external to the analytical situation. The most serious dimensions of neuroses, which psychoanalysts claim to reach, are in fact ones that they avoid for the good reason that they practically never see them in their office. There are interpretive elements that must be grasped in the mobile links of society. Crucial problems sizzle in the signifier at different levels and they are more important than the fact that one day, Greek society started to swing the other way with the Oedipus myth. It is also important to keep in mind, for example, that a giant Spaltung recently occurred in the communist world. It complicates all of our structures of reference: there is the paranoia of the Chinese, the paraphrenia of the Albanians, the perversion of the revisionists, etc. And this affects a lot of people in society! If a psychoanalyst turns a blind eye on everything of this order and claims that it does not enter the realm of analysis, it is impossible for him or her to access certain problems, not only certain political problems, but the unconscious axioms that are shared by people living in real society.

One must take a position on the question of being once the question has been raised. With madness, we are obliged to take a position on fundamental metaphysical and ethical questions: such as, what is the destiny of humankind? And what human? A real human being whose referential myths are not necessarily consistent with those found in current theology? There is a knot of problems prohibited by analytic research that it is impossible not to put back on the table...

Someone said earlier that the subject had to be put back in its place. The place of the subject, they repeat, is a hole... True, but a hole is nothing other than the nothing of the rest, and the rest counts for something! If something from the environment of the hole is poorly placed in the subject's head, it is enough for the subject to be radically decentered...

The little subject clinging to its mother, or the dazed schizophrenic who shows up, are entirely connected to this being. The subject is engaged with it and, paradoxically, it is only along the way that everything becomes blocked. This entire neurotic ball makes it so that at one point, even though it remains contingent on external determinations, there is no longer any possibility of reconnecting, of being articulated with anything that is not fantasy. The problem is to dig a few new holes *artificially* so that it can reconnect somewhere. Recourse to absolute alterity is something that, in principle, should allow it to remain connected to the foundation of all value. Yet is this absolute alterity a stone statue, the statue of the Commander, or something that does not come in one piece, something that is structured *like* a language—"in the manner of," nothing more—which is under the jurisdiction of a creationist god who has not yet been created, or, having been created, was lost the next day?

6

The Transference

J. Schotte[1] was right in highlighting the nature of signifying operations that allow us to identify transferential phenomena with those
of speech and language. This ought to help us clarify the question of
the transference outside of the strict field of psychoanalytic experience,
that is to say, of the transference as it manifests itself in the group or
institution. To the extent that we can regard the group as also "structured like a language"—to transpose one of Lacan's expressions
regarding the unconscious—the question can also be posed, perhaps,
as to how it speaks, and, above all, if it is even legitimate to consider
that it gives us access to speech. Can a group be the subject of its own
enunciation? If so, would this be by virtue of consciousness or the
unconscious? To whom does the group speak? Is the subjugated
group, alienated from the discourse of other groups, condemned to
remain prisoner of the non-meaning of its own discourse? Is there a
possible, even if only partial, way out for such a group that would
allow for it to step back a little from its own utterances and, in spite
of its subjugation, become both subject and object?

Under what sort of conditions could we hope to see a full speech
emerge from a field of empty speech—to borrow other expressions
from Lacan? Can we, for example, envisage in good faith and without betrayal that there may be "for all that something to do" in
situations as alienating as those to be found in psychiatric hospitals,
schools, and so forth? Or must we give up in sheer despair, and live

a politics where we resign ourselves to the worst possible outcome, and make social revolution the absolute precondition for any intervention in the local running of institutions by its "users"?

Or does the group and its non-meaning maintain a kind of secret dialogue—harbouring a potential alterity? In this way, could not the group be, even on the basis of its impotence, the carrier of an unconscious call that might render this alterity possible? Even if only to speak this impotence together as a group: "What does the unconscious [ça] think of all this around us?" "What good is it?" "What the hell are we doing there?" So, the subjugated group and the subject-group should not be regarded as being mutually exclusive. A formerly revolutionary contingent, that is now more or less subject to the dominant order, can still occupy, in the eyes of the masses, the empty place left by the subject of history, and may even, in certain circumstances become, despite itself, the subject of the enunciation of a revolutionary struggle, that is, the spokesperson of a discourse that is not its own, though it may mean betraying this discourse when the development of the relation of forces gives it the hope of a "return to normalcy." Thus, however subject it may be to socio-economic restraints, such a group will—as a transformation of context would reveal—unintentionally retain the possibility of a subjective cut. It is, therefore, not a question for us of conceiving the alienating and disalienating phenomena of the group as things-in-themselves, but rather as the varying sides—that would be differently expressed and developed depending on the context— of a similar institutional object.

On the side of the subjection of the group, we will need to decode those phenomena that encourage the group to withdraw into itself: leaderships, identifications, effects of suggestion, disavowals, scape-goating, and so forth. We will also need to decode anything that tends to promote local laws and idiosyncratic formations involving interdictions, rites, and anything else that tends to protect the group by buttressing it against signifying storms in which as the result of a specific operation of misrecognition—the threat is experienced as issuing from the outside. This has the effect of producing those deceitful outlooks peculiar to group delusions. This kind of group is thus involved in a perpetual struggle against any possible inscription of non-meaning: various roles are reified by a phallic appropriation along the model of the leader or of exclusion. One is part of such a group so as to collectively refuse to face up to the nothingness, that is, to the ultimate meaning of the projects in which we are engaged. This group is a kind of a syndicate or lobby of mutual defense against solitude, and of anything that might be classified as having a transcendental nature.

As concerns the other side, the subject-group does not employ the same means to secure itself. One is here threatened with being submerged in a flood of problems, tensions, internal battles, and risk of secession. This is so for the very reason of the opening of this group onto other groups. Dialogue—the intervention into other groups is an accepted aim of the subject-group—compels this group to have a certain clarity in relation to its finitude, that is, it brings into profile its distinct death, or its rupture. The calling of the Subject-group to speak tends to compromise the status and security of the group's members. There thus develops a kind of vertigo, or madness peculiar to this group. A kind of paranoid contraction is substituted for this calling to be subject: the group would like to be subject at any cost, including being in the place of the other, and in this way, it will fall into the worst alienation, the kind that is at the origin of all the compulsive and mortiferous mechanisms employed by religious, literary, and revolutionary coteries.

What might be the balancing factors of a group placed between these diverse sides of alienation; that is, between the external one of the subjugated-group, and that of the internal or borderline madness that is the project of the subject-group?

Our experience in hospitals might shed some light on this question. We know quite well that the "socialization" or reintegration of someone who is ill into a group does not simply depend on the good will of the therapists. In their attempts to reintegrate into a group or society, some of the ill in institutions encounter zones of tolerance, but also thresholds of absolute impossibility. We are here in the presence of a similar mechanism that is to be found in the rites of passage of primitive societies when initiating or welcoming into the culture a sub-group that has come of age. What happens if a person does not accept being marked by the group? If we force things to their limit, we arrive at one of two possibilities: either the group, or the recalcitrant individual, is shattered. Now, it is precisely in those groups that do not cultivate their symptoms by rituals—the subject-groups—that the risk of a face to face encounter with non-meaning is much greater, but, consequently, so is the possibility of a lifting of individual symptomatic impasses.

So long as the group remains an object for other groups and receives its non-meaning, that is, death, from the outside, one can always count on finding refuge in the group's structures of mis-recognition. But from the moment the group becomes a subject of its own destiny and assumes its own finitude and death, it is then that the data received by the superego is modified, and, consequently, the threshold of the castration complex, specific to a given social order, can be locally modified. Thus one belongs to such a group not so as to hide from desire and death, engaging in a collective process of neurotic obsession, but owing to a particular problem which is ultimately not eternal in nature, but transitory. This is what I have called the structure of "transversality."

Schotte emphasizes the fact that in the transference there is virtually never any actual dual relation. This is very important to note. The mother-child relationship, for example, is not a dual relation, at whatever level it is considered. At the moment that we envisage this relation in a real situation we recognize that it is, at the very least, triangular in character. In other words, there is always in a real situation a mediating object that acts as an ambiguous support or medium. For there to be displacement, transference, or language, there must also by necessity exist something there that can be cut or detached. Lacan strongly emphasized this feature of the object as decisive for making one's way through those questions concerning the transference and counter-transference.

One is displaced in the order of the transference only insofar as something can be displaced. Something that is neither the subject nor the object. There is no intersubjective relation, dual or otherwise, that would suffice to establish a system of expression, that is to say, a position of alterity. The face to face encounter with the other does not account for the opening onto the other, nor does it establish access to the other's understanding. The founder of metaphor is this something outside or adjacent to the subject that Lacan described under the heading of the *objet "a."*

But what about this *"a"*? One must not make of it a universal key of linguistic essence, an experiment of some new genre, or a new kind of tourism that would permit one to visit ancient Greece, for example, by effortless linguistic means. I am thinking here in particular of this perverse etymological practice brought into fashion by Heidegger. These kinds of imaginary retrospectives have basically nothing to do with Freud's genuine work on the signifier. I do not think that these etymological retrospectives are the carriers of some special message from the unconscious. In my opinion, whatever Freud borrowed, rightly or wrongly, from the realm of mythologies in order to translate his conceptual arrangements, should not be interpreted "imagingly" [*pied de l'image*]. It is the "literality" [*pied de la lettre*], in all its *artificiality*, indeed the combination which is the key to interpretation for Freud. This is clear in a book like *Jokes and their Relation to the Unconscious* wherein we see that the unconscious signifying chains in the term "joke" [*mot d'esprit*], for example, do not maintain any special relation with etymological laws. For the link can just as easily be made with a phoneme, an accentuation, syntactic play or semantic displacement. Unfortunately—and it is not by chance what was reified by Freud, and practically deified by his successors, were the mythical references that initially came to him somewhat arbitrarily in his attempt to chart out and locate the dramatization and impasses of the conjugal family. But let us not make a myth of myth! As references, the ancient myths dealing with the topic of Oedipus, for example, have nothing to do with the imaginary forces and symbolic articulations of the present conjugal family, nor with our system of social coordinates!

It is an illusion to think that there is something to read in the order of being, or of a lost world—or to think that recovering a mythical being, on this side of all historical origins, could be institutionalized as a psychoanalytic propaedeutic or maieutic. Considering the actual processes involved in the therapeutic cure or in setting up a therapeutic organization, reference to these kinds of mythico-linguistic reductions lead one nowhere except directly into the pitfalls of speculative frameworks. The important thing here is to get to the remarkable message, as well as to the object-carrier and founder of this message. But such an object would only derive its meaning on the basis of a similar retrospective illusion. We cannot hope to recover the specificity of the Freudian message unless we are able to disconnect it or sever it from its desire to return to the origins—a modern myth that established its diet for a full outpouring of sentiments beginning with Romanticism: the infinite quest for an impossible truth that supposedly lies beyond the manifest, in the heart of nature and the dark night of existence.

The remedy for this desire consists in orienting oneself in the direction of history, and the direction of the diachronic cut-out of the real and its provisional and partial attempts towards totalization—

what I would call the *bricolage* of history and social constructions. It is impossible to carry out such a reconfiguration if we do not as a precondition ask the question: where is the law? Is it behind us? Behind history? Does it fall short of our actual-situation, in which case it would lie outside our grasp? Or is it, perhaps, before us, within our reach, and potentially retrievable? As Bachelard says: nature must be pushed at least as far as our minds.[2] Who will ask this question? Certainly not the groupings and societies who establish their reason for being on ahistorical systems of religious and political legitimacy. The only groups to ask this question are the ones that accept from the start the precarious and transient nature of their existence: lucidly accept the situational and historical contingencies that confront them; accept an encounter with nothingness; and, finally, refuse to mystically reestablish and justify the existing order.

Today, a psychoanalyst would be content if his analysand overcame his anachronistic fixations; if he were able, for example, to get married, have children, reconcile himself to his biological contingencies, and integrate himself into the status quo. Regardless of the particular psychoanalytic curriculum, a reference to a predetermined model of normality remains implicit within its framework. The analyst, of course, does not in principle expect that this normalization is the product of a pure and simple identification of the analysand with the analyst, but it works no less, and even despite him (if only from the point of view of the continuity of the treatment, that is to say, often from the capacity of the analysand to continue to pay), as a process of identification of the analysand with a human profile that is compatible with the existing social order, and the acceptance [*assumation*] of his branding by the cogs of production and institutions. The analyst does not find this model ready-made in present society. His work is to create just that: to forge a new model in the place where his patient is lacking one. Moreover, and generally, this has to be his work, given that the modern bourgeois, capitalist society no longer has any satisfactory model at its disposal. It is in order to respond to this deficiency that psychoanalysis borrows its myths from earlier societies. It is thus that psychoanalysis proposes a model of drives and an ideal type of subjectivity and of familial relations that is at once new and composite; a kind of syncretism that encompasses elements of an archaic nature, and some that are quite modem. As far as the dominant social order is concerned, what is important is that the model be in a position to function in the present society. Such is the meaning of this requisite acceptance [*assumation*] of the castration complex—a kind of initiation substitution for modem societies—as the possible outcome of Oedipal impasses. This also accounts for the success and profitability of psychoanalysis.

For us the question is of a completely different kind. Our problem is to find out whether this recourse to alienating models can be limited, whether it is possible to establish the laws of subjectivity in places other than social constraint and the mystifying means of these mythical composite references. My question, therefore, is: can man become the founder of his own law?

Let us attempt afresh to resituate certain key concepts. If a totalizing god of values exists, every system of metaphoric expression will remain connected to the subjugated group by a kind of fantasmatic umbilical cord connecting it to this system of divine totalization. So as to not stretch this formulation, and in order to avoid, at whatever cost, falling into an idealist option, let us begin with the idea that we no longer need consider that such a totalizing system is to be sought at the level of *human ramification*, as if transmitted from sperm to sperm. While a *medium* of transmission certainly exists, this does not translate into it being an actual message. Spermatozoids, after all, do not speak! Also, from the point of view of meaning, this transmission eludes all the orders which are said to be "structured like a language." Taken as a system of reference, the order of human values is but an inch away from the systems of divine positionality. What is transmitted from the pregnant woman to her child? Quite a bit: nourishment and antibodies, for example. But not just these obvious things. For what is transmitted above all are the fundamental models of our industrial society. While there is still no speech here there is already a message. The message concerns industrial society; it is a specific message and differs according to the place one occupies within this order. We are here already in the signifier, though not yet in speech or in language. While the transmitted message has hardly anything to do with the structural laws of linguistics or etymology, it has a great deal to do with all those heterogeneous things that converge in the aforementioned idea of human ramification. Everything that concerns man in his relation to the most primitive demand is clearly marked by the signifier, but not necessarily by a signifier that partakes of a more or less universal linguistic essence.

All that attempts to speak in this way—though is not yet at the level of speech, but rather has to do with transference, transmission, or exchange—can be characterized as what can be cut, and as something that allows for the signifiers' play of articulation. If the objects of transmission, gestures, and glances result in rendering possible the nourishment of a child this is because, at all levels, these things have already been marked and have a direct effect on this system of signifying chains. What is the law of exchange at this level? It is impossible to avoid this question! It is played out and exposes itself anew at every turn. We are faced with a fundamental precariousness in the structure of exchange, as this signifier that is not "crystallized" like a language is clearly at the foundation of society and, in the final analysis, at the foundation of all the signifying systems, including linguistics.

If speech does not exist in the animal realm, this is because the system of transmission and of totalization of this order has until now been able to do without speech, which is not the case for the degenerate branch of humanity; this is so because the relations of speech, image, and the transference in man are tied to a fundamental deficiency which Lacan calls a "dehiscence at the heart of the organism"[3]—which, furthermore, constrains man to have recourse to various forms of social division of labor in order to survive. In the future, this survival will depend on the capacity of cybernetic machines to resolve humanity's problems. It will, therefore, be impossible to respond to the attack of a new virus without the intervention of continuously advancing computers.

If I evoke this myth of the machine, it is to highlight the absurdity of the situation. Is the computer in question God? Or perhaps it is God himself who predetermined these successive versions so that they would respond to all sons of more or less contingent problems such as, for example, the novel strategic calculations that would be required in a new cold war. After all, this myth illustrates better the impasses of present society than the staid references to the habitual imagery of familialism, regionalism, nationalism, which, moreover, suffer the disadvantage of serving to reinforce forms of social neurosis to the same extent that they are unable to respond to the goals they have set out for themselves. In fact, this traditional imagery would probably be incapable of sustaining its subjugating function were it not for the incessant work of misrecognition and the neurosis of civilization, forever condemning the subject to compulsively resort to degenerate forms of need—needs that are at once blind and without object, and addressed to a god that has become idiotic and evil.

— *Translated by John Canuma*

7

Reflections on Institutional Therapeutics and Problems of Mental Hygiene among Students

The study of mental health problems should be an integral part of anthropological research. However, the "mental thing" is generally considered to be the exclusive domain of a certain number of specialists; this "technicalization" coexists with pseudo-magical remnants that obliterate medical and paramedical functions and originate in the medieval period. (Examples: the orders of Doctors and Pharmacists, the "Hippocratic oath," the "vocation" of nurses, social assistants, etc.)

Psychiatry seems particularly affected by these archaisms due to the enormous weight of its hospital structures, the attitudes and social acts for which madness is the pretext, and the fact that scientific and technological problems have, up to the present, only marginally modified the privileged field of irrationality. Take, for example, the recent, spectacular development of chemotherapy in its psychiatric applications. Each month, new medicines are launched on the market, some of which provide vital means of therapeutic intervention. They must still be administered judiciously and in association with a range of other psychotherapeutic, ergotherapeutic, and institutional, etc., interventions. Unfortunately, this is not often the case! One reason is the disastrous situation of hospital infrastructures, which makes it impossible for doctors in psychiatric hospitals to fulfill their roles properly. But it is also due to a somewhat generalized attitude among practitioners who consider their role to be limited to investigations and prescriptions focused solely on the "ailing part" of the subject, without having to deal with other personal, familial or professional problems which a minimum of clarification reveals to be an essential condition of the success of any treatment. Along with these undeniable effects on treatment, the new medications have apparently served to reinforce mechanisms of misrecognition, avoidance, escape and rationalization towards the essential phenomena of mental disorders, and have therefore contributed to an even greater "thingification" of patients. Taken literally, the "thing" is observable in a number of services where overcoming agitation has been replaced by a generalized stupor under heavy doses of neuroleptics!

Equally marginal, on the opposite end of the spectrum, is the psychoanalytic technique that, while aiming sincerely for the heart of the problem, generally misses its mark in the domain of psychiatric practice due to an almost aristocratic, or initiatory, conception of the job of the analyst. At present, it is rare for hospitalized patients to benefit from psychoanalytic treatment. When enough analysts have been trained and accept to work full-time in hospital institutions, the question of the necessary modifications to the techniques and indications of psychoanalysis will be posed in order to adapt it to mental illnesses as they appear outside the walls of private consultation offices.

Society as a whole must be held responsible for what emerges from those places which offer a privileged chance to study moral and human values: prisons, concentration camps, barracks, psychiatric hospitals, etc. True anthropological research should propose the *recovery* of these regions, which are more or less "scotomized" from the social domain from a normative point of view, in order to reevaluate the meaning of society as creator of these "symptoms," with the aim of reaching concepts and practices that can modify the existing situation.

It would be absurd to try to determine the respective responsibilities of the different social groups involved in issues of mental hygiene. The medical profession, hospital staff, social organizations and users are all, in their own way, prisoners of the same knot of problems; the solution to them would have to come from society as a whole. At each stage in its development, society requires a particular mode of alienation corresponding to the various structures of the community: familial, academic, professional, hospital, etc. These general factors of alienation have the effect of distorting and masking the meaning of the most common individual dimensions of alienation in mental illness. Behind each "case," there is a human drama to decipher. Yet the instruments for this deciphering are to be found in the different levels of social alienation in which the subject sees him or herself "dispossessed" of his or her unique problem.

The idea of "preliminary neurosis" introduced by Couchner[1] seems to be an interesting starting point, but unfortunately it remains too general and does not allow us to measure its entire scope, which should lead, in our opinion, to a profound reworking of semiology and nosography, planes of reference and contemporary therapeutic practices. In this sense, we should consider that *analysis* cannot be limited to a specific domain: it must move through the entire field of humanity as a biological, social, historical, familial, imaginary, ethical, etc. reality.

How can we engage in reworking these ossified, invasive frontiers which are always ready to reappear and sterilize any new research: clear-cut alternatives, for example, between biology and psychology; neuroses and emotional disturbances; psychoses and neuroses; all of the preceding and psychosomatism; "treatment using neuroleptics alone" and other types, guaranteed "pure psychotherapy"; the various analytical psychotherapies and those of support, and then group therapies? How can these questions be articulated with the poorly explored world of readaptation, reclassification, recreation, etc.? How can we avoid having specialists lock themselves into their concepts and techniques like fortresses and send patients, for everything that escapes them, to other specialists without worrying much about whether they are within their "reach" or if they will be better able to respond to essential questions which are not in the province of any particular specialist as such but of a "true" subject? Doesn't this roundabout of specialists almost certainly risk "missing the subject"?

The search for group medicine, holding review meetings, etc. are a response to these concerns. Isn't there also the risk here of missing the point, and without leaving the patient with even the imaginary recourse of finding the "right specialist" somewhere else? Taking on a patient as a group is highly desirable in itself: but it still must come from a group-subject founded on concerted practices of analysis and research. It does not mean foregoing the possibility of having a specialist follow the treatment personally; on the contrary, it means that the therapist-patient relationship is articulated with a reference group that can recover everything that escapes this dual relationship.

Currently, the training of therapists is conducted on a strictly individual basis, which hardly predisposes them to future work in a team. At a certain stage, it would be essential to train therapeutic teams as teams. Instead of randomly nominating, doctors, directors or bursars with no common training to head hospital establishments, they should be under the direction of groups of technicians who have long experience studying the problems and who know each other from working together on various occasions during a number of practical training courses.

Grasping the entire interplay of problems of a mentally ill subject not only implies an exchange of information between therapists, but also an institutional environment, activities, an ambiance, etc., that are effectively under the responsibility of all of the caregiving personnel. In this way, the actions of the different persons involved would have the least chance of contradicting each other. At this price as well, the therapists themselves would have a greater assurance of not falling into the imaginary traps awaiting them, particularly in professions like these where it is normal to see the "person" be crystallized in the role of the modern mage, shaman, alchemist, etc.

For each of the therapeutic agents, accepting this involvement in, and potentially *contestation* of, his or her role and investigations, the means proposed and their efficacy, implies a radical questioning of traditional status. The existence of teamwork is already a privileged structure for receiving the mentally ill. The individuals modeled by our society are used to moving about in a field of categories that are mutually exclusive. When they "present" their troubles to people who combine therapies, without creating problems, based on the use of medicine, "logos," taking responsibility, work, play, study, etc., then a large step will have already been taken. This minimum amount of demythification of habitual categories is an important step for treatment that claims *not to miss the subject*.

In general, however, one must realize that technicians are active agents of transmission of these alienating modes of categorization. Some therapeutic practices are so valorized that they become references that tend to exclude the effects of any other mode of intervention. There is a quasi-religious hierarchy, with doctors and psychoanalysts at its summit, for example, while nurses, monitors, and social workers only "earn their salvation" to the extent that they receive some partial delegation of medical power. Nurses, instead of fulfilling their role authentically with patients, often consider themselves to be third-rate doctors, despite their privileged and often irreplaceable therapeutic power. Patients model their attitude on the attitude of their nurses, hoping to gain access to the "good word" that they may have the rare chance to receive from the "head" of the service. This master-slave dialectic does not move in only one direction: the "minorization" of nurses has repercussions on the nurse-patient relationship, with the latter becoming only an *object* of care. Correspondingly, nurses and patients tend to sterilize the role of doctors to the extent that an entire sector of the daily life of the institution escapes them completely.

What we are saying here about caregiving personnel is also true of all of the other workers of a hospital establishment, the cooks, drivers, attendants, etc. *Recovering* all of the staff of a care unit gives each one the possibility of playing an authentic human role with patients and to arrange the workplace, schedule, training, etc. to allow multiple contacts with them and provide them with the opportunity for shared activities. It represents an extraordinary opportunity to extend the therapeutic domain, which must, of course, be permanently studied and controlled by the caregiving group as a whole.

Social disparities among caregivers can never be completely eliminated, but it is essential for their pathogenic effects to be absorbed, in particular by systematically organizing a series of meetings and gatherings that would allow problems to be expressed that would otherwise disturb the purpose of the entire system. There is no institutional "formula" that should be considered primordial or recommendable; however, adopting an overall direction that aims to bring about an in-depth reworking of professional roles as they are commonly accepted, at least as they are experienced. A sustained effort is required from the caregiving team to overcome resistance from any direction. It is less a struggle than *group psychotherapy*.

We should insist on the fact that this process of analysis of the situation cannot be performed from the outside: it must be incorporated into the institution itself. Collective analysis may be led to use concepts developed elsewhere, for example in psycho-social research, but for the most part, it will have to succeed by its own means, through the different stages of its development, its accomplishments and even its failures, in building its own capacity to conceptualize, master and change situations.

When we say that there is a sort of overall key that "overdetermines" the processes of alienation in different social environments, it does not mean that we should expect each of them to be in a univocal relationship with a model that would allow us to account for it mechanically. This is what happens, for example, in a state-run hospital: the oversight committee, the administration, the doctors, etc. may be relatively homogeneous with the modalities of relationships that exist in the rest of industrial society, whereas at the level of the kitchen, cleaning, laundry and basement staff, the relationships are more feudal in type, to say nothing of the fate reserved for patients, which sometimes seems to come purely and simply from servitude.

We should note in passing that modifying the concrete conditions of existence and implementing means that are likely to facilitate the reworking of existing practices and social stratifications are not only urgent for hospitals of the old tradition: they are also required in many modern establishments. These establishments have been carefully designed in terms of comfort, but stricken from their inception by the social "diseases" that pollute the environment, ruin the atmosphere and, in a more "sterilized" context, sometimes appear even more inhuman. It may not be by chance that the first and most original of the transformations of traditional psychiatric hospitals took place in the most underdeveloped department in France: Lozère. There are parallels with the fact that new types of teacher-student relationships have been created and new types of scholastic activities have been inaugurated in small rural schools, while the few experiments of this type that have been attempted in "barracks schools" met with almost insurmountable "resistance."[2]

It is easy to imagine that problems of mental hygiene that depend on the public administration of the department of the

Seine, for example, are much more complex and present obstacles that are much more difficult to overcome than anywhere else. It is true that the importance of the stakes would justify making a special effort to try to change the current situation. Our society of Liberty, Equality and Fraternity does not, in appearance, lack good will, but it is stricken by an inability to apprehend concrete human realities in any other way than an enormous bureaucratic apparatus. Thus, since the Liberation, a certain number of ministerial circulars have proposed the generalization of different experiments in terms of ergotherapy, open services, sectorization, day hospitals, etc.

The results on the whole have been rather disappointing so far. Essential reforms cannot be instituted solely by means of administrative circulars: this is true in particular of setting up the therapeutic teams for which we indicated the necessity. Their existence depends, in the last resort, on the will of the interested parties to take charge of their creation, management and orientation. While it is true that the types of alienation that develop in doctor-nurse, doctor-patient, nurse-patient relationships are only variations of a privileged mode of alienation that exists on the level of society as a whole, it does not mean that we should passively wait for a revolutionary political transformation aimed at eliminating human exploitation of other humans in order to demystify these relationships. Changes are possible in every concrete situation: it is improbable that a therapeutic team can successfully complete its task if it does not have a precise awareness of the limits of its possibilities of intervention and of the relatively partial character of the questioning that it can hope to operate in the context of a given social situation. Unless you harbor illusions of reform, it would be impossible to expect, for example, that it would be easy to bring about conditions of labor that could radically eliminate the inherent taboos in hierarchized functions and to be able to set up a system where acceptance of reciprocal contestation would be the only rule capable of guaranteeing the emergence of truth in the fields of human sciences and techniques.

The impact of human exploitation of other humans on the imagination has received less attention than its purely economic aspects. Yet, here we have reached a nodal point where the perspective of social revolution could find an immense source of energy.

On several occasions, the social organisms put in place following victories by workers could have imposed very substantial structural changes to hospital institutions. This was the case, in particular, after the Liberation when, for a time, parties on the left benefitted from very significant liberty to adjust Social Security, investments in health and sanitary actions, conceptions and the methods to have them gain acceptance, etc. State power took this domain back under its authority with all the more ease that worker's organizations were unable to identify sufficiently clear objectives, which would have allowed the masses of users to take an informed stance. What could they have rallied persons insured under Social Security to fight for? What difference is there in their minds between what the State manages and what the various mutual associations, for example, propose?

Developing an overall perspective on these questions remains necessary, for they propose to modify existing institutions significantly while opening minds to even more radical solutions in the context of a revolutionary transformation of society.

The problems now facing the M.N.E.F.[3] deserve to be resituated in relationship to the lack of dissenting perspectives on a more global level. The problem of co-management is often raised by student representatives. It does not seem that the superficial character of issues related to management has been sufficiently clarified; these are in fact its administrative aspects. One could say, paradoxically, that the question in the domain that concerns us is the management not only of healthcare institutions, of the selection, training, and work methods of healthcare agents, but also of ill-ness itself or, if you will, its psychosocial envelope, to the extent that it can become a dominant factor, to the point of masking the true psychopathological problems of the individual "drama," as Politzer would say.

The student world is marked by *specific dimensions of alienation*. A youth, who may or may not be subject to mental disturbances, arriving at a university will see his or her personality reshaped in func-tion of the pathogenic traits of the entire environment. It is therefore not absurd to consider preventive action on this scale.

The situation of students implies a transitional mode of being, on the various levels of biological, psycho-sexual, social, intellectual, political, etc. maturation. The image of adult society obscures his or her entire intentional field. This image is experienced as external, alienating and desirable at the same time, to the extent that it underpins a series of economic values and prestige.

Once again, we find here the formalism of the *cut* in levels of reference that "measure" students based on the role that they will play when "they have finished." In the meantime, they are only embryos, poorly hatched, future "grand roles," in no way subjects "in their own right." Seen from this angle, problems of mental hygiene cannot be separated from problems of pedagogy and the necessary restructuring of current university practices. The entire current structure implies a constant crossing out of the young sub-ject's individual spontaneity, the emergence of his or her ways of cultural expression and their detours, which are sometimes difficult to understand for adults who have lost their understanding, but are often essential for the harmonious completion of his or her development. How can the mechanisms of passivity and meticu-lous blockage of a declared neurotic, his or her raptus of anxiety before exams, be absolutely separated from those that "normal" stu-dents experience and that they overcome, more or less successfully, by stereotypical behavior such as cramming, obsequiousness towards professors, or systematic opposition?

The fact that the university institution is organized in such a way that it has to respond to the needs of hierarchical promotion of private companies and public enterprises stifles the cultural and formative aspect that should be the essential part of their "apprenticeship." Students, who have to face the difficulties of their own development in the context of "interacting" with the most elaborate scientific, literary and philosophical problems of humanity, are in fact treated as extraneous, poor relatives of society. Whether they are "children of the wealthy" or not does not fundamentally change their status as "marginal."

This is all very general and relatively easy to explain. Yet these problems are embodied in an original way in each particular case, calling on therapists to interpret and understand them. These therapists also need to have some connection to the realities of the student environment. They must be cognizant of and concerned by this aspect of things, as it is certainly at least as important as the other personal and biological dimensions that can influence the state of a patient. Student organizations should have, in their own way, a "therapeutic vocation," in the sense that they have to recognize and assume responsibility, as much as possible, for the aspects of alienation in the environment they represent. Mental hygiene among students means organizing dispensaries, BAPU[4] and health clinics as well as GTU[5] and clubs, dormitories and activities in university lodgings, etc.

The organizational structures of the student movement are far from perfect, but in comparison with the sclerosis that generally reigns everywhere else, they represent a far from negligible advantage. It would not be too much to think that their capacity for human training, in the sense of accepting reciprocal contestation, is far greater than those in other areas, such as medicine and psychoanalysis, for example. The existing relationships between the student movement and the various technicians who are brought in to deal with the mental hygiene of students should be renegotiated with this in mind. This does not mean asking doctors, psychoanalysts or social workers, etc. to become militants in the student movement! Nor does it mean that militants should be giving lessons to therapists! It means putting in place organizations that are able to take advantage of the capacity for social interrelationships that are developed in the fields of student militant action in order to facilitate the development of therapeutic teams.

The doctors and nurses who took it on themselves to transform some psychiatric hospitals after the Liberation had lived through "initiatory" experiences with the Scouts, in youth hostels, with the Communist Youth, etc. or in Nazi concentration camps, where the problems of structuring, organizing and defending the environment were vital. By continuing these few initiatives, the face of psychiatry in France was profoundly changed. A similar change could come from the student movement, given the progressive role it has played in recent times, in particular during the Algerian War. It is not inconceivable that the student movement could train a certain number of young therapists who could take up the torch from those, we hope, who will be the pioneers of a new experiment and not the elements of resistance by an old system. The seeds of this establishment of therapeutic teams already exist in several places, and it would be interesting to follow and study their experiments step by step.

There is no need to develop any further here the obvious fact that the current campaign by UNEF in favor of modifying the structures of the University shares the same perspective in terms of mental hygiene. To some extent, these two perspectives rely on each other. We should focus instead on an aspect that is harder to expose, given the lack of sufficient examples at present: patients taking charge of their own illness, with the support of the entire student environment. Each care unit should have a corresponding "club" of ill and convalescing students in which students who are interested in questions of psychopathology could participate (students in medicine, psychology, psycho-sociology, philosophy, etc.). These clubs would provide students a level of socialization that would allow them to maintain their relationship with the university environment, their field of studies, and different activities for training, discussion, hobbies, etc. This structure would have to be closely associated with the care units themselves. Experiments of this type have already been carried out in other areas and have shown positive results.

The problem could also be approached from another level. In parallel to this system, and in the context of what we defined earlier as the preventive aim of student organizations, social structures could exist, at the level of general associations or on a smaller scale, that would allow students to meet up and ask for the help of their peers in clarifying, if not resolving, their problems, without waiting to reach a point, for some, where they have no other choice but to go to care institutions that, in the current state of affairs, may very well be unable to meet their needs. It is up to the student movement to take this question into consideration; however, it is not a question that should be ignored. We all know how confusing it is for students who arrive in the Kafkaesque world of the University. We know how hard it is for them to overcome all kinds of difficulties and inhibitions on their own.

The existence of University Working Groups should provide a response to one aspect of this problem. But are they enough? Isn't their focus too limited to problems of university work? Shouldn't they be changed in order to respond to a wider variety of needs? Perhaps it is better for them to remain what they are and to promote parallel organizations that could respond to other needs, ones that should be recorded and studied along with the solutions that are offered. It would be interesting to renew the analysis of the individual "ersatz" to which students turn: obsession with work, idle and guilty wandering, the role of café terraces, etc.

The systematic installation of different facilities, for example, would clearly require significant financial investment. It should therefore be formulated as a demand coming from the entire movement. Alongside the struggle to obtain the necessary credits, a series of intermediate objectives could be determined that would have immediate and significant repercussions on mental hygiene.

Some may object that this orientation carries the risk of bringing the student movement back to a corporate perspective. It would be true if these structures were not closely linked to the deeper implantation of a real student union movement. There is no vaccine to prevent "reformism" from occurring in spite of everything. The State is always ready to lay claim to and *recuperate* the most valid conquests; take, for example, Social Security, corporate committees, youth centers, sliding wage scales, youth hostels, etc. Tomorrow, the same may be true of the GTU or student wages. It is nonetheless possible to imagine how the existence of such "facilities," which would offer a large number of students the possibility to meet, work, debate, relax, could contribute to strengthening the student movement. Yet it depends, essentially, on the revolutionary dynamism of the movement, its real implantation and the relationships of the forces present.

Let's take it even further. Isn't it possible to think that this structuring of the milieu, carried out on a large scale, would allow students to get out of their "ghetto"? On the one hand, they would be led to debate a series of problems that would not be in their university curriculum anytime soon and, on the other, they would give themselves the means to enter into relationships with many sectors of society from which they are separated, for example by inviting researchers, technicians, union representatives and political representatives from different areas and inclinations, writers, artists, etc. The organization of collective surveys like those that have been perfected by technicians of active methods in schools could be envisioned, as well as meetings between students and workers from diverse companies. I have no doubt that the first result of such a survey would be to highlight the desire of many young workers to enter into closer ties with students.

The principle necessity of a struggle against the social segregation maintained between young workers and students will be easily recognized by student leaders, but the difficulty will come in terms of the means to engage in this struggle. A series of possibilities exists, however, and partial experiments could be started now. While the student movement would bring concrete testimony of its rejection of the situation provided to young workers, and in so doing would modify it to some extent, students, for their part, would have much to gain from this type of association. This approach also seems to be coherent with the demand for an allocation for studies that would position students as workers in training. Professional training, as it is now set up for young workers, implies an almost complete impossibility of expanding their cultural understanding. Here again, the results merit close examination. Luckily, we have not quite reached this point with students, despite the pretensions of industrial and technocratic groups of all types that have been trying to shape the University entirely in their own image.

This mode of alienation can be found to exist at other levels. Industrial society blindly imposes it on individual subjects who have no other choice but to rely on the existing state of things in production, institutions, the University, etc. or to run away and be more or less damaged by the feedback effects of the refusal or impossibility of being "integrated." It is a phenomenon that calls into question all social aims, at every level, and first of all those of the state. We are in the presence of certain unconscious laws that regulate the relationships between subjects and social structures, depending on the objectives inherent in production, within the framework of a system based on profit and state power dominated by a class that has long stopped playing a progressive role in the evolution of history.

The emergence of a social structure that would deliberately tend to assume its purpose as the response to the real needs of human subjects is the only way that lasting solutions could be provided that would be in the interest of no social group to question. Once again, only on the condition of being situated in a revolutionary perspective and in relation to an effective practice of class struggle can the "reforms" I have suggested here take on their full value: awareness of their precariousness is even a guarantee that they will be taken as a further stage in the struggle instead of a palliative to the "good conscience" of the established order.

8

Transversality

Institutional therapeutics is a delicate infant. Its development needs close watching, and it tends to keep very bad company. In fact, the threat to its life comes not from any congenital debility, but from the factions of all kinds that are lying in wait to rob it of its specific object. Psychologists, psychosociologists, even psychoanalysts, are ready to take over bits of it that they claim to be their province, while voracious governments look for their chance to "incorporate" it in their official texts. How many of the hopeful offspring of avant-garde psychiatry have been thus kidnapped early in life since the end of the last war—ergo-therapy, social therapy, community psychiatry and so on.

Let me begin by saying that institutional therapeutics *has* got an object, and that it must be defended against everyone who wants to make it deviate from it; it must not let itself become divorced from the reality of the social problematic. This demands both a new awareness at the widest possible social level—for instance the national approach to mental health in France—and a definite theoretical stance in relation to existing therapeutics at the most technical levels. In a sense it may be said that the absence of any common approach in the present-day psychiatric movement reflects the segregation that persists in various forms between the world of the mad and the rest of society. Psychiatrists who run mental institutions suffer from a disjunction between their concern for those in their care and more general social problems that shows itself in various ways: a systematic failure to understand what is going on outside the hospital walls, a tendency to psychologize social problems, certain blind spots about work and aims *inside* the institution and soon. Yet the problem of the effect of the social signifier on the individual faces us at every moment and at every level, and in the context of institutional therapeutics one cannot help coming up against it all the time. The social relationship is not something apart from individual and family problems; on the contrary: we are forced to recognize it in every case of psychopathology, and in my view it is even more important when one is dealing with those psychotic syndromes that present the most "desocialized" appearance.

Freud, whose work mainly developed around the problem of the neuroses, was well aware of this problem, as we can see, for instance, from the following:

> If we dwell on these situations of danger for a moment, we can say that in fact a particular determinant of anxiety (that is, situation of danger) is allotted to every age of development as being appropriate to it. The danger of psychical helplessness fits the stage of the ego's early immaturity; the danger of loss of an object (or loss of love) fits the lack of self-sufficiency in the first years of childhood; the danger of being castrated fits the phallic phase; and finally fear of the super-ego, which assumes a special position, fits the period of latency. In the course of development the old determinants of anxiety should be dropped, since the situations of danger corresponding to them have lost their importance owing to the strengthening of the ego. But this only occurs most incompletely. Many people are unable to surmount the fear of loss of love; they never become sufficiently independent of other people's love and in this respect carry on their behavior as infants.

Fear of the super-ego should normally never cease, since, in the form of moral anxiety, it is indispensable in social relations, and only in the rarest eases can an individual become independent of human society. A few of the old situations of danger, too, succeed in surviving into later periods by making contemporary modifications in their determinants of anxiety.[1]

What is the obstacle that the "old determinants of anxiety" come up against and that prevent their altogether disappearing? Whence this persistence, this survival of neurotic anxieties once the situations that produced them are past, and in the absence of any "situation of danger"? A few pages earlier, Freud reaffirms that anxiety precedes repression: the anxiety is caused by an external danger, it is *real*; but that external danger is actually evoked and determined by the instinctual internal danger: "It is true that the boy felt anxiety in the face of a demand by his libido—in this instance anxiety at being in love with his mother."[2] Thus it is the internal danger that lays the ground for the external. In terms of reality, the renunciation of the beloved object correlates with the acceptance of the loss of the member, but the "castration complex" itself cannot be got rid of by such a renunciation. For in effect it implies the introduction of an additional term in the situational triangulation of the Oedipus complex, so that there can be no end to the threat of castration which will continually reactivate what Freud calls the "unconscious need for punishment."[3] Castration and punishment, whose position had remained precarious because of the "principle of ambivalence" governing the choice of the various part objects, are thus irreversibly caught up in the working of the social signifiers. Henceforth, the authority of this *social reality* will base its survival on the establishment of an irrational morality in which punishment will be justified simply by a law of blind repetition, since it cannot be explained by any ethical legality. It is not therefore any use trying to recognize this persistence of anxiety beyond actual "situations of danger" through some impossible dialogue between the ego ideal and the super-ego; what it in fact means is that those "situations of danger" belong to the specific "signifying logic" of this particular social framework, which will have to be analysed with the same maieutic rigour as is brought to bear in the psychoanalysis of the individual.

The persistence is really a repetition, the expression of a death instinct. By seeing it merely as a continuity, we miss the question implied in it. It seems natural to prolong the resolution of the Oedipus complex into a "successful" integration into society. But surely it would be more to the point to see that the way anxiety persists must be linked with the dependence of the individual on the collectivity described by Freud. The fact is that, barring some total change in the social order, the castration complex can never be satisfactorily resolved, since contemporary society persists in giving it an unconscious function of social regulation. There becomes a more and more pronounced incompatibility between the function of the father, as the basis of a possible solution for the individual of the problems of identification inherent in the structure of the conjugal family, and the demands of industrial societies, in which an integrating model of the father/king/god pattern tends to lose any effectiveness outside the sphere of mystification. This is especially evident in phases of social regression, as for instance when fascist, dictatorial regimes or regimes of personal, presidential power give rise to imaginary phenomena of collective pseudo-phallicization that end in a ridiculous totemization by popular vote of a leader: the leader actually remains essentially without any real control over the signifying machine of the economic system, which still continues to reinforce the power and autonomy of its functioning. The Kennedys and Khrushchevs who tried to evade this law were "sacrificed"—though by different rituals—the one on the altar of the oil companies, the others on that of the barons of heavy industry.

The real subjectivity in modern States, the real powers of decision—whatever the old-fashioned dreams of the bearers of "national legitimacy" cannot be identified with any individual or with the existence of any small group of enlightened leaders. It is still unconscious and blind, and there is no hope that any modern Oedipus will guide its steps. The solution certainly does not lie in summoning up or trying to rehabilitate ancestral forms, precisely because the Freudian experience has taught us to see the problem of, on the one hand, the persistence of anxiety beyond changes in the situation that produced it, and on the other, the limits that can be assigned to this process. This is where institutional therapeutics comes in: its object is to try to change the data accepted by the super-ego into a new kind of acceptance of "initiative," rendering pointless the blind social demand for a particular kind of castrating procedure to the exclusion of anything else.

What I am now proposing is only a temporary measure. There are a certain number of formulations that I have found useful to mark different stages in an institutional experiment. I think it sensible to set out a kind of grid of correspondence between the meandering of meanings and ideas among psychotics, especially schizophrenics, and the mechanisms of growing discordance being set up at all levels of industrial society in its neo-capitalist and bureaucratic socialist phase whereby the individual tends to have to identify with an ideal of consuming-machines-consuming-producing-machines. The silence of the catatonic is perhaps a pioneering interpretation of that ideal. If the group is going to structure itself in terms of a rejection of the spoken word, what response is there apart from silence? How can an area of that society be altered so as to make even a small dent in the process of reducing the spoken word to a written system? We must, I think, distinguish between groups of two kinds. One must be extremely wary of formal descriptions of groups that define them apart from what they are aiming to do. The groups we are dealing with in institutional therapeutics are involved in a definite activity, and are totally different from those usually involved in what is known as research into group dynamics. They are attached to an institution, and in some sense or other they have a perspective, a viewpoint on the world, a job to do.

This first distinction, though it may prove difficult to sustain as we go further, can be summarized as being one between independent groups and dependent groups. The subject group, or group with a "vocation," endeavors to control its own behavior and elucidate its object, and in this case can produce its own tools of elucidation. Schotte[4] could say of this type of group that it hears and is heard, and that it can therefore work out its own system of hierarchizing structures and so become open to a world beyond its own immediate interests. The dependent group is not capable of getting things into this sort of perspective; the way it hierarchizes structures is subject to its adaptation to other groups. One can say of the subject group that it makes a statement—whereas of the dependent group only that "its cause is heard," but no one knows where or by whom, or when.

This distinction is not absolute; it is simply a first attempt to index the kind of group we are dealing with. In fact it operates like two poles of reference, since every group, but especially every subject group, tends to oscillate between two positions: that of a subjectivity whose work is to speak, and a subjectivity which is lost to view in the otherness of society. This reference provides us with a safeguard against falling into the formalism of role analysis; it also leads us to consider the problem of the part played by the individual in the group as a being with the power of speech, and thus to re-examine the usual mechanism of psycho-sociological and structuralist descriptions. It is also, undoubtedly, a way of getting back to the theories of bureaucracy, self-management, "training groups" and so on, which regularly fail in their object because of their scientistic refusal to involve meaning and content.

I think it convenient further to distinguish, in groups, between the "manifest content"—that is, what is said and done, the attitudes of the different members, the schisms, the appearance of leaders, of aspiring leaders, scapegoats and so on—and the "latent content," which can be discovered only by interpreting the various escapes of meaning in the order of phenomena. We may define this latent content as "group desire": it must be articulated with the group's specific form of love and death instincts.

Freud said that in serious neuroses there was a dislocation of the fundamental instincts; the problem facing the analyst was to reintegrate them in such a way as to dispel, say, the symptoms of sado-masochism. To undertake such an operation, the very structure of institutions whose only existence as a body is imaginary requires the setting-up of institutional means for the purpose—though it must not be forgotten that these cannot claim to be more than symbolic mediations tending by their very nature to be broken down into some kind of meaning. It is not the same as what happens in the psychoanalytic transference. The phenomena of imaginary possession are not grasped and articulated on the basis of an analyst's interpretation. The group phantasy is essentially symbolic, whatever imagery may be drawn along by it. Its inertia is regulated only by an endless return to the same insoluble problems. Experience of institutional therapeutics makes it clear that individual phantasizing never respects the particular nature of this symbolic plane of group phantasy. On the contrary, it tries to absorb it, and to overlay it with particular imaginings that are "naturally" to be found in the various roles that could be structured by using the signifiers circulated by the collective. This "imaginary incarnation" of some of the signifying articulations of the group—on the pretext of organization, efficiency, prestige, or, equally, of incapacity, non-qualification, etc.—crystallizes the structure as a whole, hinders its possibilities for change, determines its features and its "mass," and restricts to the utmost its possibilities for dialogue with anything that might tend to bring its "rules of the game" into question: in short, it produces all the conditions for degenerating into what we have called a dependent group.

The unconscious desire of a group, for instance the "pilot" group in a traditional hospital, as expression of a death instinct, will probably not be such as can be stated in words, and will produce a whole range of symptoms. Though those symptoms may in a sense be "articulated like a language" and describable in a structural context, to the extent that they tend to disguise the institution as subject they will never succeed in expressing themselves otherwise than in incoherent terms from which one will still be left to decipher the object (totem and taboo) erected at the very point at which the emergence of real speech in the group becomes an impossibility. The bringing to light of this point, at which desire is reduced to showing only the tip of a (false) nose, cannot give access to desire itself since that will remain, as such, unconscious as the neurotic intends, refusing completely to let itself be demolished by exhaustive explanations. But clearing a space, keeping room for a first plane of reference for this group desire to be identified, will immediately place the whole statement of the problem beyond chance relationships, will throw an entirely new light on "problems of organization," and to that extent obscure attempts at formal and apparently rational description. In other words, it is the trial run for any attempt at group analysis.

In such an attempt, a fundamental distinction will emerge from the very beginning between curing the alienation of the group and analyzing it. The function of a group analysis is not the same as that of setting up a community with a more or less psycho-sociological orientation, or group-engineering. Let me repeat: group analysis is both more and less than role-adaptation, transmitting information and so on. The key questions have been asked before likes and dislikes have hardened, before sub-groups have formed, at the level from which the group's potential creativity springs—though generally all creativity is strangled at birth by its complete rejection of nonsense, the group preferring to spend its time mouthing clichés about its "terms of reference," and thus closing off the possibility of ever saying anything real, that is, anything that could have any connection with other strands of human discourse, historical, scientific, aesthetic or whatever.

Take the case of a political group "condemned by history": what sort of desire could it live by other than one forever turning in upon itself? It will have incessantly to be producing mechanisms of defence, of denial, of repression, group phantasies, myths, dogmas and so on. Analysis of these can only lead to discovering that they express the nature of the group's death wish in its relation to the buried and emasculated historic instincts of enslaved masses, classes or nationalities. It seems to me that this last aspect of the "highest level" of analysis cannot be separated from the other psychoanalytic problems of the group, or indeed of individuals.

In the traditional psychiatric hospital, for example, there is a dominant group consisting of the director, the financial administrator, the doctors and their wives, etc., who form a solid structure that blocks any expression of the desire of the groups of human beings of which the institution is composed. What happens to that desire? One looks first at the symptoms to be seen at the level of various sub-groups, which carry the classic social blemishes, being set in their ways, disturbance, all forms of divisiveness, but also at other signs—alcoholism among one lot of nurses perhaps, or the generally unintelligent behavior of another (for it is quite true, as Lacan points out, that stupidity is another way of expressing violent emotion). It is surely a kind of respect for the mystery embodied in neuroses and psychoses that makes those attendants in our modern graveyard degrade themselves and thus pay negative homage to the message of those whom the entire organization of our society is geared to disregarding. Not everyone can afford, like some psychiatrists, to take refuge in the higher reaches of aestheticism and thus indicate that, as far as they are concerned, it is not life's major questions that they are dealing with in their hospital work.

Group analysis will not make it its aim to elucidate a static truth underlying this symptomatology, but rather to create the conditions favorable to a particular mode of *interpretation*, identical, following Schotte's view, to a transference. Transference and interpretation represent a symbolic mode of intervention, but we must remember that they are not something done by an individual or group that adopts the role of "analyst" for the purpose. The interpretation may well be given by the idiot of the ward if he is able to make his voice heard at the right time, the time when a particular signifier becomes active at the level of the structure as a whole, for instance in organizing a game of hop-scotch. One has to meet interpretation half-way. One must therefore rid oneself of all preconceptions—psychological, sociological, pedagogical or even therapeutic. In as much as the psychiatrist or nurse wields a certain amount of power, he or she must be considered responsible for destroying the possibilities of expression of the institution's unconscious subjectivity. A fixed transference, a rigid mechanism, like the relationship of nurses and patients with the doctor, an obligatory, predetermined, "territorialized" transference onto a particular role or stereotype, is worse than a resistance to analysis: it is a way of interiorizing bourgeois repression by the repetitive, archaic and artificial re-emergence of the phenomena of caste, with all the spellbinding and reactionary group phantasies they bring in their train.

As a temporary support set up to preserve, at least for a time, the object of our practice, I propose to replace the ambiguous idea of the institutional transference with a new concept: *transversality* in the group. The idea of transversality is opposed to:

(a) verticality, as described in the organogramme of a pyramidal structure (leaders, assistants, etc.);

(b) horizontality, as it exists in the disturbed wards of a hospital, or, even more, in the senile wards; in other words a state of affairs in which things and people fit in as best they can with the situation in which they find themselves.

Think of a field with a fence around it in which there are horses with adjustable blinkers: the adjustment of their blinkers is the "coefficient of transversality." If they are so adjusted as to make the horses totally blind, then presumably a certain traumatic form of encounter will take place. Gradually, as the flaps are opened, one can envisage them moving about more easily. Let us try to imagine how people relate to one another in terms of affectivity. According to Schopenhauer's famous parable of the porcupines, no one can stand being too close to his fellow-men:

> One freezing winter day, a herd of porcupines huddled together to protect themselves against the cold by their combined warmth. But their spines pricked each other so painfully that they soon drew apart again. Since the cold continued, however, they had to draw together once more, and once more they found the pricking painful. This alternate moving together and apart went on until they discovered just the right distance to preserve them from both evils.[5]

In a hospital, the "coefficient of transversality" is the degree of blindness of each of the people present. However, I would suggest that the official adjusting of all the blinkers, and the overt communication that results from it, depends almost automatically on what happens at the level of the medical superintendent, the nursing superintendent, the financial administrator and so on. Hence all movement is from the summit to the base. There may, of course, be some "pressure from the base," but it never usually manages to make any change in the overall structure of blindness. Any modification must be in terms of a structural redefinition of each person's role, and a reorientation of the whole institution. So long as people remain fixated on themselves, they never see anything *but* themselves.

Transversality is a dimension that tries to overcome both the impasse of pure verticality and that of mere horizontality: it tends to be achieved when there is maximum communication among different levels and, above all, in different meanings. It is this that an independent group is working towards. My hypothesis is this: it is possible to change the various coefficients of unconscious transversality at the various levels of an institution. For example, the overt communication that takes place within the circle consisting of the medical superintendent and the house-doctors may remain on an extremely formal level, and it may appear that its coefficient of transversality is very low. On the other hand the latent and repressed coefficient existing at department level may be found to be much higher: the nurses have more genuine relationships among themselves, in virtue of which the patients can make transferences that have a therapeutic effect. Now—and remember this is still hypothetical—the multiple coefficients of transversality, though of differing intensity, remain homogeneous. In fact, the level of transversality existing in the group that has the real power unconsciously determines how the extensive possibilities of other levels of transversality are regulated. Suppose—though it would be unusual—there were a strong coefficient of transversality among the house-doctors: since they generally have no real power in the running of the institution, that strong coefficient would remain latent, and would be felt only in a very small area. If I may be permitted to apply an analogy from thermodynamics to a sphere in which matters are determined by social lines of force, I would say that the excessive institutional entropy of this state of transversality results in the absorption of any inclination to lessen it. But do not forget that the fact that we are convinced that one or several groups hold the key to regulating the latent transversality of the institution as a whole does not mean that we can identify the group or groups concerned. They are not necessarily the same as the official authorities of the establishment who control only its official expression. It is essential to distinguish the real power from the manifest power. The real relationship of forces has to be analysed. Everyone knows that the law of the State is not made by the ministries; similarly, in a psychiatric hospital, *de facto* power may elude the official representatives of the law and be shared among various sub-groups—the ward, the specialist department, even the hospital social club or the staff association. It seems eminently desirable that the doctors and nurses who are supposed to be responsible for caring for the patients should secure collective control over the management of those things beyond rules and regulations that determine the atmosphere, the relationships, everything that really makes the institution tick. But you cannot achieve this merely by declaring a reform; the best intentions in the world are no guarantee of actually getting to this dimension of transversality.

If the declared intention of the doctors and nurses is to have an effect beyond merely that of a disclaimer, their entire selves as desiring beings must be involved and brought into question by the signifying structure they face. This could lead to a decisive re-examination of a whole series of supposedly established truths: why does the State withhold grants? Why does Social Security persistently refuse to recognize group therapy? Though essentially liberal, surely medicine is reactionary when it comes to matters of classification and hierarchy—as indeed are our trade-union federations, though they are in theory more to the left. In an institution, the effective, that is unconscious, source of power, the holder of the real power, is neither permanent nor obvious. It has to be flushed out, so to say, by an analytic search that at times involves huge detours by way of the crucial problems of our time.

If the analysis of an institution consists in endeavoring to make it aware that it should gain control of what is being said, any possibility of creative intervention will depend on its initiators being able to exist at the point where "it should have been able to speak" so as to be imprinted by the signifier of the group—in other words to accept a form of castration. This wound, this barrier, this obliteration of their powers of imagination leads back, of course, to an analysis of the objects discovered by Freudianism to underlie any possible assumption of the symbolic order by the subject: breast, feces, penis and so on, all of which are—at least in phantasy—detachable; but it also leads back to an analysis of the role of all the transitional objects[6] related to the washing machine, the television, in short all that makes life worth living today. Furthermore, the sum of all these part objects, starting with the picture of the body as the basis for self-identification, is itself thrown daily onto the market as fodder, alongside the hidden Stock Exchange that deals with shares in pseudo-eroticism, aestheticism, sport and all the rest. Industrial society thus secures unconscious control of our fate by its need—satisfying from the point of view of the death instinct—to disjoint every consumer/producer in such a way that ultimately humanity would find itself becoming a great fragmented body held together only as the supreme God of the Economy shall decree. It is, then, pointless to force a social symptom to fit into "the order of things," for that is in the last resort its only basis; it would be like taking an obsessional who washes his hands a hundred times a day and shutting him up in a room without a sink—he would displace his symptomatology onto panic and unbearable attacks of anxiety.

Only if there is a certain degree of transversality will it be possible—though only for a time, since all this is subject to continual re-thinking—to set going an analytic process giving individuals a real hope of using the group as a mirror. When that happens, the individual will manifest both the group and himself. If the group he joins acts as a signifying chain, he will be revealed to himself as he is beyond his imaginary and neurotic dilemmas. If, on the other hand, he happens to join a group that is profoundly alienated, caught up in its own distorted imagery, the neurotic will have his narcissism reinforced beyond his wildest hopes, while the psychotic can continue silently devoting himself to his sublime universal passions. The alternative to an intervention of the group-analytic kind is the possibility that an individual would join the group as both listener and speaker, and thus gain access to the group's inwardness and interpret it.

If a certain degree of transversality becomes solidly established in an institution, a new kind of dialogue can begin in the group: the delusions and all the other unconscious manifestations which have hitherto kept the patient in a kind of solitary confinement can achieve a collective mode of expression. The modification of the super-ego that I spoke of earlier occurs at the moment when a particular model of language is ready to emerge where social structures have been hitherto functioning only as a ritual. To consider the possibility of therapists intervening in such a process is to pose the problem of an analytic control which would, in turn, presuppose to some extent a radical transformation in the present psychoanalytic movement-which has certainly not up to now been much interested in re-centering its activity on real patients where they actually are, that is, for the most part, in the sphere of hospital and community psychiatry.

The social status of medical superintendent is the basis of a phantasy alienation, setting him up as a distant personage. How could such a person be persuaded even to accept, let alone be eager, to have his every move questioned, without retreating in panic? The doctor who abandons his phantasy status in order to place his role on a symbolic plane is, on the other hand, well placed to effect the necessary splitting-up of the medical function into a number of different responsibilities involving various kinds of groups and individuals. The object of that function moves away from "totemization" and is transferred to different kinds of institutions, extensions and delegations of power. The very fact that the doctor could adopt such a splitting-up would thus represent the first phase of setting up a structure of transversality. His role, now "articulated like a language," would be involved with the sum of the group's phantasies and signifiers. Rather than each individual acting out the comedy of life for his own and other people's benefit in line with the reification of the group, transversality appears inevitably to demand the imprinting of each role. Once firmly established by a group wielding a significant share of legal and *real* power, this principle of questioning and re-defining roles is very likely, if applied in an analytic context, to have repercussions at every other level as well. Such a modification of ego ideals also modifies the introjections of the super-ego, and makes it possible to set in motion a type of castration complex related to different social demands from those patients previously experienced in their familial, professional and other relationships. To accept being "put on trial," being verbally laid bare by others, a certain type of reciprocal challenge, and humor, the abolition of hierarchical privilege and so on—all this will tend to create a new group law whose "initiating" effects will bring to light, or at least into the half-light, a number of signs that actualize transcendental aspects of madness hitherto repressed. Phantasies of death, or of bodily destruction, so important in psychoses, can be re-experienced in the warm atmosphere of a group, even though one might have thought their fate was essentially to remain in the control of a neo-society whose mission was to exorcise them.

This said, however, one must not lose sight of the fact that, even when paved with the best intentions, the therapeutic endeavor is still constantly in danger of foundering in the besotting mythology of "togetherness." But experience shows that the best safeguard against that danger is to bring to the surface the group's instinctual demands. These force everyone, whether patient or doctor, to consider the problem of their being and destiny. The group then becomes ambiguous. At one level, it is reassuring and protective, screening all access to transcendence, generating obsessional defences and a mode of alienation one cannot help finding comforting, lending eternity at interest. But at the other, there appears behind this artificial reassurance the most detailed picture of human finitude, in which every undertaking of mine is taken from me in the name of a demand more implacable than my own death—that of being caught up in the existence of that other, who alone guarantees what reaches me via human speech. Unlike what happens in individual analysis, there is no longer any imaginary reference to the master! slave relationship, and it therefore seems to me to represent a possible way of overcoming the castration complex.

Transversality in the group is a dimension opposite and complementary to the structures that generate pyramidal hierarchization and sterile ways of transmitting messages.

Transversality is the unconscious source of action in the group, going beyond the objective laws on which it is based, carrying the group's desire.

This dimension can only be seen clearly in certain groups which, intentionally or otherwise, try to accept the meaning of their praxis, and establish themselves as subject groups—thus putting themselves in the position of having to bring about their own death.

By contrast, dependent groups are determined passively from outside, and with the help of mechanisms of self-preservation, magically protect themselves from a non-sense experienced as external. In so doing, they are rejecting all possibility of the dialectical enrichment that arises from the group's otherness.

A group analysis, setting out to reorganize the structures of transversality, seems a possibility—providing it avoids both the trap of those psychologizing descriptions of its own internal relationships which result in losing the phantasmic dimensions peculiar to the group, and that of compartmentalization which purposely keeps it on the level of a dependent group.

The effect of the group's signifier on the subject is felt, on the part of the latter, at the level of a "threshold" of castration, for at each phase of its symbolic history, the group has its own demand to make on the individual subjects, involving a relative abandonment of their instinctual urgings to "be part of a group."

There may or may not be a compatibility between this desire, this group Eros, and the practical possibilities for each person of supporting such a trial—a trial that may be experienced in different ways, from a sense of rejection or even of mutilation, to creative acceptance that could lead to a permanent change in the personality.

This imprinting by the group is not a one-way affair: it gives some rights, some authority to the individuals affected. But, on the other hand, it can produce alterations in the group's level of tolerance towards individual divergences, and result in crises over mystified issues that will endanger the group's future.

The role of group analyst is to reveal the existence of such situations and to lead the group as a whole to be less ready to evade the lessons they teach.

It is my hypothesis that there is nothing inevitable about the bureaucratic self-mutilation of a subject group, or its unconscious resort to mechanisms that militate against its potential transversality. They depend, from the first moment, on an acceptance of the risk—which accompanies the emergence of any phenomenon of real meaning—of having to confront irrationality, death, and the otherness of the other.

— Translated by Rosemary Sheed

9

Reflections on Institutional Psychotherapy for Philosophers

You have asked me to situate our experience with institutional psychotherapy in relation to the human sciences, its relationship to philosophy, etc. This may be a question for us to ask you, since our object is not fundamentally theoretical: a fair reworking of the division of labor could lead to you being responsible for appreciating the scope and the pertinence of the concepts that we put into action and their coherence with other disciplines. It would also be up to you to determine whether the response to these questions should come from philosophy and what that implies for philosophy in return. Not having the leisure nor the necessary qualifications to venture very far in this domain, I will only note that the question here is not the traditional classification of the sciences, even if it has been brought up-to-date by refocusing on the human sciences.

Philosophers *cannot avoid* making pronouncements about the status of each one of these sciences. Yet while they are asked not to content themselves with studying the notions introduced by the Freudian experience, for example, from the outside, some will object that they are stepping outside their field, getting lost in the study of monographs, practicing analysis for their own sake, etc. Some philosophers have thought to remove this difficulty by calling for the development of purely theoretical psychoanalysis. Their attitude implies a certain misunderstanding, or even disdain, for the concrete problems of psycho-pathology. In fact, it can only lead to drying up theoretical production. It is obvious that the theoretical field, while it carries with it a unique requirement of coherence, cannot be separated from the pragmatic field.

In parallel to the development of the experimental sciences, the history of philosophy has long been inhabited by the fantasy of creating a homogenous, complete and definitive "system" of concepts that could serve as a reference for all scientific disciplines, etc.

After the Hegelian exploit, this fantasy had to stop for breath: a phenomenological "period of latency" led to asking once again whether, after all, philosophy should not finally accept to "sever" itself from the idea of having to be, in one way or another, a "science of the sciences" and to begin a specific process within each science that would lead it to play the role of assistant during all of the times when their internal theoretical approaches threatened to lead them astray, due to the lack of sufficient refinement of their conceptual tools.

I will only mention a few reference points related to our practice of institutional psychotherapy to give an account of the types of problem we encounter.

The original discovery of institutional psychotherapy, the one that we always come back to for strength when faced with "heresies," is the recognition that the place of existence, for example a psychiatric hospital, carries out a radical modification of anything, of any order, that appears there. A therapeutic technique carried out against the "background" of a psychiatric hospital becomes essentially other. For example, it is not possible for a traditionally trained psychoanalyst to start treatment in a hospital service without radically changing not only his or her technique, but also his or her theoretical goals in terms of psychopathology, which he or she generally refuses to do. This is well-known, but what we find to be new is that we do not think Freudian techniques are impossible in a hospital. I cannot list (and I could only do it all too superficially here) all of the effects of "transmutation" that take place relative to any translation of individuals and techniques to the psychiatric field.[1] To define these phenomena, we were led to propose the concept of an *institutional object* as an object specific to the technical and scientific field of institutional psychotherapy.[2] In doing so, our intention was not to situate ourselves in the tradition of research inspired by psychosociology. In fact, problems of group dynamics do not, in practice, hold our attention very much. The experience of hospital institutions, "therapeutic clubs," group psychotherapy techniques, the establishment of collective analyzers, etc. allowed us to develop a sufficient mastery of it and to dispense, in most cases, with the need to refer to cumbersome experimental materials. However, it also allowed us to realize the lack of potency of the hypotheses and methods of group dynamaticians. Operating daily in the "praxis" of a living institution, we notice that the reason for our efficacy or our failures escapes us and that the theoretical references that have currency in universities generally fail to respond to problems. Many "authors" create explanatory systems from a causal order that, although called dynamic, is nonetheless mechanical and incompatible with any dialectic of human speech.

Once the step has been taken to assert that there is an "institutional object" that is specific to our research, we come to a theoretical precipice: understanding this object in terms of a "group subjectivity" that we would have to differentiate according to diverse "subjective positions,"[3] group fantasies and ideals, resistances and superego mechanisms, derivation, repetition and displacement, compensatory activities, the emergence of an erotic or fatal group passion adopting speech that allows it to get out of its circular totalization by connecting with the outside of the group and reworking its principles of conservation in spatial-temporal and imaginary terms as well as in institutional and historical signifying chains…

In this somewhat eclectic way, we came to recast a series of notions from various sources for our *institutional* use… Some of these notions, like the superego and fantasy, were easier to adapt due to the ambiguities of Freudian doctrine, which does not differentiate between their use at the level of individuals or groups. Other notions, like transference, involved a deeper reassessment. In classical analytical doctrine, this notion seems inextricably linked to the person and the speech of the analyst. In what way could a group or an institution serve as the support for a relationship of transference? Can a group *interpret*, in the same way as a psychoanalyst, the "material"—symptoms, parapraxis, etc.—that occurs within it due to "latent content" related to complexes of unconscious significations? It is an important question: we accept everything it implies. Even if it means having to abandon the use of the term "transfer" outside of the strict relationship "on the couch" and to condemn its extension to the categories of lateral transfers (Slavson), institutional transfers and counter-transfers (Tosquelles and Sivadon), etc.

There is nothing extraordinary in the recognition that the group serves as a mirror and concentrates some individual reactions that can serve as a support for the expression of group drives; it attenuates specific disparities, reinforces mechanisms of suggestibility, etc. Let me repeat, these are not the phenomena that prompted our school of institutional psychotherapy to introduce new vocabulary. Our concern is to determine the conditions that allow an institution to play an analytical role in the Freudian sense. We know that psychoanalysts are not regularly in a position to intervene in cases of psychosis, especially in the case of committed patients. For several years, our attention has therefore been entirely focused on a reevaluation of analytical notions that give a therapeutic group[4] the means to move beyond its role of basic assistance. Asking the question of the existence of a group subject, a group unconscious, that cannot be reduced to the simple addition of individual subjectivities, is not only of theoretical importance for us, but it also has considerable practical impact.

How can a group begin to speak in a given institution and at a given moment of its history without reinforcing the serial and alienating mechanisms that generally characterize groups in industrial societies? At the level of an institution that provides care, is it possible to place an individual in a situation that is radically different from the doctor-patient bond, impasses of identification related to the status of the traditional family, socio-professional relationships of subjugation, etc.?

Is an individual who "tells him- or herself" that he or she is troubled by the desire for an object the same as someone who makes the same confession to a parent, psychoanalyst or friend? If it is true that shame and guilt "precede existence" such that they lead to death more surely than any other passion, one must also admit that there are institutional shame and guilt. It is a *certain type* of incest, in a certain group, that will lead me to die of shame. But then what am I, *as an individual*, if not an "institution" where laws, prohibitions, interdictions, ideals, etc. intersect, a subset of the institution of the family, age group, social class, etc.? An entire philosophical tradition has had to take vast detours, starting with the individual *res cogitans*, to miss all or part of the *res publica*. If it is true that the individual is the implacable support of the *utterance* of words, the group is no less the depositary and initiator of all language and of the efficacy of utterances.

Be that as it may, we consider group subjectivity to be an *absolute precondition* for the emergence of any individual subjectivity. From the perspective of certainty of the individual cogito, group subjectivity seems unstable. Yet when considering it from the angle of the production of value systems, in other words, symbolic structures polarized by the existence of others, it constitutes the only guarantee for grasping the meaning of even the slightest human gestures and words. A mentally ill individual will turn to the language spoken in his or her environment to seek not only the means to express his or her call to the other when suffering, but the somatic presentification of this suffering as well. If it is true that an unconscious "structured like a language" exists behind symptomatic nonsense, that a signifying chain and a potential interpretation capable of reworking the articulation of over-determined pairs—symptom and unconscious subject, language and speech, demand and desire, superego and ego ideal, social persona and individual responsibility in history, etc.—exist behind the bureaucratic absurdity of institutions for the mentally ill, then the analytical domain will tend to overflow the field of significations that are constantly refocused on the assumption of the ego.

Treating the institution as a subject leads to introducing the principle of an "ordination" of nonsense beyond individual symptomatology. The unique position of institutional psychotherapy comes from the fact that its starting point, helping individuals who have been rejected by society, or more exactly individuals whose history of development and its accidents were such that they were unable to find a place in society, leads it to question all human institutions, their proclaimed goals, their definitions of different types of individuals, roles, social functions, norms, etc. This possibility is undoubtedly linked to the fact that the social space reserved for madness, not to say the "madness reserve," escapes some of the "rationality" of institutions reserved for normal individuals. It could make it easier for us to read the signification and fate of industrial societies (state monopoly capitalism or bureaucratic socialism) to the extent that, up to now, they have not been in a position to produce economic, social and political institutions capable of making the speech and social creativity of the popular masses operative—masses who remain *objects* of the economic machine.

Psychiatric hospitals give us the best example of "institutional objects" radically diverted from their apparent social aim; these giant imprisoning machines increase the opacity of disturbances, the solitude of the patients, the nonsense of their existence. The reaction they provoke is a social pathoplasty[5] of mental illness, causing them to harden and close in on themselves. This social alienation is superposed on the more specific instances of a psychopathological alienation. An accurate reading of its impact, however, reveals the possibility of another status for the therapeutic institution: reflecting on itself, this institution will not only tend to recapture the meaning of the enterprise of producing care collectively and interpret each particular case through an analytical process, but in each of these occasions, it will identify the effects of global society, accompanied by a social critique that can be articulated with other currents of thought and struggles. In particular, it seems that a reexamination of the foundations of political economy of industrial societies that starts with the question of social subjectivity and that aims to situate the problem of the adjustment of the production of merchandise in institutions adapted to users and consumers of every nature, would allow a way out of the already stereotyped framework of debates on "the morselization of work," the emergence of "new working classes," etc. The subjectivity of industrial society, from a science fiction perspective, once took the form of a giant calculating machine defining a response for each need, not only for existing individuals, but also for future generations! The Cartesian meditation, under these conditions, could have been expressed in this way: "Of course, I think, but in terms of existence, it is best to ask the supreme subject directly, the machine that is the foundation of my desire and producer of every response. Never again will I know, when I think I am, what existence might be, and even when I claim to know that I exist from the fact that I say I think I am, I will not grasp anything more than a refrain that comes from somewhere else and that speaks about me in terms of many other gadgets… Never again will I have a guarantee of *truly* existing, outside the universal machine." And our human, behind the steering wheel, waiting for the horse racing results, or in the company of some other evil demon, would be easily convinced that, despite everything, without a doubt, he or she does exist and no one can prove the contrary, since the supreme economic God is incapable of deception, since he or she is a prisoner of the universe and unaware of any irruption of desire, lies or truth, with the expansion of consumer society and the widespread use of neuroleptics…

The concept of group subjectivity implies the development of a theory of the signifier in the social field or it risks falling into Jungian metaphors on the collective soul, Moreno's "tele," etc. It requires asking whether the interactions that we have described between psychoanalysis, psychiatry, the social and legal sciences, ethnology, linguistics, etc. allow us to dispense with answering the question of the ontological status of said subjectivity.

It is no more possible to give self-contained definitions in this area than in any other. Making statements today about the nature of the state in modern society, for example, implies performing a differential analysis of its current forms and the various ways in which they evolve. This analysis would allow the common term to be found, the aria that makes this "state" object appear each time at the intersection of various and more or less effective attempts to establish regulatory bodies that claim to ensure the seamless development of productive forces and neutralize class antagonisms. The state, as an institutional object, has become a signifying machine, systematically reifying social processes. Its aspect as an operative of demand in the symbolic order tends to stifle any possible representation in the imaginary order, in other words on the order of human desire—except in its atypical forms: guilt, perversion, "pathology" or revolution.

The fact that existing economic systems, if they are not reclaimed by a social class capable of surpassing its own interests and imposing the creation of a classless society, are therefore constantly secreting social institutions that transform individuals into the cogs of a vast machine, poses the problem in return of assuming social subjectivity to be the inevitable final term of the process of production. Is it possible to conceive of a social force taking power that has norms that are compatible with the minimal exercise of authentic human language? Will all social evolution move in the direction of an ever-increasing oppression of human desire? By advancing the concept of social subjectivity, are we giving new life to myths of the redemption of the lost subject and its counterpart, the god who died in reality but still speaks in dreams? These questions are all the more telling because industrial societies, in their race for exploits, death, madness and stupidity, are still frighteningly dynamic!

The existence of an increasing correspondence between social symptomatology and individual modes of mental alienation can be seen when wild and spontaneous forms of sociality emerge, especially in the formation of groups of adolescents who try to resolve, in their own way, the identificatory impasses inherent in oedipal triangulation and specific to the contemporary crisis of the traditional family. Studies of this process have served as the occasion for reinvigorating myths of the collapse of the "paternal function," of family deficiencies as the "root of all our problems," etc. Without a respectable army, church and recognized god, or a stable social order, can the passage to adulthood only take place by indulging in the drugs of consumer society?

The type of car, partner or role I covet determines the way in which the "I" escapes me. *I is an other*. But this other is not a subject. It is a signifying machine that predetermines what will be good or bad for me and those like me in a potential area of consumption. Yet wouldn't the only response to this overwhelming of the subject be to return to circulation the model of the Father-President, the totem raised at the head of the state, in the absence of being able to reestablish the religious legitimacy of a King too radically castrated by history? In this area, Freud's theoretical constructs and those of *Totem and Taboo* do not appear, at first glance, to offer much progress. We must, however, turn to Freudianism, despite its myths or because of them, if we truly want to explore these problems. University philosophical research remains dry and desiccated on these questions. It has even constructed a system to resist access to them. To say nothing of some crucial notions like the "death drive" that they have simply ignored. It has long discredited basic notions such as the "unconscious," the "unconscious subject," which are considered aberrant, a contradiction in terms, an abuse of language, the insolence of a scientific mindset, etc. Following the work of Jacques Lacan, the idea has spread that these notions could, on the contrary, cast retrospective light on the formula of philosophers from Descartes to Husserl who were concerned with the foundation of the subject.

For our part, we think that the concept of group subjectivity is an extension of Freudian theory. Freud, in all innocence, does perform a constant shift in plane that makes him regularly miss social reality, but like a modern Oedipus, his blindness leads us to paths that may be more reliable than any others. He left us the means to define the relationship between the subject and others outside of idealist hypotheses. While Lukacs remains stuck with "class unconscious" and the role of "indeterminateness" in the historical process and never leaves the imaginary problems of consciousness, Freud turns directly to the status of the subject. He describes it as fundamentally unconscious, escaping individual determination for the most part and marked almost indelibly by the structural relationships of the social group and its various modes of communication. The next step leads to considering that this subjectivity, manifested at the level of the institution, possesses its own laws, its group or individual "interpreters," its operatives; it develops specific systems of resistance, misreading, certain types of fantasy that are relatively autonomous from individual fantasies. While the latter refer to an imaginary structural order subjected to the human organism, group fantasies are articulated with the totality of signifiers and social structures. Because of this fact, they are the seat of an entire series of clashes and impasses between the individual and the group.

If you remember my warning that I am not a philosopher, you will not begrudge me for not asserting anything that is not based on the simple collection of reflections emerging from institutional practice. Each problem advanced remains in suspense! What is this thing-subject that, from one individual to another, is supposed to embody the group's speech? Where would one look for an *interpretation* on the level of the group? Wouldn't a leader automatically become its spokesperson? How can the legitimacy of the "order word" of a particular group have a basis in historical truth? Aren't speech and the subject essentially "stuck" to the individual, etc.? Only the individual proffers one word or another. Let me repeat, not only does language refer to the totality of what is said in every place by every individual, but it also refers to everything that is articulated by all *economic machines*. Who speaks when the Finance Minister modifies the discount rate by one percent and, by doing so, changes the direct buying power of consumers and affects millions of individual projects? The Minister, of course, or at least the Ministry! Yet who is the subject of this signifying chain? Through what links of communication, through what webs of language can one find the key or the truth of a Ministerial order? A minister's words obviously do not refer intimately to the person but to the relationships of production and the contradictions that regulate industrial societies, to something that might be happening between Moscow, Washington, Beijing, Leopoldville… Would it then be an abuse to speak of the subject at the level of a class or a state? One might object that it is not something that is as transparent to itself as the subject is supposed to be. Self-consciousness is certainly a guarantee of being conscious, but not of being a subject when there is a *meaning* to being a subject, in other words, in the register of the other established by speech. In social terms, things may be more certain. A group, party or caste that claims to be the subject of history, called on to perform an historic mission, may only be, in fact, an institutional object moved by external circumstances, the conjunction of forces in presence, etc. In terms of social subjectivity, nothing is a foregone conclusion. Some have repeated that social facts are not things, and yet they first present themselves as things. The fact that they can leave their status as objects does not depend on humanist observers.

The rise of social subjectivity depends very precisely on the capacity of groups, institutions, classes, etc., to articulate their totalization in function of historical phenomena and natural laws. Any research in this domain is therefore placed in an intersection of political and social problems that extend far beyond the field of a specific practice. When it is a question, for example, in political economics, of adjusting the process of consumption with the process of production by means of adequate institutions, questions arise that are similar to the ones we have tried to delineate in terms of social subjectivity. This institutionalization of relationships of production is treated, in capitalist countries and "socialist" ones alike, either blindly, or in the framework of bureaucratic-type planning. How can institutional models that can be articulated with a "logic of nonsense" emerge at this level? Who in industrial society could serve as a guarantor for human existence? Traditional religious and political institutions are now manifestly incapable of doing it. It is up to philosophical research to determine the concepts that could establish a field of reference that could respond, on the one hand, to the demands of the objective sciences and, on the other, to those of the "technologies" of concrete human existence. If this is not the case, a series of awkward doctrines will tend to reemerge in many different forms: theories of parallelism, perception-consciousness systems, theories of form and their structuralist derivatives, reflexology, without mentioning the famous debates on superstructures subjected to infrastructures, etc. The philosophical institution, in this case, serves as the head curator of the museum of outmoded concepts. In fact, it generally remains at a safe distance from any innovation, as is still generally the case with Freudism. It is not inconceivable that this situation could change. The problem is not only to put new concepts into circulation to move other types of research out of their impasse, but also, which is the same thing, to reclaim hold of the fundamental concepts of philosophy as they give themselves to us through the edge of their truth. From a certain point of view, we can see that Hegelian thought is far from fertilizing anthropological research in the way that would be necessary. A systematic review of this thought remains of primordial importance. From another angle, the inability of philosophical thought to develop a doctrine of existence that is not subjugated to the individual, which does not imply a "deduction" of the existence of others, and correlatively, the establishment of theories of intersubjectivity that lead to an endless quest for social order instead of starting from it, have considerably bogged down the average fields of reference for students and researchers in all of the human sciences. For its part, the "Marxist institution," stricken with sterility for decades, has not helped them to move away from mechanicist methodologies either. Let me repeat, the question is not only the functional adjustment of the various human sciences but also an appropriate appreciation of the status of the subject of scientific utterances in his or her relationship with the individual desire of the researcher and the historical drives with which he or she is faced. Depending on whether a therapist, for example, considers that his or her field is closed, without a common border with other disciplines, and reifies philosophy as a foreign body, he or she will implicitly deny all human sciences access to the social subjectivity that, according to us, is implied at the level of each institutional sub-set. This seems to apply to even the most technical research. We think that no interpretation (be it psychoanalytical, psychosociological, etc.) leaves anyone exempt from having to respond to the critical questions raised by history. No political "region" is autonomous from a technological or philosophical "region." Does authentic philosophical research exist that can determine the status of the subject independently of the nature of contemporary historical subjectivity in one situation or another? Doesn't postulating the existence of social subjectivity and institutional objects, like we do, lead to asking the question of the nature of the philosophical object?

Does a mode of philosophical apperception exist that can rightly allow itself to be enclosed in individual subjectivity? The same question can be raised in the realms of artistic production. The possibility of engaging in a real reconfiguration of social, political, esthetic and moral, etc. problems, in a way that brings them out of their current disjunction depends on how we respond to this question. If we think that the philosophical institution must become the *interpreter*, the grammarian of the languages that are spoken in the different technological, scientific and literary fields at different periods, then it may be possible to consider that the object of philosophy comes down precisely to grasping the social subjectivity that we said was only given through manifest content that demands decoding and interpretation because it escapes historical accidents, academic contingency, technical specifications, etc. The philosophical institution would then be defined as needing to recapture a structure of reference, playing the role of the "analyzer," by means of a maieutic that perpetually reestablishes itself through the conceptual production of the various human sciences. It would have to recognize, first of all, that psychoanalysis, as well as institutional therapy, ethnology, linguistics, etc. have shown in counter-relief the need for a redefinition of philosophical research. It remains to be seen whether its current institution will be able to "speak" from this lack, or whether several generations and a few philosophical crises will be necessary before reaching that point. Will the day ever come when President Schreber's and Artaud's definitions of God are studied with the same attention and same rigor as those of Descartes or Malebranche? How long will we maintain the separation between theoretical critique and the concrete analytical activity of the human sciences? Can the damage caused by this divide at the heart of anthropology be equated to the circumstances that split the world with an iron curtain? And isn't it being split again in many other regions according to the nature of the development of the state?... Speaking of which, is the study of these successive schisms in the contemporary universe the exclusive domain of professional politicians, diplomats and specialized journalists? We are well placed to know that each individual is experiencing these cuts today on an imaginary level that is much more charged than the antique myths with which psycho-sexual complexes are generally associated.

Philosophical research would therefore have to concern itself not only with a constant conceptual reordering, but also with developing, in the "field," conditions for establishing and maintaining a logic of nonsense as it emerges in every domain, updating the register of the possibilities of signification of human existence, here, elsewhere and now.

10

Nine Theses of the Left Opposition

Summary

Thesis 1: Capitalism and the State

In analyzing the development of capitalism and the politics of the labor movement, it is important, from the beginning, to consider all economic and political phenomena as a *structured totality*, a concrete whole, the result of historical development, defined as a set of *determined relationships*. Vital theoretical consequences ensue: the refusal to cut the world in two, capitalism and socialism; the refusal to consider capitalism as the juxtaposition of national capitalisms, of which some would be advanced and some would be behind; the refusal to think that the advancement of some is not organically connected to the delay of others.

This Marxist point of view is tending to disappear completely from the communist movement, under the pretext, for example, that the development of productive forces in the USSR requires a superior stage of relationships of production. As big as the USSR is, productive forces do not develop there independently of socialist countries, or even of the capitalist world. There is no abstract outline of capitalism, with one country or another representing the model that the others would tend to follow. The general outline of capitalism is not a universal structure to which individual nations would be added; it is a structure existing in this very diversity and inconceivable without it. This is what led Trotsky to criticize the creation of proletarian internationalism: it is not based on the general characteristics of capitalism, on its abstract structure, but on its particular form, not on the similarity of the conditions of struggle but on their interdependence.

Capitalism's fundamental contradiction between the development of productive forces and relationships of production must be analyzed on a global scale. The end of capital (producing surplus-value, enhancing capital) is in contradiction with the means for achieving this enhancement: the unlimited development of productive forces, the unlimited production of use values. The extension of capitalism to the entire planet has given rise to a global division of labor between different nations, and the process of reproduction of capital is now a global process. Almost all goods are the product of several partial labor processes divided between several countries. Yet capital has not been able to break the national framework and the state inside which it developed, which are now an obstacle to the development of productive forces. While the global division of labor would require the elimination of all customs barriers, a rational redistribution of the means of production and consumption, and planning on a global level, capitalism can only survive by maintaining relationships of production within a national framework, with state intervention, which has become an instrument for enhancing capital.

The state plays a vital role in the process of circulating capital, notably by allowing the rotation of capital to be accelerated and the realization of the surplus-value contained in the goods produced. In the domain of distribution and production, the state assumes the part of capital that only has a weak profit rate, which, in compensation, allows the profit rate of private sector monopolies to rise. Capital circulates between the private and the public sector in many ways: *monopolies and the state are joined in an organic whole, state monopoly capitalism*. State monopoly capitalism appeared during crises: the First World War, the Great Depression, the Second World

War. These three stages marked the significant reduction of international exchanges of capital and goods, the closing of national markets, the withdrawal of capital towards the state as supreme savior. The state then tried to restart the process of adding value to capital and producing surplus value, the process halted by the crisis. The process of "nationalization of capital," however, does not disappear with the end of the crisis: it remains and sometimes develops with phases of growth that correspond to an opposing process, the globalization of relationships of production and circulation.

Each of these two movements implies its opposite. The capitalist world is not a juxtaposition of several, more or less developed state monopoly capitalisms. The types of monopoly capitalism are determined by their place in the international division of labor; they imply this division and cannot exist without it. Inversely, the monopoly internationalization of productive forces implies state monopoly capitalism and does not happen outside of states; internationalization occurs through nations. *The relationships between states therefore appear to be the expression and the mode of realization of the internationalization of economic life at the stage of state monopoly capitalism.* Yet these national and state structures, through which internationalization occurs, are also the obstacle to internationalization; states represent historical archaisms opposed to the development of productive forces on an international scale.

Relationships of production are maintained at the national level as the result of a compromise. Marked by its historical traditions and social particularism, the bourgeoisie is not internationalist, while the modes of capitalist production grow increasingly international each day. The compromise requires, on the one hand, that the bourgeoisie keep their domination over the state apparatus and, on the other, that organized political society institutionalizes and integrates the working class as much as possible. The latter's struggles are thus kept in the margins of the real places of decision concerning capitalist economy. The centralization of capital and "capitalist expropriation within capital" are such that the bourgeoisie has lost all of the power that allowed it to overcome archaic structures, starting with the state itself. The bourgeoisie needs the nationalist state to survive. It is a prisoner of its own class reality: the limit of the bourgeoisie is the bourgeoisie itself.

In summary, we can say that:

The development of capitalism is the basis for two contradictory movements: on one side, the globalization of productive forces and therefore of relationships of production; on the other, a qualitatively new role for the state in its economic interventions (mechanisms of state monopoly capitalism). The fundamental contradiction of the mode of capitalist production (between relationships of production and productive forces) is expressed as a contradiction between economic structure and state structure, allowing the structure to survive. This contradiction occurs again within the state, pulled on one side towards the globalization of relationships of production, and on the other towards the need to keep relationships of production in a national framework and strengthen the mechanisms of state monopoly capitalism. Institutional relationships are flooded with economic relationships and tend to break under pressure from them. This break cannot occur spontaneously. It requires the proletariat to create its own institutions: in other words, the intervention of a *revolutionary subjectivity*. Its non-emergence in history is the reason why bourgeois institutions have been maintained.

Thesis 2: Capitalism and the Strategy of the International Labor Movement

The history of capitalism is the history of class struggle. We should not fall into the pseudo-objectivism of the current analyses of the official communist movement, which always present physical and cultural phenomena as the result of a mechanical necessity imposed from the outside on class struggle. This method "authorizes" it to clear the labor movement of all historical responsibility in the development of capitalism. Capital is not external to the proletariat, it is the surplus value produced by the proletariat's work: in the same way, the structures and institutions of capitalism are the result of the economic and political struggles of the proletariat; and its organizations have a direct responsibility for it.

The responsibility of social-democracy in strengthening the state in 1914 and putting in place structures of state monopoly capitalism is flagrant. It is the result of chauvinistic nationalism, patriotism and the support of national defense. Everything happens as if the nationalism of the labor movement gave the bourgeoisie back the instruments of domination that it had lost. This process has been regularly repeated in the communist movement, which always upheld the idea that the constant growth of productive forces would be impossible in the framework of capitalism and would inevitably lead to an internal breakdown of the system. Communists were waiting for the explosion of a final crisis for capitalism. It was therefore up to the leaders of the Communist Parties to stifle any revolutionary tendencies that would prevent this destiny from occurring… While it is true that the expropriation of the bourgeoisie by capitalism comes from the development of productive forces, it does not mean that bourgeois states are incapable of secreting "regulatory mechanisms" that would allow capitalism to overcome the difficulties of adaptation to the development of productive forces, investments, the division of markets, monetary problems, "planning," the integration of the working class, etc.

Modernist currents favor accelerating the proletariat's integration into the state and foresee an alliance between the working class and the driving forces of capitalism to neutralize the reactionary bourgeoisie and make capitalist society evolve progressively. Communist parties that are faithful to the USSR, however, are still hesitant to move in this direction. All political ideologies are the product of the same type of error, which consists of combining forces of a different nature: social classes and state or economic decision-making centers. The result is to slow class struggle on an international level and to paralyze it when faced with showdowns that could challenge the power of the bourgeoisie. The working class has the following choice to make: either assist modern capitalism according to the wishes of the modernists, the apostles of the "new working class"; or put itself on the front line of a hypothetical rallying of nationalist and reactionary forces, reducing it to a supporting role serving the interests of the petit and grand bourgeoisie. In each case, the working class is condemned to lose the goal of its struggle at every step.

It was only yesterday that proletariats didn't have a country! For the communist movement, the struggle against reactionary nationalism remains a fundamental task, inseparable from a reworking of the relationships between the avant-garde of the party and the popular masses. In fact, when communist parties play the game of parliamentarianism and the defense of national interests, when their goal is the struggle against the power of monopolies, they encourage the reconciliation of all social classes and make the party apparatus the only political recourse of the working class. As struggle and combativeness are worn thin on these illusions, the omnipotence of the bureaucratic infrastructure of the labor movement grows. The Leninist tactic of a *status quo* between social forces, a tactic adopted in function of an unfavorable relationship of forces at the time of the NEP, was transformed by the Stalinist dictatorship into an ideology of the *status quo*. The compromise agreements imposed by the imperialists at the end of the civil war were changed into a philosophy of coexistence and peaceful coexistence between capitalist and socialist states. Stalinist ideology opened the way for a reactionary myth of a *necessary defense, by the working class, of the development of national productive forces against "cosmopolitan trusts."* The proletariat became the objective ally of monopoly capitalism in its endeavors to dismantle and liquidate traditional economies; in fact, it contributed indirectly to accelerating the process of relative and absolute underdevelopment to which the majority of the globe's population has fallen victim.

In this objective context of monopolist internationalism and in the absence of any international strategy for proletarian struggle, the Soviet state was able to impose the dogma of the necessary equation of its interests and those of the masses. The Soviet state became the international advocate of the masses before the global bourgeoisie. In reality, this system is founded on the principle of *give and take* with imperialism and maintaining the *status quo*: Soviet bureaucracy negotiates its influence over the communist movement with capitalism.

Rebuilding a revolutionary avant-garde that has the function not of *representing* the masses but of *structuring* them, coordinating their struggle according to a collectively developed strategy, transforming the relationship of forces, with the fundamental objective of suppressing the capitalist mode of production and overthrowing the bourgeoisie in power, was blocked during the period of Stalinist hegemony. The new international situation of post-World War Two, marked by the extension of the "socialist system" in several European states, and especially by the rapid extension of anti-imperialist revolution after the Chinese Revolution, progressively modified the conditions that had allowed the Soviet state to impose its hegemony on the international communist movement. Along with spectacular conflicts with the Yugoslavian, Polish and Hungarian communist parties, the USSR developed new types of relationships with all communist organizations, on the basis of relative independence negotiated according to the interests of the parties present and sometimes their respective power.

Thesis 3: Inter-Imperialist Contradictions

The theme of inter-imperialist contradiction holds a major place in the current ideology of the communist movement. Yet it is an "ideological" theme par excellence, in other words, it remains at the level of appearances of reality without trying to grasp the political causes that led to the development of this theme.

The economic power of the United States is such that it appears to be the defender of the entire capitalist system. This power developed from particularly favorable factors: a vast internal market without customs barriers, an abundance of capital and labor. The Second World War, which ruined Europe, doubled American industrial production and increased the reserves of the United States to the point that it came to own 80% of the world's gold reserves. The creation of the International Monetary Fund consecrated the supremacy of the dollar as the currency of reference. By offering capital to a dismantled Europe, the United States put European capitalism back on its feet while giving American industries an outlet when threatened with overproduction. The US appears to be the promoter of free exchange and international movements of capital and goods. It has become the principal agent of the international division of labor. The entire economic and political strategy of the United States is aimed at deepening and expanding the capitalist division of labor between nations, which explains why it is systematically favorable to establishing large markets, notably a large Atlantic market.

While the United States defends the interests of the capitalist mode of production as a whole, it runs into contradictions that result from the diversity of national situations in terms of relationships of production, class struggles, etc., and it encounters heavy setbacks. These setbacks are not due to any aspiration of independence on the part of the supposedly national monopolies. They are due to the impossibility for the bourgeoisie to overcome the national fixation of relationships of production (relationships with the proletariat, petit bourgeoisie, farmers, etc.)—because this national structuring is necessary to its class existence.

We have already insisted on the historical responsibility of proletariat organizations in the resurgence of the national question in the 20th century. Yet this historical regression ends up situating historical causality in such archaisms as the state or even pre-capitalist structures. It is a fact that the question of agriculture is an obstacle to a vast Atlantic market. The French Communist Party has highlighted the weakness of French monopolies in comparison to their American competitors; however, you would have to be blind not to see that these monopolies support this large market. It is in their interest to shed expensive agriculture which raises the value of the labor force and prevents a more rational international division of labor for agricultural production. The French state only started to try to rid itself of this burden in 1958, supporting an increased rural exodus since the 1950s. The bourgeoisie, however, no longer has any historical capacity; integration in the global market has come too late for it not to be obliged to make difficult compromises with farmers and the proletariat. Other countries, like Germany, have also had to make these compromises despite their greater orientation towards a global market. *The central point is therefore that, in the absence of a global structuring of the proletariat's revolutionary struggle, no social force is capable of overcoming national, regional and pre-capitalist archaisms that block the realization of the capitalist ideal of a rational division of labor on an international scale.*

If the state is the connecting point between the internationalization of capital and the national specificity of relationships of production, class struggle, etc., then it represents the geometric location of the contradictions of capitalism. Inter-imperialist contradictions are all the more accentuated that classes, and first of all the proletariat, isolated in the national stranglehold and incapable of a universal point of view, lead the state to make compromises that constantly bring it back and reduce it to a national context, even when it makes efforts towards internationalization. That small farmers and small business owners do not have an internationalist vision is a surprise to no one; the real incapacity of the bourgeoisie to overcome its pre-capitalist structures is much stranger. Yet for the national particularism of the bourgeoisie to come from the national particularism of the proletariat is something that would shock the communist strategists! Inter-imperialist contradictions are the mystified flip-side of the national fragmentation of the proletariat's struggles, the apparently objective expression of what we could call *inter-proletarian-contradictions*. The internal division of the bourgeoisie is merely the expression of the proletariat's division.

The explanation behind the mystery of these contradictions is the following: they have an objective reality, an objectivity, but this objective reality is absolutely not independent from the politics of the international communist movement, which is also an objective reality! Here we find the same mechanism as the one underlying the set-up of the structures of state monopoly capitalism: the communist movement, integrated in the structured system of capitalist institutions, develops a policy that is an integral part of the "objective reality" of this system. Then, switching hats, it claims to engage in a theoretical analysis of this objective reality by forgetting that it contributed, often decisively, to its existence. It made this objective reality unconsciously; but its theoretical consciousness completely forgot it and is unable to understand it. The system of institutions of the capitalist mode of production works like a language, and the communist movement, because it has refused to situate itself as breaking with the system as a whole, now represents an objective element of the rules of its functioning.

It should be noted that the importance we give to the state, to the policies of communist organizations, etc. in the explanation of the objective structures of capitalism raises the question of the degree of reality of the institutional level, the level of the superstructure and its relationship with the economic structure in Marxist concepts. The problem of the reality of superstructures has always represented a real puzzle for Marxist theorists, who are torn between a Hegelian-type solution (the superstructure is the materialization of class consciousness) and a mechanist solution (the superstructure is a pure reflection of the economic structure). Some think that they have resolved the contradiction by declaring that they are equally real, but characterizing superstructure as "real-ideal" and structure as "real-material." They only prove that they have overcome the contradiction in an imaginary way. After endlessly repeating that state and superstructure have an "objective reality," that they have a "distinct efficacy," etc., not one step has been made in resolving the problem, because they have simply forgotten to *pose* it correctly, in other words in the relationship between the objective reality and the subjective reality of proletarian organizations. All of the analyses we have developed reveal, in relief, the problem that revolutionary Marxism must resolve at all costs on the level of theory and on the level of practice, if it wants to move beyond the alternative between vulgar materialism and Hegelian idealism: the problem of the subject.

Thesis 4: The Third World

Capitalism's inability to remove pre-capitalist structures is flagrant in the Third World. What characterizes the Third World is not that the countries in it are underdeveloped, but that they are exploited and dominated. The notion of underdevelopment is insufficient, because it refuses to see the organic connection between the delays in certain countries and the advancements in others, just as it refuses to consider the place of Third World countries in the organic whole of the international division of labor in the capitalist system. The main points are:

a) Third World countries have deformed economies (capital is invested in spheres of production determined by the monopolies of industrial nations);

b) the imbalanced exchange of goods and capital is analyzed as an enormous drain on the surplus value produced in these countries in favor of international capital.

As a result, only a narrow sphere of production is inserted into the global process of reproducing capital; the rest of the vast masses of people in the Third World are subjected to pre-capitalist, feudal relationships of production. Moreover, with Third World states being controlled by international capitalism, the latter blocks all possibility of development by strengthening archaic structures and by making compromises with the old ruling classes, showering them with dollars to consolidate their position. This leads us to examine the theses of the Chinese Communist Party. Its principal reaffirmation of the need for revolutionary struggle to drive the overthrow of imperialism is an important challenge to the reformist theories of Soviet leaders who have abandoned the perspective of international revolution. But in reality, the opposition of Chinese communists to the policies of Khrushchev and his successors is not based on Marxist analysis. It arose from the empirical recognition of the lack of revolutionary struggles outside the margins of imperialism. This pseudo-theorization of a state of fact coexists eclectically with maintaining Marxist-Leninist principles in a mainly verbal purity. The CCP seems to have taken its position, once and for all, based on the fact that class struggle in capitalist countries cannot be expected to be anything more than reserve forces for the anti-imperialist struggles in the so-called storm belt.

Consequently, the CCP and the pro-Chinese have not developed any critical theory nor offered any international revolutionary strategy and, although in a different way than the Soviets, they *develop their international relations according to the rules and modes imposed by imperialism* (for example, the diplomatic alliance with De Gaulle). Taking a closer look, the policies of the Chinese CP are not fundamentally different than those of the USSR. They also aim to capitalize on and profit from the raw material of the revolutionary struggles of the hungry people of the world, by means of negotiations with the imperialist powers.

To the extent that the international communist movement has allowed most struggles for emancipation to develop under the lead of petit bourgeois movements of liberation, it is not surprising that we can see the reemergence of a series of particularisms, the survival of colonial defects in the form of false national questions. This limits the possibilities of moving beyond the institutional frameworks established by imperialists and makes establishing a front of mass struggle with revolutionary goals all the more difficult.

By justifying the national aspect of struggle, by theorizing the need for these states to have an intermediary phase called "national democracy," and which is in fact a voluntary abandon of all potential class struggle, the Chinese communists have not distinguished themselves from Soviet communists on this point. Compare, for example, the attitude of the Indonesian CP, of pro-Chinese persuasion, and the completely similar attitude of the Indian CP, of Soviet persuasion; and notice, in each case, the magnificent results of their class collaboration policies! For Chinese communists, defining the struggles of the storm belt as the driving force behind international class struggle is an excuse for not making them revolutionary. They use these struggles without engaging in a political critique of their *spontaneous* character; we find here the same mechanism of anti-dialectical realism and objectivism as in their analysis of the situation of the working class in capitalist countries. *Class struggle is characterized by its universality.* The communist movement must distinguish itself from nationalist struggles in underdeveloped countries, especially since no viable socialist model is likely to be established in them. This is not only true of countries led by a coalition of "national democracy," but also for those that are led by a communist party: the examples of China and Cuba illustrate the limits of the most sizeable endeavors in this domain.

The Chinese Party and the Soviet Party share their over-estimation of the scope of petit-bourgeois struggles concerning:

1) *their offensive effectiveness against the bourgeois state*: it is unfortunately the case that the United States is capable of recovering its influence in regions that it considers to be key. When that option proves impossible, it slips on the mask of peaceful coexistence and imposes its solution at all costs.

2) *the alignment of the proletariat's struggles with petit bourgeois objectives*: this is the thesis of the union of all anti-monopolist layers. Because of this, the struggles of the working class and its allies are not aimed at their real enemy, the bourgeoisie in power in each country, but against something that only tends to be considered a symbol by the Soviets and the Chinese: monopoly power. As if the United States, in Vietnam for example, was not acting in the name and place of all international capitalism! Today, the French Communist Party supports De Gaulle's foreign policy, under the pretext that it would help move towards peace. As if De Gaulle was not acting as a subtle advocate of the Americans! Imperialists know how to share roles! However, isn't the only way to fight effectively against the war in Vietnam for the working classes in every place and by every means possible to strengthen their struggle against each

bourgeois state without dwelling on the contradictions that take them temporarily away from American imperialism?

The Chinese and the Soviets are avoiding the difficulty for the revolutionary proletariat to overthrow the bastions of capitalism. Not only in theory but in their opportunistic practice, in their defense of marginal and sometimes reactionary demands, the leaders of the communist movement have shown that they have given up developing a revolutionary strategy on an international scale. They are only guided by the moment, circumstances, imperialist divisions, a potential world war. Their passivity in the face of a state of affairs, the *status quo*, in the face of spontaneous conflicts, the inevitability of historical standoffs is a repudiation of the very foundations of Marxist-Leninist theory and practice. Overestimating the ability of petit bourgeois movements to carry out democratic and socialist tasks successfully tends to lead to the logical result of eliminating the communist movement as a movement (for example, the elimination of the CP in Iraq or the suppression of the Egyptian and Algerian CP by the communists themselves).

While it is true that the origins of the Sino-Soviet conflict can be found in the opposition between *international strategies of the state* and violent conflicts with no specific class perspective, only the rebuilding of an international communist avant-garde would be able to overcome these contradictions based on revolutionary theory and practice, prevent sectorial squabbles from falling directly into particularism, and offer objectives and perspectives to the oppressed masses that cannot be appropriated by class enemies.

Thesis 5: Socialist States

The Soviet state is all the more incapable of serving as a model and guide for the international communist movement that it is caught in the play of political and economic contradictions imposed on an international scale by the mode of capitalist production.

The inability of socialist states to find their way in building a classless society does not only come from the ideological deficiencies of their leaders and the mode of bureaucratic relations between the apparatus of power and the popular masses. In large part, socialist economies grew in function of similar global market data and objectives as capitalist economies. The social antagonisms that remain in socialist countries are therefore the indirect reflection of the contradictions that exist between different types of industrial societies. The ideology of peaceful coexistence and economic competition (Khrushchev's command had already been formulated by Stalin) is merely an expression of acceptance of the hegemony of the capitalist mode of production. In fact, there is a certain symmetry between the evolution of capitalist and socialist industrial societies. On one side, capitalism and free enterprise have been led to make state capitalism play a decisive role, to turn, at least in their words, towards national and regional planning, to picture the integration of national and regional economies in large international markets, to discuss global plans of support for underdeveloped countries, etc. On the other, the USSR and its allies have loosened their planning systems in terms of decentralization, turned progressively to the criteria of market economies, the profitability of investments and profit as a means of individual and collective motivation for increased production, etc. Soviet leaders seem resigned to giving private property a role and accepting the return of agriculture to individual, if not ancestral, forms of production.

Inter-socialist contradictions have continued to grow. Already in 1959, in economic terms, they formed the backdrop of the Yugoslavian breakdown and inaugurated a chain reaction of crises in the international communist movement, the effects of which are still being felt in popular democracies. Sino-Soviet differences were economic at first: intense negotiations with Stalin over Manchuria, railway lines, Sinkiang, etc. After the death of Stalin, a compromise was concluded that was supposed to bring substantial economic assistance, but everything was cast in doubt by the great crisis of the communist movement in 1956. Differences, especially economic differences, took a scandalous turn, with the massive withdrawal of Soviet technicians, the cancellation of industrial development plans, etc. The Chinese people paid a heavy price for these ideological divergences which, in the framework of real proletarian internationalism, would never have been dealt with on that level.

In general terms, economic relations between the USSR and its allies have always been established on the model of the international relations of global capitalism and regulated by the "might is right" principle, the same law that has presided over the development of capitalism since the 19th century. Economic exchanges have always taken place based on international market prices, and often at rates that are less favorable for dependent economies. During the Stalinist period, there was a systematic exploitation of popular democracies. The recent history of East Germany, Hungary, etc. would be incomprehensible without reference to this attitude by the USSR. The result has been a massive return of religious archaisms, nationalism, the passivity of the working and agricultural masses, a legitimate suspicion of socialism, a tendency to be seduced by the creations and ways of life in capitalist countries...

Take, for example, the chronic crisis of the USSR agricultural economy. The fate of agricultural workers was not determined according to socialist norms, following the principle of *to each according to his or her labor*, but using methods similar to capitalist economy, that could be summed up as: *to each according to his or her capital, or to each according to his or her initial situation.* Considerable differences therefore exist and grow worse between the more favored state enterprises (sovkhozy) and the cooperatives (kolkhozy), as well as between wealthy kolkhozy and poor ones. The result is well known: insufficient production, an increasing use of individual parcels for feeding cities, cereal imports, etc. Another result: the discouragement and disgust of a large portion of the Soviet populace which, while disapproving of this regime, probably condemns communist ideology itself.

Should we conclude from its current evolution that the USSR is in the process of returning to capitalism as Chinese communist theorists and some bourgeois theorists claim? This is an old problem raised by Leon Trotsky in compelling pages of *The Revolution Betrayed* (1936). For him, the USSR was involved in an *incomplete process*. In the case where the Russian working class, with support from the international working class, was unable to eliminate Thermidorian bureaucracy from power, this bureaucracy would come to form a social class. From 1925 to 1940, the year of his assassination, Trotsky continued to defend the idea that nothing was definitively over in the USSR. He defined the USSR as a "proletarian state" where political power had escaped the working class, requiring it to engage in an intense struggle for "political revolution." But he considered that bureaucracy had not shown itself strong enough to liquidate the foundation of the proletarian state. His entire analysis was based on the prediction of a permanent and growing instability in every domain of Soviet society. And the historical evolution of the USSR has not occurred without obstacles and internal difficulties! Nevertheless, the incomplete process described by Trotsky did not lead to the appearance of the alternatives he predicted. Other aspects of Trotsky's descriptions remain invaluable instruments for interpreting the internal contradictions of the Soviet economy, the development of its current crisis and the ongoing reform projects: especially when Trotsky describes the opposition between the problem of quality and technical or cultural creativity, and the imperatives of a bureaucracy and a state that do not want "to die."

As irrefutable as Trotsky's analyses seem in economic terms, the political and social consequences that he deduced from them seem more problematic to us. Bureaucracy was not overthrown, workers were integrated into a political society made up of compromises and have not been pushed into the type of impasse that would have made them rise up en masse to accomplish this famous political revolution. Bureaucracy has progressively changed the nature of its insertion in society, abandoning the system of Stalinist dictatorship by stages, to pass into a regime where technocracy and ideology tend to replace apparatchik bureaucracy and the doctrinal ideology of the epigones of Marxism. Yet a fundamental characteristic of this evolution remains that, as a whole, no matter what the twists and turns, the masses are no longer marching along. While they did not engage in the Trotskyist path of political revolution, they did not respond either to the lyrical appeals of the Krushchevists: to consecrate all of their energy on edifying the *state of all the people*. On the other hand, the bureaucracy shows no inclination of committing hara-kiri; on the contrary, it is developing its conservative ideology: defending the national and international status quo, refusing any analysis in function of class struggle, rehabilitating pacifist myths, petit bourgeois moralism, practical disinterest in revolutionary struggles developing throughout the world, etc. Nothing leads one to think that it is reestablishing capitalism as Marx defined it: it appears capable of adapting to the current relationships of production and profiting from them.

Soviet leaders now foresee the decentralizing of the power of economic decision-making. Will this reform be a step forward and will it benefit workers? It is unlikely, but reforms in the sense of more flexible planning imposed by the contradictions in which they are caught do not necessarily mean the start of a return to capitalism. The Chinese communists' condemnation of the current direction taken by Soviet economists in favor of criteria of profitability for companies, criteria that are similar to capitalist political economy, remains dogmatic and in the end may miss the point. Seen from the angle of a formal description of economic mechanisms, we can accept the need for a system to calculate investments, make provisions in terms of profitability, etc. This system would have its own requirements and logic that ideological considerations of any order would be unable to improve. But when socialist economists forget that value is nothing other than crystallized social and human labor and that prices, money, and capital profitability are only translations of the separation between producers and means of production, that they favor the persistence of mechanisms like in capitalist merchant production where, through the intermediary of the monetary system and economic mechanisms social labor finds itself at the disposition of a minority social category that uses it according to its own criteria and institutions. In western industrial societies, it is a power of compromise between state capitalism, oligopolies and the bourgeoisie; in the Soviet system, it is the power of bureaucratic social categories structured in an original way, playing a function of regulation, for their benefit, of processes of production, circulation and distribution.

While it is not serious to equate the social structures of socialist countries and those of capitalist powers overall, it is interesting to note the existence of a certain symmetry in the responses that they each bring to global economic problems. The current evolution of the USSR has its counterpart, to some extent, in the fact that the state in capitalist societies no longer fulfills its function as an instrument of the *dictatorship* of the bourgeoisie in the same way and, moreover, now plays a key role in *integrating* salaried classes, supporting different archaic layers of the bourgeoisie, and, in short, relatively regulating all capitalism on the national and international levels. The USSR's policy of peaceful coexistence, for its part, has an economic correlate in its increasing integration into global markets.

For example, the agricultural crisis of the USSR and the imports that it requires "relieve" the chronic overproduction of the United States, and even "international tension" follows this symmetry by "programming" in complementary fashion the leading industrial sectors of arms production in the United States and the USSR: missiles, atomic bombs, etc.

The fundamental task of the revolutionary avant-garde is to stop the constant self-mutilation from which the communist movement has been suffering since it was required to follow the Stalinist policy of "defending the first socialist state." In the name of the superior interests of the "camp of socialism and peace," with the complicity of the social-democrat and communist bureaucratic labor movements, class compromises have been established throughout the world and a permanent process of reinforcement of the structures of capitalism has been developed. Bureaucrats have taken advantage of it to strengthen their hold over labor states. Soviet theorists have postponed indefinitely the necessary "degeneration" of the state in favor of the reformist myth of a "state of all people." Their approach parallels the western modernists who claim that capitalism will lead to an expropriation of the bourgeoisie and the establishment of a neo-socialist society. In their plans, they each "do without" the need for direct political control of power by the workers. They sidestep this difficulty in the name of realism, the myth of the working class's maturation, the preservation of peace, etc., clearly showing that they have broken with the Marxist analysis of class struggle.

Structuring class struggle on an international scale is the only way to eliminate the foundation of state politics. This politics can only take place with a true antagonism towards international monopoly relations and tends to *suppress* them. It presupposes the suppression of political societies that serve as the support for the different levels of their differentiation: in imperialist metropolises, in underdeveloped countries and also in bureaucratic socialist states. The development of the first stage of the socialist mode of production now raises, on an international scale, the question of the revolutionary passage to the second stage of the socialist mode of production by the international proletariat. This can happen on the condition that the revolutionary movement regains its cohesion and its final goal, which is to lead class struggle to its conclusion: the overthrow and destruction of states as the instruments of class domination and the suppression of classes themselves.

Thesis 6: The State and Modernism in France

The policies of the organizations of the French labor movement have made a decisive contribution to the establishment of the current structures of state monopoly capitalism; they have allowed the French economy to regain the ground it had lost over several decades. For one hundred and fifty years, the French bourgeoisie has remained in power by allying itself with the petite bourgeoisie and farmers, justifying protectionism that clashes with the free exchange of the English bourgeoisie. In terms of investments, the politics of the bourgeoisie led to a delay in industrial investment until the end of the 19th century. Capital was abundant, but it was invested much more in state funds than in industrial value. A large portion of the capital was also placed in foreign funds. Not only was three-fourths of the capital placed abroad erased by the First World War, the departure of capital led to a great weakening of investments in France.

During the war, state intervention (control over foreign commerce and exchange, agreements with industrial leaders for sharing raw materials, increases in the public debt) represented the beginnings of state monopoly capitalism, mainly in the direction of helping it catch up. Yet it was primarily the arrival of the Popular

Front in power, bringing the support of the proletariat to the bourgeoisie, that allowed more profound state intervention to begin, contributing to saving the bourgeoisie from its disarray in the face of the Great Depression. There is a connection between the fact that the Popular Front restored the power of the bourgeoisie and the development of the structures of state monopoly capitalism. The agent of this process was primarily the communist movement. The same mechanism occurred after the Liberation. The bourgeoisie, which failed in 1940, lost power in 1944 and was discredited because of its collaboration. The Communist Party, the only political force firmly implanted in the country, quickly returned the bourgeoisie to power after perfecting its instruments. The structures of state monopoly capitalism made such a leap forward that they left behind some processes of the same type in other capitalist countries. Key sectors of industry, transportation, communications, and credit were nationalized. More than half of the investments were financed by public funds. Finally, the structures of the Monnet Plan, destined at first to coordinate basic sectors, were created.

The structures put in place or supported by the labor movement after the Liberation and used by the bourgeoisie allowed the latter to overcome a very serious economic and political crisis; however, the results were characterized by disparities and imbalances. French agriculture was unable to move out of its archaic structures; regional disparities increased; the misery in areas previously ignored by private capital grew; finally, state capitalism was unable to satisfy social needs, which by their very nature cannot be expressed as solvent demands on the market, requiring a complete transformation of institutions: housing, professional and technical training, sanitation infrastructures, planning, etc.

The specific role of the state in economic development in France led to a particular differentiation of economic ideologies. Three economic ideologies have developed in France:

On the far right, a traditionalist-bourgeois ideology persists. It is the free market approach of the 20th century, favoring free economic and financial mechanisms, the return of the gold standard on an international level, the adjustment of interest rates in function of supply and demand and not in function of arbitrary state decisions. This anti-state perspective is nuanced by moderate interventionism, since absolute economic liberalism is nonsensical in contemporary structures.

Modernism, which stretches from Gaullism to the PSU [Unified Socialist Party], including part of the SFIO [French Section of the Worker's International] and the left-wing Christians, favors: 1. Modifying the structures of capitalism in function of the evolution of productive forces; 2. State intervention to change these structures, resolve economic crises, etc.

A third ideology is shared primarily by the CP [Communist Party] and part of the SFIO; it is a kind of economic traditionalism on the left. This ideology awaits the imminent arrival of a catastrophic economic crisis, without really believeing it will come. It sees concentration and centralization as scandalous and defends all archaic forms of the French economy.

Our assessment may not seem to fit with the fact that the Communist Party contributed to putting the structures of state capitalism into place in 1936 and 1945! It is appropriate to recall some forgotten historical facts, notably that at the same time as the FCP was helping establish these structures, it always tried to limit their scope, insisting on the political necessity of an alliance with the merchant and agricultural petit bourgeoisie. This is how it justified its refusal to apply the program of nationalization proposed by one wing of the Popular Front, a program that was finally reduced to immediate demands. Less well known is the reticence of the Communist Party in 1945. However, when the modernist Mendès-France proposed a program of nationalization to the provisional government that included Communists, they attacked it. Subsequently, Thorez and Mollet opposed the reforms of distribution channels. The policy of defending familial agricultural property and small businesses has been a constant line for the CP since 1936.

For the bourgeoisie, modernism is the ideology that expresses acceptance of state monopoly capitalism and the integration of the proletariat in its structures. The myth of the state, public service, the common good, etc. goes along with the myth of uniting all classes that belong to a common whole: the nation. Yet modernism in its various forms has deeply infiltrated the ranks of the working class. While pure technocratic ideology can be considered to be the extreme right of modernism, it leaves a series of nuances on the left. Technocrats on the left speak of the need to confide power to the "experts" but place a greater emphasis on "participation," "dialog," "conciliation," and "compromise," on the peaceful solution of conflicts with the proletariat. Modernism rejects all concrete nationalism, to the extent that it accepts the structures of bourgeois political society, enlists the proletariat to establish itself as a pressure group and proposes a "progressive" intervention of the state in capitalist relationships of production. Fundamentally, the modernism of the PSU is no different than the modernism of senior officials and certain "avant-garde" bosses.

Modernists have introduced the *new working class*, one that no longer fights in the name of the same objectives as the traditional working class, being less oriented towards salary negotiations and more oriented towards the many aspects of labor processes and production processes. It would be the working class of the era of "consumer society." It is indisputable that the working class has changed, but the ideological formulation of these transformations by the modernists tends to make it into a new myth; in reality, it leads to a reinforcement of alienation, because there is not a *modern* and a *traditional* working class. There is only one working class in which civil servants, employees and agricultural laborers should be included. The revolutionary movement must rely on this real unit, without seeking empty alliances with a dying petit bourgeoisie. Nonetheless, *this myth of a new working class remains operative and expresses the current impossibility of real unification: the powerlessness of the unions to emit unifying order words and to offer an image of the proletariat in which it can be recognized as a whole.* In the union movement, the modernists speak of a possible insertion in "decision centers," of "cracks" in the capitalist machine, etc. The fundamental limit of this strategy, however, is the acceptance of the pre-established framework of the state and the nation. It is better to be suspicious of these kinds of "transitory demands." In any case, only the interested parties could develop their programs, from modes of organization more closely related to the reality of the working class, and within what we will call "subjective units"[1] that dialogue between one industrial branch to another. If the working class does not restructure itself, which implies an entirely different conception of party-union relationships than the "transmission belt," these transitory demands risk being emptied of their revolutionary content and becoming the justification of the most bland reformism.

Here, we are only offering a new formulation of basic Marxist-Leninist tenets. For example, it is not enough for the working class to have a party and revolutionary unions, but it is decisive for it to be structured with an organizational framework adapted to its level: committees, soviets, etc. through which it can express its deepest desires, that will also give avant-garde organizations the means to recognize the true combativeness of different sectors, their level of awareness, their understanding of advanced order words, etc. This type of on-the-fly organization also represents an indispensable antidote to the temptation of manipulation by bureaucratic apparatuses and leaders of the labor movement. In the pre-revolutionary period, a network of basic committees in factories, in neighborhoods, among youths, and the army constitutes a double embryo of power, developing a kind of spare proletarian legality whose subversive position towards state power makes it an irreplaceable strategic weapon for overthrowing the bourgeoisie.

Thesis 7: Political Society

Is Gaullism the power of monopolies? Gaullism appeared at a time when the bourgeoisie saw its means of political domination fading and had to confront a revolutionary situation that threatened its existence as a class. Gaullism represents an attempt to establish a new form of state, a new type of political domination. Its great feat is to have successfully concluded a series of successive compromises, the results of which cannot be purely and simply assimilated to reactionary policies from the point of view of the bourgeoisie. It is true that in 1944 and in 1958, de Gaulle was only able to accomplish the near-impossible feat of bringing different factions of the bourgeoisie together because of the indirect support from the labor movement, in the context of Stalinist or neo-Stalinist strategy. It would be wrong to define Gaullism as the "power of the monopolies," simply because *monopolies, with or without de Gaulle, are not capable of holding power by themselves.* There is no coherent social force behind Gaullism.

The strategy of Gaullism consists of aspiring towards a formation on the right, the UNR [Union for the New Republic], other formations like the Indépendants or the MRP [Popular Republican Movement] and creating a pole of opposition to the FCP, which therefore has the possibility of "elevating" itself to the rank of ringleader of the opposition. The UNR has tried to establish itself as a veritable federation of fiefs, a decentralized party on the American model, not the British. Compromises are made, not at the central level between political headquarters, but at the regional or municipal level, while no one can say that the UNR is the exclusive representative of any local bourgeoisie.

The limits of Gaullism appear in that its solutions, while they suppose the complicity of the communist movement, are limited to a national context, like any bourgeois solution. Kennedyism could have been a type of Gaullism at the international level, but it did not happen because there is no possible international solution for capitalism. It is precisely this inability to find global solutions, to produce global institutions that are capable of resolving the problems raised by the development of productive forces that condemns capitalism as a mode of production. Gaullism, like Kennedyism, like any other solution of this type, is only the expression of a dying bourgeoisie trying to hold on to its dreams.

The contradiction between the high level of "maturity" of productive forces and relationships of production in France, and the immaturity of the class consciousness of the proletariat is the problem of the French Communist Party, and is capital for the avant-garde of revolutionary militants. Moving to a superior stage in revolutionary processes on an international scale depends on unblocking the "over-maturation" of revolution in Western countries (weighed against the "premature" revolutions of 1905 and 1917 in Russia). While it is true that the Party played an openly counter-revolutionary role in certain decisive periods, how can one explain the almost hegemonic control that it continues to exercise over the labor movement? We would have to study the complex historical mediations through which the spontaneous class consciousness of the proletariat was caught in the snares of an organization that bound it, sterilized it and diverted it to serve objectives that were foreign to the proletariat. From its creation, the FCP has been placed in an ambiguous position when the de facto strategy of *socialism in a single country* was developed after the defeat of the German revolution. The party, born in Tours, which only gave lip service to the "21 conditions" of the International, had kept the structures and the people of social-democracy: it was not an instrument of revolution. The choice of a numerous and muddled CP would play the role of "diplomatic pawn" for the Soviet state and contribute to releasing the pressure of the interventionists on Russia, while bringing the authority of the October Revolution to those remaining after the failure of French social-democracy.

It would be an oversimplification to explain what followed by this original flaw, especially since the compromise between the Communist International and the Social-Democrats tactically rallied to the cause did not last. Yet as soon as the right was chased out of the party, the left was beaten and excluded in turn after the death of Lenin—all within the context of a sectarian political position that appeared ultra-leftist, but where verbal and physical violence replaced perspective. In fact, the first appearance of the communist left, in the 1920s, quickly split from the workers' avant-garde. Contact was never reestablished. As for the Party, which despite its gesticulations consolidated its hold on the most revolutionary wing of the labor movement, it was able to calmly execute its turn to the right in the policies of the Popular Front. The support that this first communist movement was able to provide to the primary struggles of the proletariat was not completely ineffective. Despite its theoretical mediocrity and the decline in the level of militants, the Party was able to navigate between both ideological terrorism (defending the USSR, a necessity of monolithism) and official political institutionalization, during periods of collaboration with governments. It did not hesitate to ally itself with conservative forces or employ nationalist and chauvinist demagogy on occasion, while staying close enough to the reality of the labor movement that it could continue to monopolize its expression.

Over the past decade, the foundations of this hegemony have started to shake. The leaders of the FCP are worried that the monolithic façade of the international communist movement has been shattered; without the cohesive element of a façade of cooperation between parties on a global scale, the only things that remain are tradition, an empty organizational discipline and completely vulnerable propaganda themes. This may explain the FCP's rush to condemn heresies, its preference for excommunication, and its hesitation to accept Italian-style polycentrism.

The entire history of opposition groups of all stripes, however, shows their misunderstanding of the degree of Stalinist implantation in the French labor movement. The entire strategy of these groups until now has been to see opposition activities as a way to recruit militants who would then be organized elsewhere. In short, they put in place structures they believed capable of leading the movement through crises and revolutionary situations that would lead to the collapse of party hegemony by entire sections. The construction of an "organization of leaders" destined to become the future center of a new revolutionary party became a sterile groupuscular activity, and also a caricature of the defects of the organizations they criticized. As long as the Left Opposition continues to waver between abstract, necessarily dogmatic, critique not verified by militant policies, and underground *entrist* activities, the political monopoly of the FCP in the labor world will never be threatened.

Thesis 8: Revolutionary Organization

The working class will never be able to modify capitalist relationships of production spontaneously and transform state power while respecting bourgeois legality. The internal contradictions come from the fact that the working class does not currently have the means to develop its struggles in a framework other than the one predetermined by the relationships of capitalist exploitation of national states.

Capitalism, however, has given itself the means to transfer and resolve in part on the international level the crucial problems posed by these struggles on a national level. Therefore, each of the sectorial struggles of the proletariat tends to call the international framework of capitalism into question, but given that the labor organizations have enclosed these struggles inside the borders of the state, they are condemned to powerlessness.

Monopoly internationalization is nothing more than the international placement of capital, the crystallization of surplus value extracted from the social work of the proletariat by the structures of capitalist exploitation. We can therefore say that the fruit of the proletariat's labor, as a productive force, is opposed to the historical and political development of the proletariat as a class. The proletariat, however, effectively holds vast power. It is no longer an interchangeable resource; its avant-garde has the means to paralyze production radically. It can contribute to making crises arise that could lead to revolutionary situations. This potential is so threatening that unions have accepted the *contractualization* and *institutionalization* of strikes. Socialist revolution, however, will only occur in highly developed industrial nations with a new type of revolutionary party and a new type of organization of the masses, including a radical change of their reciprocal relationships. The communists have not yet performed a scientific reexamination of Leninist standards of organization. Some think that they have done it, but they have only returned to social-democrat methods, abandoning any revolutionary perspective.

The current centralism of the communist parties is technically absurd. The same leaders—in fact the same handful of leaders—are entrusted with multiple, complex tasks: elaborating the political line, supervising the organization, the press, labor and agricultural union struggles, youth organizations, etc. Without denying the leadership role of the party, we can assert *the need for an effective decentralization of the direction of mass struggle at its various sectoral levels.* Only under this condition will these struggles stop being bogged down in national, regional, racial, corporatist, etc. archaisms that the bourgeoisie strives to keep artificially alive in the framework of capitalist relationships of production. It means repeating the obvious fact that there is no other means for a "transitional program" of the working class to be developed by itself and according to objectives that it can set at any time. The role of the revolutionary avant-garde is to contribute to unifying struggles, to *interpret* each stage in the perspective of the whole, to propose order words that enable movement to a higher level of struggle. To exist, to "speak out," the working class needs a *place*, an institutional *object* specific to it and from which it can take its place in the signifying web of history. The irreplaceable *signifying chain* is the texture of its organization, its internal workings, its public expression, its work methods, etc. everything that will mark it as radically different from the ideology and the practices of the dominant class. This does not mean that it will be able to constitute itself as *signifying something for itself and by itself,* that it will be able to signify its alliances and compromises for others.

In industrialized developed nations, the working class would be perfectly capable of taking over the leadership of a socialist state, but the syndical and political order words of the current communist movement only refer the struggles of workers to their permanent formation as a *revolutionary social class*, and to their national particularities. There are shared roles between bourgeois *ideology* and reformist *practices*: they each *sociologize* the different wage classes, ages, genders, technological conditions, cultural conditions, etc. The policy that claims to unite the so-called anti-monopolist layers around the working class divides it, dispersing its action and neutralizing its revolutionary effectiveness. While Marxist research should participate in creative development and formulate responses that go beyond the solutions of the bourgeoisie in every domain, the "research" of the FCP, for example, is nothing more than a droning repetition of empty formulas and imaginary promises. The revolutionary party should examine economic, cultural and social problems in depth and express them by means of order words, so that its daily practices never break the *fundamental historical chain* for partial and transitory goals. The working class cannot and should not engage in a dialog with the petite bourgeoisie, farmers, monopolies, etc. like the leaders of communist parties claim to do in its name. Its only interlocutor is itself, to the extent that it is marked by a historical finality that sets it apart as a class, the only one that is not closed in on itself and its own interests. Because the working class carries its own subversion within it, because it is the only class capable of imposing the end of class divisions on the other classes, the primary task of the revolutionary party is to protect it from all outside ideologies and its primary duty is to extract everything outside it that seems to carry a trace of truth. The working class can only engage in a "dialog" with itself through the intermediary of currents and organizations that are intrinsically part of itself.

Despite the unequal development of struggles, they share the potential to end in global revolution. Leon Trotsky already recognized this fact when he developed his theory of permanent revolution from an indication in Marx. No repetition of history can be imagined at the level of one country or another. Coming out of feudalism, Yemen, for example, did not encounter a future punctuated by the emergence of a bourgeois royalty, then a "French-style" revolution allowing the harmonious development of commercial, financial and then industrial capitalism. Yemen moved *directly* to "rootless cosmopolitan" oligopolies, to use Stalinist terminology. The stage of bourgeois revolution is missing, or it is only a historical sham, an artificially maintained archaism allowing the oligopolies to develop. Communist support of Aref, Ben Bella and

Soekarno shows the same blindness. This is why social revolution is the only possible result in every current situation of class struggle: the *objective conditions* are ripe for every democratic and national struggle to lead to the stage of the industrial and agricultural proletariat taking power. However, this does not exempt us from analyzing as clearly as possible why the *subjective conditions* do not allow us to expect this revolutionary deluge from the proletariat of industrial powers, which is stuck in a "permanent immaturity."

When we are so quick to "liquidate" the historical foundations of the existence of social-democratic parties and national liberation parties, aren't we taking our dreams for reality? Aren't these parties thriving and retrenched behind the state powers of the bastions of capitalism and the countries subjected to neo-colonialism? Doesn't our insistence on having the working class express and establish the truth of the revolutionary party lead to rehabilitating the myth of spontaneism and bringing anarchist and populist themes back in favor? Placing the accent on these themes unconditionally could lead to giving credence to the idea that there is a "good working class" (like Rousseau's "good savage") whose intelligent, revolutionary and pure nature, whose revolutionary penchants are diverted by the evil stewards of large organizations. There is no doubt that the working class, in large majority, is much closer to the way bureaucrats of all categories of the labor movement picture it than that fantasy! The foundations of our challenge to the "models" of political and syndicalist organization, and to their reciprocal relationships that are inadequate to the real situation of workers in developed capitalist countries can be found less in a philosophy of freedom or in humanist or psycho-sociological considerations of democracy in general than in the *development of industrial societies itself.*

No matter what the neo-capitalist or socialist bureaucratic regime, one cannot expect to see any fundamental problem resolved using the current modes of organization and types of institutions. The only real possible outcome is the establishment of planning on a global scale, since it is true that any provision, coordination, elaboration and division of the factors of production and means of financing requires the possibility of an uninterrupted collection of means. Yet what sense do the planning pretensions of modern capitalism have when it appears that, for political and economic reasons, it will never be able to take charge of all of the zones "left behind" by imperialism in a rational way? Global socialist planning could offer not only to organize developed sectors but also and *in the same way* the straggling, archaic, etc. sectors. All of these spots of misery and meaninglessness that rot society, that are condemned in the name of "non-profitability" would be recaptured by means of a plan that would remodel international social space and human ways of life.

The needs and the desires of human beings, however, at different times and in different situations, their misery, their anxieties, their failures, etc., do not, for the most part, come from this level of rationality. It is up to people to be able to express them and up to society to remedy them in the most coherent and least alienating way possible. Political society in bourgeois democracies is only the marketplace of the various factions of capitalism. Political society in a socialist democracy would be a place of dialog between technological and scientific forces of production on the one hand and human institutions on the other, in that they are adjusted to respond at all times to both the material needs of each individual and also his or her deepest aspirations and demands to give meaning to his or her existence. While the increase in productive forces tends to lead to increasing concentration, no central organism will ever be able to respond to differentiated social needs. This shows the need for different sectors of the "masses" to speak out, for them to be given the means to express themselves in forms that are not automatically antisocial, non-integrable, absurd and, in the end, alienating. *In other words, it is not a question of only considering planning from the perspective of production, circulation and distribution, but also planning the "production of institutions," of all of the forms of social organization capable of serving as a "guarantor" of industrial society.*

A current with sociological aspirations is now endeavoring to show that the working class is also marked by bourgeois ideology. On the level of consumption, it seems that only quantitative factors separate a bourgeois from a proletarian, but in their relationships related to production, in the mode of their relationships with professional, social, etc. "supervision," on cultural, ethical and even unconscious levels, bourgeois and proletarians are truly *two distinct races*. The impetus of class struggle is the fact that capitalist society is arranged in function of the particular needs of a dying class. Despite progress, the working class can never feel at home in it. You only have to look at the way urban planning, hospitals, and universities are conceived of in a culture conditioned by television to find this constant: nothing is arranged to allow creative social activity to exist. On the contrary, all of these structures are calculated so that each individual is channeled into isolation, social seriality, herd instincts and access to "calming" leisure activities for workers.

Order words such as "Bread, Peace and Freedom" have become notions as abstract as the bourgeois emblems of "Liberty, Equality, Fraternity." The revolutionary movement can and should initiate another type of response. It should take a stand against the reduction of the working class to a simple function of production and consumption. It should always put the common trait forward, the fundamental goal of struggle, the only one that is capable of giving some cohesion to workers and reconstituting them as a revolutionary social class. This common trait, this "institutional object," is the state. The key to the situation still remains the need to overthrow state power. For the FCP, the common denominator of various struggles is the monopolist hydra. It has a hundred faces and as many responses that divide people. The only way to unify the struggles is to update objectives and give workers the possibility to take aim at the fundamental objective: bourgeois control of state power. On these questions, the gap between the FCP and the CGT is obvious. Take an example: a group of revolutionary militants in the mining sector would have to confront not only the political and organizational aspects of day to day struggle, but also to articulate its problems with those of all of the national mining regions and adjacent branches, to enter into relationships with the militants of corresponding unions in the EEC, etc. If it were the petroleum industry, a series of problems would be raised with the popular organizations of producing countries, etc. Developing this program on a national, regional and also international level, however, presupposes significant transformations of the syndicalist movement and consequently in the communist movement.

Some might object that the central committee of the FCP has been gathering commissions together around it for a long time, commissions comprised of "competent and devoted" comrades in every domain. Consulting the work of these commissions is the best proof of the inability of a central headquarters to provide answers to a multiplicity of problems. With startling regularity, these "specialists" miss the essential. This is due less to incompetence than to a "conditioning" to the work methods of party leaders, such that the slightest indication by a high-ranking leader is enough to determine an orientation and impose the sterilization of all research. The same is true of the congress "exercises" that consist of empty speeches on pre-established themes. Nothing separates these methods from those of the traditional bourgeoisie. Yet the revolutionary avant-garde must also look at its own work methods, because, unfortunately, there is often little to distinguish it from large organizations! A revolutionary party will not emerge by miracle; it is a synthesis to be won, not in the ideological domain, but in the reality of class struggle. The new weapon, the prototype of the party that the working class needs to engage in revolution in capitalist countries can only be radically different from the parties that currently exist and those that have existed until now.

The centralist disease of communist parties is due less to the ill intentions of their leaders than to the false relationships they establish with mass movements. The Marxist movement does not follow the same rhythm and does not have the same type of understanding of events as the masses. Yet it is vital for both that the signification of the progress and retreats in class struggle be constantly explained. Without this explanation, a victory like the one in June 1936 could quickly turn into a defeat. Inversely, a disaster like the Paris Commune allowed the global working class to clearly identify its future possibilities. Some theorists think it is inevitable that the Party will turn into a bureaucratic outgrowth of the labor movement and they have returned to libertarian ideas in terms of organization. Yet because of the increasing integration of the working class, whatever institutional system is developed within it will always risk being "recuperated" by capitalism.

Under the pretext of unity at any price, no syndicate could claim the vocation of being the "people's syndicate" for all people. Revolutionary syndicalism is something other than consumer protection, cooperatives, etc. Recently, just as the Communist Party has integrated bourgeois parliamentary system, unions have had the tendency to betray their fundamental vocation to gather together the dynamic forces of the working class, change its internal relationships of force to the detriment of reformist currents and strengthen its cohesion against employers. Exceptionally, in periods of heightened struggle, a union can reveal itself capable of bringing the entire working class with it; but this occurs in pre-revolutionary periods. This type of objective, in normal periods, can only mean that the revolutionary current is aligned with the average level of the masses and leads inevitably to reinforcing reformism and the dominant ideology.

Mass revolutionary politics would consist of helping the youth avant-garde, for example, acquire the means to develop its own politics *by itself*, train militants at each sectional level, make them better able to take initiatives that could attract a majority of the youth masses, etc. These communist youth could then establish alliances with other movements!

Leading the way for this politics is inseparable from putting into place a mode of organization that is very different than the communist-bureaucratic ideas in terms of organizing the masses, which have shown themselves incapable of capitalizing on the various forms of spontaneous struggle. A politics of unified action, without support from the masses, mechanically leads to "manipulations" at the top and cartels blindly developing their compromises on the basis of the reformist "greatest common denominator." A final example: without a correct orientation on the question of abortion, and without a revolutionary work method, the UFF[2] has become a coterie of "old wives' tales" when it could be pushing a sizeable national campaign for the defense of the hundreds of thousands of women who have to resort to clandestine abortions every year...

Thesis 9: The Regrouping Stage

It is not part of our project to define specific lines of action and modes of political intervention for bringing revolutionary militants together under the current conditions in France, or to imagine what forms and at what rhythm this regrouping could contribute to advance conditions favorable to the creation of a revolutionary party.

We propose to define a general outline of the conditions of possibility of this project. At the present stage, revolutionary militants and the groups that they can make, while they may be desirable and indispensable, are unable to form even the embryo of this type of party. When a "revolutionary current" has started to emerge and begin its theoretical and political progression, when it is sufficiently implanted in the mass organizations controlled by the FCP, when the crisis that the Party is undergoing has reached the point that communist militants on the left start to detach themselves and pursue their own politics, then the later stages can be considered.

The passionate fervor of small groups on the far left and their blindness do not contribute anything to this process. Neither does the "conspiratorial" style of militants in most opposition groups today.

Is it enough to say that the objective will be met the day that the working class has regained "consciousness" of its power? In reality, the avant-garde of the working class is aware, in a certain way, of the impasse of its current struggles. The majority of workers have the impression of "going in circles." They know that political and syndicalist organizations offer them no alternatives. Yet the working class, as such, does not have any means at its disposal other than existing organizations to express itself and to be represented. Without any other alternative, the working masses feel almost forced to remain faithful to them, if only to preserve a minimum of unity and maintain a minimal demarcation between them and the enemy.

Would it be enough to create a new party and new unions to clarify the situation? All attempts in this direction have ended in failure. A revolutionary organization must be introduced into the working class *beforehand* to be able to catalyze the phenomenon of transforming and eliminating existing organizations. The nature of their entanglement in the current political and social system of the bourgeoisie, and the way that the working class passively assumes the reformist image they propose for it determine, in large part, the *means to employ* and the *intermediate stages* needed to give structure to a revolutionary avant-garde that is not seen as foreign by the masses and in which they gradually recognize themselves as their struggles develop. For a revolutionary party to be in the working class "like a fish in water," it is not enough to assert its necessity and to start listing the elements of a program. The consciousness of the working class itself must be changed in correlation to a revolutionary politics led by the avant-garde party: updating revolutionary *situations* and exploiting them coherently. A certain number of preliminary conditions must therefore be met for this party to be created. The historic decision to create it cannot come from the "voluntarist" pretentions of a small group of revolutionary militants. (The disorganized attempts to keep the old 4th International alive sometimes raise extra obstacles to the construction of a revolutionary party. While it is already absurd to want to create a revolutionary party from scratch without any basic militant establishment, the same operation attempted on the scale of a centralized international party is purely and simply an aberration that has the appalling practical results of tarnishing the theoretical contributions of L. Trotsky in the eyes of ill-informed militants.)

It is one thing to initiate an overall perspective on struggle, to imagine its possible phases and inevitable ordeals, to discuss the means needed in the short term, etc. It is another thing to establish straight away the catalog of demands that could "hook" the masses. Depending on the way that a party with a revolutionary vocation gives itself the right to engage in this type of development, which will only be valid *if it is accepted immediately by a significant part of the working avant-garde*, a certain type of relationship of subjugation will be predetermined between the party and the masses. (E.g. taking up the theory of unions as a "driving force" as if it were self-evident.) Slowed down by these obstacles during decisive trials, the so-called revolutionary party will reveal itself incapable of living up to its historic task. To get around this difficulty, it is not enough to declare "good resolutions" against bureaucracy and to swear allegiance to the Leninist norms of democratic centralism.

Small revolutionary groups, with their misunderstanding of the real nature of this problem, tend to recreate ideologically and support indirectly the structures and functioning of the political and syndical apparatuses of the "large organizations." Without sufficient clarification and questioning, they come to explain the bureaucratization of the labor movement uniquely from the political errors and betrayals of its leaders or because of unfortunate circumstances, generally described from the perspective of a historical philosophy. This leads to two basic notions: "the period of ascent" that "comes from the base" and the "period of decline" where revolutionaries have to work against the current!

When the conditions for its creation are met, the revolutionary party will immediately be "recognized" by a notable part of the working avant-garde as an indispensable instrument in its struggle. Verification of its reality will therefore occur *on the level of class struggle.* Its very creation will cause a change in the relationship of forces. And the bourgeoisie will react! Misunderstanding the need for this "counter-ordeal" would mean losing the essential part of Marxist-Leninist scientific teaching. The creation of the Bolshevik Party took place under given historical conditions after a long political fight within social-democracy. It gave rise to entirely new forms of organization. Bolshevism developed on the basis of certain types of struggle, which saw their objectives and methods changed in return. Claiming to create from scratch a proletariat revolutionary organization in a predictable timeframe in France today, claiming to be able to unite the first core group and begin defining a program, are the claims of a utopian perspective that presupposes a characteristic ignorance of Marxism-Leninism and the history of the labor movement.

Alongside several objective factors—conditions of social struggles, political crises, etc.—certain international factors enter into the equation and could play a determinant role. The triumph of a socialist revolution in no matter what capitalist power would cause a chain reaction in the evolution of the labor movement. In the same way, the reemergence of proletarian revolutionary currents in socialist countries would have an incalculable effect on this process. We will have to take a more detailed look at the possibilities of intervention by a group of communist revolutionary militants in different social and political sectors. Yet we can only do it after acquiring a certain amount of practical results. We would like to avoid adding our names to the all too long list of avant-garde currents and organizations that were unable to do more than formulate critiques and promises, while in reality they were despairingly reduced to turning in circles.

Nevertheless, supposing that history will condemn us to a similar fate, we would prefer to remain silent, for what is to come, and retain... the benefit of the doubt.

11

From One Sign to the Other (excerpts)

Can a *stroke*, a check, be properly taken as a minimal sign? Scoria of an instrumentality, point or knife, movements that delimit space too squarely, they only become signifying material to the extent that they are used in another system. On their own, they have no coherent way of articulating themselves with those like them.

A *point*. What is it? How can it be defined except by reference to something else? A crossing of lines. It goes adrift…

A *spot*. A spot of random shape lending itself to any infinitesimal reduction that the imagination lends it, to the point that it refuses to consider any scissiparity that would transform it into a multiplicity of spots. In short, a point.

A spot meets another spot… What do they say to each other?… An impossible encounter. Impossible to imagine that another claims to exist.

Let us assume that an evil demon forces them to confront each other… Their immediate and merciless marriage would result in the negation of their multiplicity.

We return to the swamp of spots.

Here are spots; by convention or indifference, one would say that they are one and the same spot. Is a notebook more stained by receiving a multitude of spots or by being purely and simply dunked in a bucket of ink?

Let's let the spot take precedence and forbid the one and the multiple from signifying anything by themselves.

What do the contents matter as long as we have the contour?

Unless the universe is suddenly plunged in infinite ink-black night.

Police emergency squad: *cogito ergo sum.* The bright siren saves me whenever some imperfect contour leaves hope of a response to my call…

Does God have a contour?

If He is light, then there is no doubt: our interloping silhouettes receive their nuance from His perfection.

But if He is pitch black?

Police emergency squad: *cogito ergo sum.* The affair is in the bag. What do the contents matter, we'll have the contour. It has been this way too long for us to come back to it validly. Statute of limitations: a year and a day would have sufficed, yet it has been understood for three hundred and thirty years.

Here are spots that I place around I under the radiant eyes of God. I will take care to only grasp them by their contour; with kid gloves; a delicate operation requiring regular phenomenologico-mathematical training… I digress. It is impossible to isolate a contour of spots from its support. It is a truth of experience and I think that no one can change it. Maybe God! But do the demands of his perfection authorize him to deal with things as insignificant as spots?

Special treatment for the black of the spot: preserving the contour, it gives the content temporary autonomy, allowing it to be used as a simple support of the contour, just for the time of a few transpositions, then it is erased and transferred to the exterior...

Things are arranged more or less this way: I take a spot, I put it on another, gap to gap, their contours vibrate, hesitate, then blend in a curious twist. It allows us to verify in passing the law according to which emptiness, unlike being, is identical to empty space at any point on the area to which it is related.

With a bit more pedantry, one would say that the empty space of their intersection tends, at the limit, to be identical to the union of their non-shared parts—this composition of the whole being is designated by some logicians as an extension.

Now we are equipped with a curious instrument that we will call the *point-sign*, which has the following characteristics:
  —it is unique and indivisible,
  —it was engendered by two mother spots first treated with emptiness,
  —an examination of its morphology allows several false trails to be distinguished in its false interior, including:
        —an anti-cavity, common to both the father and mother
        —two distinct anti-cavities, one coming from the father and the other from the mother
        —the two latter ones being one and the same as the first and, moreover, indistinguishable from the so-called external area

Here is the sign. The sign of nothing. A sign that, referring only to itself, refers to nothing. It carries nothingness within itself. And for this reason, it connects without difficulty to other signs that carry the same nihility. While it is still impossible to distinguish between them, they may be delineated by virtue of an inexistence solely established outside themselves.

Is it the same one each time? Not even the movement of same to same is guaranteed in its identity. It is not only a univocal passage from void to void, but also an accent, a trembling of being on its passage. Nothing is determined in repetition: neither the fate of nothingness, nor the salvation of an outside meaning.

Let's review our acquisitions. Spots contaminate each other irreversibly, point-signs exist by themselves and we can try to mark them with each other. Their false internal parts give them a pseudo-field that lets them take an illusory distance while protecting them from the narcissistic relationship of annihilation.

Unlike with spot-points, a *chain of point-signs* is possible.

With spots, the one and the multiple lost their features and were globally sent back to the alternative between being and non-being. It was the Manichean triumph of the spotted.

With the point-sign, interior and exterior being one and the same in the heart of nothingness, the one and the multiple were made possible in written form. It opens the era of the signifier.

An emptiness hollowed out by an anti-hole. The materiality of the sign is only the support of this essential organ.

Two point-signs mate without resulting in the mortal effusion that we know is inevitable with spots. Here the *unary trait* is established. Can it be articulated with another unary trait? They can link together to form, for example, a line, a uniform and featureless trail on which all the points are equivalent. Except for two points: those marking the beginning and end of the chain. Although one can posit the equivalency of a solution of continuity and circularity because of the law that identifies the cavity from the inside and the lack of determination from the outside. Under these conditions, any point on the line could be taken indifferently as a point tangent to a cut.

Which goes to show that narcissistic passion can be expressed as both circular repetition and a death sentence.

What is a point-sign other than this circularity, except that it is intersected by itself, in its heart?

Being able to indicate alternation and the breaks in it provides the means for transcribing all languages. More and less, white and black, etc., are usually enough for us to operate in binary systems. At the moment, however, we are looking at the heart of the sign and not to its systematic use. Moreover, aren't plus and minus archaic instruments? Each one external to the other, they are separated by a blank space that plays, without appearing to, an essential role: it veils the fundamental sign that we are trying to pin down.

Let's let the line wander and picture the case where a unary trait, composed of two point-signs, is crossed by another unary trait. A complex operation!

Four point-signs face to face: each one hesitating to pair up with its two immediate neighbors or, diagonally, with the one across from it. All four of them lean on the central bar, like holding hands at a bus stop.

This axial repartition around a point that does not exist raises a few questions.

Does a single crossing require the involvement of four point-signs?

Let's look at each case separately.

1. No point-sign coupled with axial nothingness gives: nothing of nothing.

2. A single point-sign coupled with axial nothingness, and the latter is immediately incorporated in the reserves of nothingness of the point-sign. Correlatively, the nothing of nothing in the first case has a support.

3. Two point-signs make a unary trait.

4. Three point-signs combine in a single unary trait, or are able to create an intersection. And if they are unable to do so as three, there is no reason that they would be better able to as four. In the same way that we had to accept the "cogito" and the contour without discussion, we will admit by axiom that there is "intersection." Three signs are therefore enough.

5. Four signs or more are superfluous; every point above the third can fuse with one of the first three without problem. Unless we want to make several intersections.

We know that for a square to function as an intersection, it must necessarily eliminate one of its poles. It is like death; or at least the kind of death that gives a bridge player the possibility to play with another player's hand. Here death is relegated without difficulty to axial nothingness.

I have forgotten the case where negative numbers of point-signs are spread around the empty axial point. I will let curious and informed readers explore this case.

A unary trait marked by a point-sign: this is the basic sign.

The marking, or castration, as you wish, of the primitive stroke constitutes an external reduplication of the internal marking of the point-sign.

A *plus* is now possible. A plus with three points or, if you prefer, a plus amputated of a quarter of itself.

We can now move forward more quickly. Let's take a *minus*. What is a minus other than an uncrossed plus? In summary, a minus would be worth less than a plus?

Among the essential characteristics of signs, we are told, the most important are their differentiation and distinctive oppositions. I do not wish to contradict the authorities on the matter here, but just propose, more modestly, a unique prototype of the sign that would be able to account for all creation on its own.

Searching for the God sign.

A blinking red light in the night marks alternation on the background of an absence that is nowhere asserted positively. It could lead one to think that a minus is much less than a plus!… Indeed!

Emptiness, absence absolutely require a specific signifying support.

In fact, binary notation always relies on three elements, if we take into consideration the existence of the separation between the signs. Adjacent to the plus and minus, the blank is a constitutive part of the sign. It is the sign of the sign. Could we reduce it beyond a signifying battery? Could we, for example, identify the minus with the plus?

Take a chain of point-signs, circular or not. Let's try to indicate a position using crossed plus and minus in such a way that the continuity is not altered. We should note that, so far, the coordinates of inside and outside for the point-sign, no more than those for above and below for a chain of points, are not irreversibly orientable.

Let us form a chain of crossed point-signs: the three points positioned symmetrically in relation to a base line constituted of mediating points that cannot be made symmetrical will indifferently represent the alternatives "plus followed by minus" or "minus followed by plus" or the sequences of "plus followed by plus" or "minus followed by minus."

We will write plus as ... and minus as ... or vice versa.

The three starting signs of the binary battery have been converted into three new elements:

1. A unique basic sign formed of three point-signs.

2. The possibility of the two point-signs being adjacent, in other words, suppression of the *blank sign*.

3. A sequencing rule stating that the adjacency of two basic signs can only take place in one point, since each one of them cannot be immediately connected to more than two other basic signs, which makes the formation of chain intersections impossible and prohibits the development of diverging networks.

The point-sign can be both here and elsewhere at the same time, distinct or agglomerated. As the raw material of the sign, it does not signify by itself. The positionality of symmetry and dissymmetry is only possible, at any level, in a complex structure that immediately puts *three basic signs* into play—or at least six point-signs along with all of their complications!

The same ternary structure can represent a point-sign, a basic sign and a chain of three basic signs closed in on itself. Taken by themselves, each of these elements is nothing: a single point-sign oscillates in the imbalance between being and nothingness, a basic sign threatens to agglutinate its three point-signs or disperse them and a triangular chain of three signs can, at any moment, fall back on two signs, one sign or nothing.

We can only specify the nature and the identity of the structure under consideration with the arrival of a *fourth term* that initiates its law of recurrence.

Law, death, closure and indetermination are retroactively involved with the existence of this fourth term. The combinations are closed: it must be taken elsewhere, always beyond.

The point-sign probably remains open because of the elimination of its quaternary pole.

The point-sign projects its system of internal-external cuts on a zero dimension of space.

With the basic sign, a neutral axis serves as the foundation of the possibility of the ambivalence of the third pole. While the first dimension is frankly used in scriptural linearity, the same is not true of the second dimension. Its use is marked by a deep ambiguity.

When the two valences of the end of the chain swing like the waving eyes of a caterpillar, and then opt for one or the other of the possible articulations, an irreversible determination is made for the link in question. It brings about a modification, a specification, a new possible meaning for the entire chain. What happens then to the second dimension? It remains confined to a thin outgrowth, a palpitation running down the line in the first dimension.

Under these circumstances, can we even honestly say that it is used?... At an ornamental level, maybe! Yet look at what remains in Morse code!

The rosaries of basic signs have no other choice in their diachronic hitching but to choose, once and for all, between even and odd. The conception of their signifying world is much different than the chains of organic chemistry, for example. The prohibition cast on the second dimension should be related to the one against the first dimension for point-signs: marking can only occur there in an anti-dimension.

The *chain effect* of basic signs in the first dimension may only be an external consequence of the primary process at the level of point-signs. There is a series of related requirements here for which the reasons escape me.

Maybe one of the mysteries of "transversality" implies that the shortest path, and the only path, between two points is a non-existent third point.

Can we say of the desire to be plus or minus, or to be plus for the minus, or minus for the plus, can we say that the phallus can only be deployed in a space that prohibits, for example, any non-ambiguous response to the nevertheless inevitable demand for an additional dimension?

Yet if the written sign remains intrinsically linked to the space it catches on and cuts into according to a perpetual movement of retention, is the same true of sound signs? What is their support? Is their nature such that it is enough for them to bring into play a void space that is peculiar to the subject? Wouldn't it have been more elegant for us to imagine our basic sign in a less repulsive form than the triangle: a curve, for example, the essence of a turn? Our writing would have been closer to the one used by physicists to transcribe phenomena of alternation in wave effects and would have been more conducive to dreaming... Sun broken on the horizon, a ray twisting to recover its lost unity by connecting to another broken sun...

Once again, the basic sign drifts towards the point sign: contour cut by a spot. But cut in two distinct and non-exchangeable ways: cut from above, cut from below... cut inside, cut outside...

Don't the cutting of the point-sign and opening of the ternary basic sign as cutting and opening develop in the dimension of non-being that is supposed to double space at every point?

Is the fourth dimension anything other than this zero dimension? Can we conceive of a dimension "minus something" as the place of the unconscious: the navel of the dream as the point of passage from subject to being.

How can we avoid the temptation of reifying the dimension of lack? How can this relay be preserved from any ambiguity constituted by the to-and-fro between "no being" and "no meaning"? How can we avoid a great reconciliation under the auspices of the God-Nothing between the apostles of nothing and those of the Holy Trinity?

With constituted languages, there are hardly any surprises: from code to message, the space of signification—the epitome of civilized terrain—is furrowed, squared off in every direction; even the finest poetic subtleties are ordered in the implacable signifying battery…

Any over-determination of meaning could, in principle, be rigorously articulated in a system of signs in which all possible variants could be encoded.

Consider, for example, the phonetic chunks shared by the following two sentences:

—Le BORD JOLI de la rivière.[1]

—Le sénateur BORGEAUD LIT dans son lit.[2]

Let's transcribe them using a very primitive binary system (in reality a simple coded transcription), using the following code:

BOR = +
JO   = + +
LI   = + + +

Separation between the syllables = −

Separation between the two words   = – –

We can then write the part in capital letters of the first sentence as:

+ – – + + – + + +

and the part of the second sentence as:

+ – + + – – + + +

But by changing the code in this way:

BOR   = + or + –

JO   = + +

LI   = + + + or – + + +

separation between the syllables   = –

separation between the two words   = – –

we can also read the part of the first sentence and the second sentence (as well as a third "sentence" that would be composed of three taken separately as words) in a single binary text:

+ – – + + – – + + +

We should note that in more developed cases that we cannot address here, where a certain amount of interval data would enter into the translation, we would reach problems of interpretation that call into question cuts that pass not only through the inside of words but also inside groups of syllables, opening the possibility of taking charge of elements that have ambiguity of a different nature.

Our new code is composed of four additional + and two –. The fact that something had to be added to combine the translations of the imagined variants can be balanced against the need to remove something from the point-spot and from crossed unary traits to have them function in a signifying way. Phenomena of multivalence of meaning in a constituted text seem not to come from the anti-dimension of the cut that comes into play with point-signs and basic signs.

However, a passage between these different orders must exist!

The example chosen here may have seemed childish! We can admit, however, that a mechanism like the one for which it served as the pretext, allows *any type* of ambiguity concerning rhythms, accents, intonations, letters, phonemes, monemes, morphemes, semantemes, riddles, puns, etc. to be articulated in binary chains.

Imagine someone who enjoys a particular genre and who, at a symphony concert, only pays attention to the timpani, cymbals and triangle. Stopwatch in hand, he or she carefully records each of their successive appearances. It is not impossible that he or she would be able to reconstitute a rigorous reference to the musical text, from which a good musician could find the title of the piece, the author and, why not?, the general texture of his or her writing…

To pass this test with success, a certain number of conditions would have to be met:

—the information the musician possesses about the musical codes in circulation is: 1. sufficiently coherent to allow him or her to decipher an orchestral text from one of its weakest sub-ensembles, 2. sufficiently extensive that it includes the proposed sample;

—the information provided by the music lover in question is sufficient in quantity and in coherence relative to the structure of the text that there is a margin of security so that conjectural factors such as noise, fatigue, luck, intuition, etc. can be reduced.

It goes without saying that these various elements of indecision could almost be completely eliminated by replacing listening to the musician with an electronic calculator! The progress of machinism has not ceased to surprise us! We have no idea what bulldozer work will soon take place in the hedges of literary space, leaving phonemes inanimate and soulless, and incapable of being attached to our soul.

Most transcription systems continue to neglect the codification of many signifying elements that are interpreted according to custom or personal understanding.

This is the case, for example, of musical writing, for which we know the elements of intervals, silence, rhythm, etc. were the result of a long historical evolution, one that still relies on oral tradition to transmit essential indications related to interpretation.

In truth, signifying rationality only exercises its hold with real tyranny today on the most exposed sectors of mass production and consumption.

Yet there is every reason to believe that with the development of computers, systems of rigorous formulation will gradually impose themselves in every domain of human existence, making each of the old use values undergo a scientific and technological treatment.

The individual subject would then have completely lost its natural right to "consume meaning," the conquest of which culminated in the Enlightenment.

The question would remain of a possible relay, from another status of subjectivity, to various familial, political, cultural, etc. levels, in a society that has reworked the relationships of production existing in contemporary industrial societies from top to bottom.

Within the circularity of processes of human existence and social mechanisms, the potential of a cut is preserved along with the reemergence of a group desire that is not actualized anywhere on the order of determination.

History only appears to be saturated with causes and effects.

The image of the passage from same to same, reflected in the mirror of an imminent emergence of the same to the nascent other, increases its inertia up to the point of a possible breakdown of the structures that support it.

Every thing that could not authorize anyone to expect that the same to the same could go beyond its specular status by itself to open a ternary order.

Dialectic only functions with its third term, which in truth is its only real time, since the two others are only retrospections of meaning.

We must recognize that it does not have the assurance nor the majesty that some attribute to it. It is, let's not forget, an untransportable, perishable commodity. Both precarious and unavoidable, it is played out in trifles, accidents, pustules of nonsense emerging on the great body of signifying determinations of all orders.

Effects of multiple meanings, problems of translation, tastes and colors are a direct function of the *amount that univocal determination is lacking* in the different code systems—a differential quantity. One could ideally situate them on a scale, and at its extremities, there would be, on one side, an absolutely empty system of transcription where a lone sign would be charged with representing everything and, on the other, an absolutely rigorous encrypted transcription leaving no room for any freedom of interpretation.

The reader—individual, group or machine—can only unify the different systems of reading he or she faces to the extent that he or she differentiates and enriches the keys to his or her interpretation.

No response, no gesture tends to be self-evident anymore: each calls for interpretations on multiple levels.

Despite appearances, economic growth seen over a long period of history does not lead to draining the signifying batteries of reference of individuals.

The uniformization, mediocrity and monotony that swamp consumer societies are not inherent to technical progress, but to a social order incapable of developing production in a framework that renews its own subjective purposes.

When it is over, we will be able to say of assembly line work that it was only a stage where human gestures were used in place of signifying articulations, just for the time it took the socio-industrial machine to find the way to utter it, situate it, interpret it and integrate it.

In the face of the prodigious expansion of science and technology, the position required for human collectivities in the process of production is the position of the subject.

Misunderstanding this requirement comes from the persistent antagonism between the development of productive forces and relationships of production inherent to societies divided into classes and bureaucratized societies.

Improvements, the rise in the standard of living only exacerbate the unconscious demand for subjective parity between the all-powerful object of production and systematically disqualified human desire. A scandal that is increased by the inequality of the process according to the respective positions of diverse social groups in the field of economic relationships.

The scientific community provides a glimpse of a possible mode of subjective re-appropriation of objectal signifiers. *Collective utterance* in theoretical physics, for example, constantly composes and recomposes a giant signifying machine where the machines themselves and the signifier are inextricably enmeshed, capable of intercepting and interpreting all of the theoretically aberrant manifestations of elementary particles. They manifest not only the inability to provide a plausible explanation of their behavior but, in recent cases, it appears that their emergence into existence depends on the technological-theoretical enterprise itself.

They differ in this way from the alchemy of desire that prefers giving up its objects to annihilating itself in them; signifying surrationality recreates its objects as it destroys them.

Institutional objects, produced and maintained due to the hegemony of one class over others, do not have the same plasticity: their life and death do not depend on a rational analysis but on tensions, tests of strength, that cannot be described in a satisfactory manner without relying on a dialectical logic capable of integrating effects of nonsense.

The human sciences, faithful to an outdated scientific ideal, make excessive efforts to build conceptual apparatuses capable of anchoring their object beyond the waves of irrationality. In practice, their scientists can scarcely protect themselves from every face to face with the discrepancies and singularities of the subject. Freudianism aside, they generally avoid the problem of bringing forth their own specific methodology.

A better listening position would give them the possibility of measuring the radical and inexorable impact of the subjective fact on each of their objects of research. While some have said the world is not mathematized but only "mathematizable by our mind if we accept the necessary latitude" (Robert Gérard), then we must admit that unlike elementary particles, human subjects have an auto-referential capacity that gives them the possibility to play with their own normative systems, to move from one to the next, to evade the ones that might confine them, to choose the ones that help them dream.

Anthropological laws will only gain assurance and coherence with history to the extent that their axioms leave the place of honor to the unpredictable but always imminent possibility of opening onto a space of nonsense and to the possibility of an other—or third—

subjectivity to foresee their acts, to counter their repeated effects, in short to reshape them in a different way.

The reader can constantly be read. The subject is transferred to all of the missing intersections of the signifier. This pursuit has no end, not even in death. Only the imagination can deliver us bound hand and foot to the subject in itself such as God would have created it, if only he had not been in such a bad mood that day!

Compared to such a fundamentally perverse subject, particles look like angels. Even when they pretend, they are beyond reproach; it is not their fault. They expect nothing from anyone and the nothing they offer is something else altogether. They are docile and blameless before the law, at least in as much as the law takes care to leave them the famous "necessary latitude." In cases where a conflict arises, they push the spirit of conciliation to select their advocates from within the theory that targets them, leaving naysayers to their own devices.

All things considered, the comparison draws particles closer to the subject than individuals to objects with ordinary, realistic and archaic meanings inherited from the Cartesian expanse. Despite being of a different mode than the object of human desire, defined as desire of the other, the objects of theoretical physics are no less equally regulated by a principle of alterity that prevents any possibility of intersecting with themselves without destroying their own identity.

In short, they only lack speech! Yet considering how we use them, it may not be essential! At least in terms of creating a symbolic order that aims to explain the strategy of desire. Once the thread of university psychology's causalist explanations is broken like a pearl necklace, it may not be too much to hope that a connection will occur one day between the methodology of the "New Scientific Mind" and anthropological semiology.

Before acceding to discourse, a child only has a few distinctive oppositions to situate his or her world and navigate the thicket of his or her native language. In the relationship with the other, several equivalent or ambivalent significations correspond to each element of his or her reading. Speech only emerges on the level of symbolic overdetermination. He or she is only a subject of unconscious relationships woven around and from him or her.

The child will only be constituted in the opacity of him- or herself and the already seen when he or she incorporates or reifies ambient relational and linguistic ambivalences, and when he or she takes as his or her own the bad law of the group that gives force of law to its contingent prohibitions and structural demands. His or her true birth coincides with a time when, relying on the social order, he or she closes and fills the gaps of nonsense that opened in the faulty space we detected at the heart of the sign.

Only in the trials of desire, dreams and death will he or she risk another furtive, anxious glance beyond the mirror of significations.

At every one of the dangerous intersections of the imagination, the question of the fundamental duplicity of the subject in its relationship with the signifier is raised again.

While with reality, all readings, with equal rights, are related to the same factual texture, incapable of serving as foundation for any freedom of indetermination; the place of interconnection between text and listening, the signifying chain, constantly incised by the principle of indecision, bleeds so much that the subject is temporalized there.

Neither of these two faces could be opposed to the other. They follow the same extension. Here we find a new betrayal of the demand for another space: the third dimension is struck at the moment when human behavior believes itself assured of having a depth of field.

There is no guarantee that inside and outside will not be inverted, leaving it without recourse in the ordeals of anxiety and madness.

Unlike machines, the vocation of structure is not to refer to the subject. The lack of internal articulations is self-sufficient: it does not open onto anything in particular, it simply remains available in the limits of its internal logic. Structural phenomena oppose the ordeal of the subject with the inertia of repetition or seek paths of deformation that do not modify them fundamentally. Unlike machines and living organisms, the principle of their transformation is not written in the heart of the law that founds them, but in a law articulated outside them. The alterity of their exteriority is not of the same nature as the one that is at the root of subjectivity. The space underlying them is sterile, no more or fewer dimensions can be elicited from it. The nonsense of their daily existence is not of the same nature as that of desire. Their world of everyone at home and everyone for him- or herself develops mortal fantasies that involve a death that is not of the same nature as the one that awaits us at the root of desire.

Human existence, once it is thrown on the market, cannot be taken back. It is therefore legitimate to seek to found the order of collective and individual significations on economic and social bases and to relate myths and fantasy to structural analyses of elementary relationships of parentage or unconscious psychic causality.

Yet nothing, not even dialectic, can account for the capacity of a subject to articulate itself with one code starting from another code.

In the matrix of all rationality, there is a logic of alterity where everything can depend on nothing or not much and where the *ex nihilo* creation of the signifier constitutes the absolute precondition for any insertion of fact or being into an unimpeachable field of determination.

The same signifying chain informed by a child, adult, "primitive," artist or mathematician deploys a set of significations that penetrates each fact, reworks it, negates it or even recreates it without guaranteeing its existential status in any way.

Being and nothingness, in themselves, have absolutely nothing to say about it. The signifier speaks out on their behalf using totalizing-detotalizing sets that are capable of metabolizing them in an infinite game of references from one structure to another.

Being for the sign constitutes the only tipping point where determination can, under certain conditions, be replayed. One phoneme more or less, and my fate is completely changed. One word on love or death and other logics and other spaces appear.

Would we say that the existence of the sign precedes the essence of the intersubjective relationship? It is useless to approach this question from the logic of déjà vu where the same has the vocation of identifying itself with the same, the other with the other and where the relationships between same and other are transcribed in a system with the primary claim of excluding desire. The sacrosanct principle of the excluded third seems to correlate to the necessity for signifying chains to keep the third-point of the minimal signal in check and to develop themselves only in the negation and exteriority of the space of the cut.

Signs strangle their magic; words and sentences saturate absence; the remedy of their kaleidoscopic significations seeps into the wounds and cuts of the body of human and natural law.

The unconscious takes fright and closes down. Being-for-structure reclaims its rights and people speak, again, as if nothing had happened. The arrival of the sign in language is the most hard-working operation of all: a bandage on the wound of desire.

To be honest, the subject does not dislike being scorned by the sign. It pretends to forget its relationship with the dimension minus one of desire and imitates its conversion to the visible and audible dimensions of writing and language. This trick allows it to reconstitute itself partially as desire in that it leads to seek out compulsively a transgression of the law of signs and enjoy the punishment in return.

The subject is never completely prisoner of its—translucent, aseptic, imputrescible and timeless—signifying chains; it is never completely at ease there. It is only in its element with less noble objects. Its favorite place is the less than nothing and to sustain it, its favorite consort is failing flesh, even a little gamey.

The "I" defies nothing.

Deceitful speech only suits it in its prime truth, as soon as it is tied down in becoming a necessary deceit; taking on the force of a law, it turns away and devotes itself, provocatively, to virtue.

Casually, the devil was posted there to satisfy every need in this matter: his resources drained, he had to recognize his impotence and abandon his vocation in a world that long ago integrated his effects of reversal in every chain of daily life.

Let us only mention here the respect with which the musicians of the 12th century avoided the "Diabolus in musica" and what later happened with the Ars Nova and the dodecaphonists!

All eternity in one, nipped in the bud, in no time at all.

Grasped by the other on the edge of myself, I ebb to the other end of the chain. The coordinates cross. The I for I was only a possible mirage in the intimacy of the other for me. But this other, to the extent that it refers to an other for the other, from which any orientation is impossible, forbids me any security related to the true position of the subject and leaves me beset by the vertigo of an eternal return to my first effusions with death.

The subject dreams of annihilating itself in the object of desire like the sign escapes itself in nothingness.

Decanted from its exteriority and brought back to its essential cut, is the sign fundamentally different from the desiring subject? Aren't they both led to seek a borrowed identity from the other, allowing them, sometimes, to distinguish between them? Necessarily articulated to establish a signifying chain, don't they have the same principle of immanence that saves them from disappearing?

Alternating between one and multiple, in a space that is neither alternative nor exclusive, the sign of the subject and the subject of the sign are articulated below the before, during and after, at the root of all temporalization.

One foot on the same, I stumble towards the other. Just the time to ensure myself an illusory permanence. A light hold on the last touch leaves trailing behind it a stroboscopic line, like a ribbon in the spokes of the bicycle of a conscript on leave.

Desire for nothing. The recollection of everything that doesn't hold up. An approximation of death like the flip side of the slide from the same to the other. Another world where death decided to be the subject and the subject decided to be death.

Pains of the I in the face of death. Emotion of the words of death at the limit of the death of words. Phallus and mummy, pathetic heraldry of the chivalry of despair.

The effusion of the subject and the partial object: humble and pitiful resurrection. Unlike the encounter between the unary trait and the third point, it supposes an irreparable crack in the field of codifiable demands. With a sort of indifference, the subject accepts falling into dimensions that are foreign to it and in which it will be bundled up and consumed according agencies] from which it will be hard to remove it.

Isn't the reconciliation of the sign and the subject in a third object something that could satisfy even the most demanding minds in dialectical terms?

We want to celebrate the peace concluded between spots and points, being and nothingness, God and a few other characters. Looking closer at the operation, however, one cannot avoid seeing it as grotesque mystification: everyone is working for him- or her-self—despite the impossibility of self—and nothing is ever assured except by endless recourse to pseudo-alterity.

The exclusivism of signs is such that alterity is condemned to only being able to express itself through the intermediary of signs. We have seen, for example, how it is impossible to signify the alterity of the sign without taking it from the sign itself.

The last entrenchments of alterity are just pure seriality.

Alternative, pretense, evasion … in its search for a foundation, human existence finds no more salvation in itself than in others, who despite appearances are never authentically disposed to putting themselves at the service of same to same.

To attempt to trigger the famous chain reactions of desire, the subject forays into illusions: more or less mythical triad games.

Copulated-copulating, we go before being, taking great care of the integrity of the singular support of universalism that the God of wrath and the Fall, suddenly repentant, is supposed to have provided us at the last moment.

Lost paradise of the plane of reference of an alterity that does not depend on me, of an Other for the other that cannot be reduced to the categories of identification, of something in the heart of the other and the I that categorically prohibits the dissolution of alterity…

Nothing remains of this epic other than permanent bitterness and two gold rings, the unimpeachable witnesses of another origin: the cut, preserved as a concept, and dreams. It would be very hard for the arranged marriage between sign and subject to make us forget the impossible passion between same and other. Dowry of the subject or ransom of the sign, the compromise is not negotiated on a copula foreign to one or the other but relies on both to exist. It allowed the establishment of a pagan cult of icons with the vocation of incarnating alterity. It led to forbidding all pleasure from same to same, of one for the other.

Signs are not frank; they conceal their true intentions with regard to being, which, despite everything, is forced to pass through them! Only the "I" is capable of foiling their little game. It calls them on the very point of the cut that is the basis of their deceit: "Evil demon if you want, your lie is my foundation in that the truth of your uncertainty is the only one in which I can recognize myself."

Signs resent the subject for not submitting to them without reserve. They miss no opportunity to remind it of the lack of nobility of its origins. On the strength of their grasp of being, they disorient it in the register of knowledge. They abuse their privilege of being the only ones to have access beyond common sense.

Whatever their honorific position, the dead resent their mutilation in the name of the greater interests of the signifier.

Sex also has its word to say on this point. But it does so in such an untimely manner that it must be reminded to respect the established order. Things are so much easier to arrange with it when it is persuaded to work for the public good. And yet, it would have the poor taste to complain; didn't its appearance of eternity give it an enviable authority?

Sometimes madmen, perverts and cranks identify themselves with the insignia of the subject and break their law of silence. Setting off to bear witness to a truth beyond the principle of the sign, we find them, sooner or later, heart in hand, definitively occupied with the affairs of the mind.

Under these conditions, how can you expect the same and its kind to be tempted to go further? Like the signifying chain, they refuse depth. They hardly dare develop in more than one dimension!

The backworlds sink into the primordial cut of the sign. The pulses from same to other are barely felt as they catch on the edge of discourse and shroud desire.

Nothing returns to nothing. Everything offers itself as something. Truth is suspended on the scar of non-return. Impossible to gamble everything for nothing!

Exceptionally, the subject will be recovered at the point where all signification is rendered inoperable, when the fog of meaning reaches saturation. The reign of clouds and spots: all distinctions once again become unworkable; the duplicity of totalization returns to an impasse.

A wrinkle, a crevice, a vacuole on the surface of nothing, the feeling of futility. Inconspicuously, nothing turns up again; it sets a stage and puts itself on display using fantasies that keep desire in suspense by means of an imaginary space of polyvalent and infinitely expandable coordinates.

Some have said that being is full of holes.
They immediately thought of cave-dwellers or Swiss cheese.
Not even close!
At best, an anamorphose on the hackneyed theme of "Trompe-l'oeil" accompanied by Trompe-la-mort [Trick-death].

12

The Group and the Person

A Fragmented Balance-Sheet

To follow so many other speakers on the theme of society, the responsibility of individuals, militants, groups and so on, creates a certain inhibition. It is a minefield, with questioners hidden in fortified dug-outs waiting to attack you: what right has he to speak? what business is it of his? what is he getting at? And professional academics are there too, to recall you to modesty, and systematically to restrict any approach to these problems that is remotely ambitious.

Not even ambitious, necessarily, but related to responsibility. For example, we may study this or that text of Marx or Freud, we may study it in depth, seeing it in the context of the general trends of the period; but very few people will agree to pursue that study into its bearing on the present day, on its implications for, say, the development of imperialism and the Third World, or a particular current school of thought.

In different places and different circumstances I have put forward different ideas. For instance I have spoken of the "introjects of the super-ego," of the capacity of dependent groups to allow the individual super-ego a free rein. I have tried to suggest procedures for institutional analysis, seeking more or less successfully to introduce flexibility. Today I want to go further, but once again there is this inhibition. The best way to tackle it is, I think, to try to express my ideas just as they come into my head.

The first question is: what can it possibly do for "them"? Do I really need to say any more, and to expose myself yet again? The people and groups I have known and argued with go about their business with little concern for institutional analysis: history takes its course, and all groups tend to follow their routine until their path is diverted in some way or other by an obstacle, whether from within or without.

No, that is not precisely true: the militant groups with whom I am still in touch, institutional therapy groups and the groups in the FGERI,[1] have not been without interest in the subject; it is just that they take it for what it, on the whole, is—ideas picked up here and there from Marx, Freud, Lacan, Trotskyist criticism and so on. Some indeed think that quite enough is already going on, and that the time spent absorbing those ideas could well be used for thinking about something else.

It seems to me, on the contrary, that if our theories are not properly worked out, we are in danger of floundering about, wasting our efforts at collective thinking, and letting ourselves be carried away by psycho-sociologically inspired trends of thought or be caught up by the demands of the super-egos of hard-line militant groups.

Take one hard-liner, Louis Althusser:

The proletarian revolution also needs militants who are scholars (historical materialism) and philosophers (dialectical materialism) to help to defend and develop its theory... The fusion of Marxist theory with the workers' movement is the greatest event in the whole of human history (its first effect being the socialist revolutions). Philosophy represents the class struggle in theory. The key function of the practice of philosophy can he summed up in a word: tracing a line of demarcation between true and false ideas. As Lenin said, "The entire class struggle may at times be contained in the battle for one word rather than another. Some words fight among themselves, others are the cause of equivocation, over which decisive, but undecided, battles are fought..."[2]

Amateurs keep out! I still want to say things as they come to mind without being on guard all the time, but I have been warned. Without realizing it, the class struggle lies in wait at every corner—especially since intellectuals lack what Althusser calls "class instinct." It seems that the class struggle can come down to a collision between classes of words—the words of "the class" against the words of the bourgeoisie. Does it really matter so much what one says? One Trotskyist group did me the honor of devoting over half of a sixteen-page pamphlet to a vehement denunciation of my tedious theories of group subjectivity. I almost collapsed under the weight of their accusations: petit-bourgeois, impenitent idealist, irresponsible element! "Your false theories could mislead good militants."[3] They compared me to Henri de Man, a Nazi collaborator sentenced in his absence to forced labor when the war was over. It makes you think...

To return to the point. My inhibitions, as you can see, can be expressed only by being dressed up in external statements, and now that I am using quotations as weapons of debate, I will offer some more in the hope of salvation:

Where a powerful impetus has been given to group formation neuroses may diminish and at all events temporarily disappear [says Freud]. Justifiable attempts have also been made to turn this antagonism between neuroses and group formation to therapeutic account. Even those who do not regret the disappearance of religious illusions from the civilized world of today will admit that so long as they were in force they offered those who were bound by them the most powerful protection against the danger of neurosis. Nor is it hard to discern that all the ties that bind people to mystico-religious or philosophico-religious sects and communities are expressions of crooked cures of all kinds of neuroses. All of this is correlated with the contrast between directly sexual impulsions and those which are inhibited in their aim.[4]

As you *see*, Freud did not dissociate the problem of neurosis from what is expressed in the term "collective grouping." For him there is a continuity between the states of being in love, hypnosis and group formation. Freud might well authorize me to say whatever I liked from a free association of these themes. But the hard-liners once again seize the microphone: "That's all very well when you're talking of neurosis or even institutional therapy, but you have no right to say whatever you please in the highly responsible field of the class struggle…"

The point upon which I feel most uncertain, and militant groups are most intransigent, is that of the group's subjectivity. "… production also is not only a particular production. Rather, it is always a certain social body, a *social subject*, which is active in a greater or sparser totality of branches of production."[5] Oh yes, I am well aware that when Marx talks like that of a social subject he does not mean it in the way I use it, involving a correlate of phantasizing, and a whole aspect of social creativity which I have sought to sum up as "transversality." All the same, I am glad to find in Marx—and no longer the "young Marx"—this re-emergence of subjectivity.

Well now, this quotations game has repercussions on a register of the unconscious level. I have only to read them out, and the spectre of guilt recedes, the statue of the Commander the victim of intemperance, all is well—I can now say whatever I like on my own account. I am not going to try to produce a theory basing the intrinsic interlinking of historical processes on the demands of the unconscious. To me that is too obvious to need demonstrating. The whole fabric of my inmost existence is made up of the events of contemporary history—at least in so far as they have affected me in various ways. My phantasies have been molded by the "1936 complex," by that wonderful book of Trotsky's, *My Life*, by all the extraordinary rhetoric of the Liberation, especially those of the youth hostelling movement, anarchist groups, the UJRF,[6] Trotskyist groups and the Yugoslav brigades, and, more recently, by the saga of the "Communist menace"—the Twentieth Congress of the Communist Party of the Soviet Union, the Algerian war, the War in Vietnam, the left wing of the UNEF,[7] and so on and so on.

Yet I also like that kind of inwardness I see in Descartes, seeking to find strength from within himself, and the ultra-inward writing of people like Proust and Gide; I like Jarry, Kafka, Joyce, Beckett, Blanchot and Artaud just as in music I like Fauré, Debussy and Ravel. Clearly, then, I am a divided man: a petty bourgeois who has flirted with certain elements of the workers' movement, but has kept alive his subscription to the ideology of the ruling class. If Althusser had been there, I should have had to make my choice, and I might well have found myself in the serried ranks of those indispensable agents of any social revolution—the theory-mongers. But this brings us back to square one—the same problem has to be faced all over again. For whom do I speak? Am I really only one of those pathetic agents of the academic ideology, the bourgeois ideology, who try to build a bridge between the classes and so contribute to integrating the working class into the bourgeois order?

Another figure to whom I owe a lot is Sartre. It is not exactly easy to admit it. I like Sartre not so much for the consistency of his theoretical contribution, but the opposite—for the way he goes off on tangents, for all his mistakes and the good faith in which he makes them, from *Les Communistes* or *Nausea* to his endeavors to integrate Marxist dialectic into the mainstream of philosophy, which has certainly failed. I like Sartre precisely because of his failure; he seems to me to have set himself against the contradictory demands that were tormenting him and to have remained obsessed with them; he appears to have resolved no problem, apart from never having been seduced by the elegance of structuralism, or the dogmatism of some of Mao Tse-tung's more distinguished adherents. Sartre's confusions, his naïveties, his passion, all add to his value in my eyes. Which brings me back to the slippery slope: humanism, preserving our values and all that.

Of course, that is only as long as the individual unconscious and history do not meet, and the topology of the Moebius strip as delineated by Lacan is not a means of getting from one to the other. As far as I am concerned, posing the question is something of a device, for I am convinced—as experience of psychoses and serious neuroses makes absolutely clear—that, beyond the Ego, the subject is to be found scattered in fragments all over the world of history: a patient with delusions will start talking foreign languages, will hallucinate history, and wars and class conflicts will become the means of his/her own self-expression.

All this may be true of madness, you may say, but history, the history of social groups, has nothing to do with such madness. Here again, I show my fundamental irresponsibility. If only I could content myself with itemizing the various areas of phantasy in which I can find security! But then I would remain condemned to going back and forth in a dead end, and would have to admit that I have merely yielded to the external constraints that were part and parcel of each of the situations that made me. Underlying my different options—being-for-history, being-for-a-particular-group, being-for-literature—is there not some search for an unthinking answer to what I can only call being-for-existence, being-for-suffering?

The child, the neurotic, every one of us, starts by being denied any true possession of self; for the individual can only speak in the context of the discourse of the Other. To continue with the quotation from Freud I gave earlier on,

If he is left to himself, a neurotic is obliged to replace by his own symptom formations the great group formations from which he is excluded. He creates his own world of imagination for himself, his own religion, his own system of delusions, and thus recapitulates the institutions of humanity in a distorted way which is clear evidence of the dominating part played by the directly sexual impulsions.[8]

The established discourse of the groups of young people that I belonged to, the established discourse of the workers' organizations I encountered in the fifties, the philosophical discourse of the bourgeois university, literary discourse, and all the other discourses, each had its own consistency and its own axioms, and each demanded that I adapt myself to it in order to try and make it my own. At the same time, these successive attempts at mastering discourses actually formed me by fragmenting me—since that fragmentation itself was, on the plane of the imaginary, simply the first beginning of a more profound reuniting. After reading a novel, I would find a whole new world opening up before me in, say, a youth hostel, quite another in political action and so on. My behavior was thus affected by a kind of polymorphism with more or less perverse implications. Different social bodies of reference were expecting me to make a decision on one level or another, and to become established in some identifiable role—but identifiable by whom? An intellectual? A militant? A professional revolutionary? Perhaps, but in the distance I began to hear something saying, "You are going to be a psychoanalyst."

Note, however, that these different orders must not be seen on the same level. A certain type of group initiation has its own special imprint: real militant activity in a reified social context creates a radical break with the sense of passivity that comes with participation in the usual institutions. It may be that I shall later on come to see that I was myself contributing a certain activism, an illusion of effectiveness, a headlong rush forward. Yet I believe that no one who had the experience of being a militant in one of those youth organizations or mass movements, in the Communist Party or some splinter group, will ever again be just the same as everyone else. Whether there was real effectiveness hardly matters; certain kinds of action and concentration represent a break with the habitual social processes, and in particular with the modes of communication and expression of feeling inherited from the family.

I have tried to schematize this break, this difference, by distinguishing between the subject group and the object group. This involves to some extent reopening the question of the distinction between intellectuals and manual workers, a slight chance of taking up the desire of a group, however concealed it may be, a chance of escaping from the immutable determinism whose models come from the structure of the nuclear family, the organization of labor in industrial societies (in terms of wages and of hierarchy), the army, the church and the university.

A small group of militants is something apart from society; the subversion it plans is not usually directed to something in the immediate future, except in such exceptional cases as that of Fidel Castro or the Latin American guerrillas. Its horizon is the boundary of history itself: anything is possible, even if in reality the universe remains opaque. Something of the same sort exists in institutional pedagogy and institutional psychotherapy. Even in impossible, dead-end situations, one tries to tinker with the institutional machinery, to produce an effect on some part of it; the institutions acquire a kind of plasticity, at least in the way they are represented in the sphere of intention.

Castro, at the head of hundreds of thousands of Cubans, unhesitatingly went to war against what he called "organigrammism," or planning from the center. This is something that is a problem throughout all the so-called socialist societies. A certain concept of the institution, which I should call non-subjective, implies that the system and its modifications exist to serve an external end, as part of a teleological system. There is a program to fulfil, and a number of possible options, but it is always a question of responding to specific demands to produce—production here being taken in the widest sense (it can refer to entertainment or education as well as to consumer goods). The production of the institution remains a sub-whole within production as a whole. It is a residue, suggesting what Lacan calls the *objet petit "a."* What are the laws governing the formation of institutions? Is there not a general problem of the production of institutions?

One could say that revolutions produce institutions; the creative rumblings that unleashed the French revolution were luxuriant in this respect. But beware of spelling revolution with a capital R. Things happened by way of successive modifications, and any master plan remained entirely abstract and never put into effect: this is evident in, for instance, the successive constitutions drafted by the French revolution. Only with the history of the workers' movement since Marx have we seen a conscious plan setting out to produce non-utopian institutional models for reorganizing the structure of the State with a view to its future withering away—for starting up a revolutionary power, for setting up political and trade-union bodies aiming (at least in theory) to fulfil the demands of the class struggle. It is noteworthy that organizational problems have often more truly engendered splinter groups, major battles, even schisms, than have ideological divergences; and with Leninism, the problem of organization became the primordial one. Debates about the party line, the signified and the signification were very often no more than a front to conceal what was at issue at the level of the organizational signifier, which at times went down to the tiniest detail. Who should control this or that authority? How should the unions be related to the party? What was to be the role of the soviets?

There is of course a general problem about the subjective processes of "breakthrough groups" throughout history, but for the moment I want simply to focus the idea of the subject group on the birth of revolutionary groups.[9] These groups make a special point of linking, or trying to link, their organization options very closely with their revolutionary program. Historically, we can point to one great creative event that was stifled by the hegemony of Stalinism in the USSR and in the Communist International. Even today, most revolutionary tendencies still see organizational problems in the framework within which they were formulated fifty years ago by Lenin. Imperialism, on the other hand, seems to have been capable of producing relative institutional solutions enabling it to escape from even the most catastrophic ordeals. After the crisis of 1929 it produced the New Deal; after the Second World War it was able to organize "reconstruction" and re-mould international relations. These were, of course, only partial measures, effected by trial and error, since the dominant imperialism had formulated no consistent policy or aims. But in the terms of production, they have enabled imperialism to remain considerably in advance of the so-called socialist States in its capacity for institutional creativity. But in the socialist States none of the major projects of reform since 1956 has yet seen the light of day. In this respect it is the difference that is crucial. At the time of the first Five Year Plan, Russia was introducing capitalist production plans into its factories. Even today, in both the technological and the industrial fields, the organization of production and even the internal structure of companies are still largely dependent on the models set up by capitalism. We are also seeing the importation into Russia and Czechoslovakia of the capitalist pattern of mass consumption of cars. It looks as though the planned structure of the socialist States is not capable of permitting the emergence of any form of original social creativity in response to the demands of different social groups. Very different was the situation after the 1917 revolution, before the Stalinist terror took over. Though the soviets rapidly degenerated at the mass level, there were some intensively creative years in a number of specific areas—cinema, architecture, education, sexuality, etc. Even Freudianism made considerable progress. The 1917 revolution is still charged with a powerful group Eros, and it will long continue to exercise that power: the vast forces of social creativity unleashed by it illuminated the field of research in all spheres.

We may well be witnessing the dawn of a new revolutionary development that will follow on from that somber period, but we are still too close to the daily events of history to see it clearly. The extraordinary way that bureaucratization took place in the Bolshevik Party and the soviet State under Stalin seems to me comparable to neurotic processes that become more violent as the instincts underlying them are more powerful. The Stalin dictatorship could never have taken so excessive a form had it not needed to repress the fastest-flowing current of social expression the world has ever known. It must also be recognized that the voluntarism of the Leninist organization and its systematic mistrust of the spontaneity of the masses undoubtedly led it to miss seeing the revolutionary possibilities represented by the soviets. In fact there never was any real theory of soviet organization in Leninism: "All power to the soviets" was only a transitional slogan, and the soviets were soon centralized to suit the Bolsheviks' determination to maintain absolute control of all power in view of the rise of counter-revolutionary attack from both within and without. The only institutions that remained important were the State power, the Party and the army. The systems of organizational decentralization established by the Bolshevik Party during the years of underground struggle disappeared in favor of centralism. The International was militarized willy-nilly, and the various organizations in sympathy with Bolshevism were made to accept the absurd "Twenty-One Points."

Enormous revolutionary forces all over the world thus found themselves arbitrarily cut off from their proper social context, and some Communist bodies never really recovered. (The Communist movement was unable, above all, to become established and organized in vast areas of what we today call the Third World—presumably to indicate that it is "a world apart.")

The same pattern of organization (Party—Central Committee—Politburo—secretariat—secretary—general; and mass organizations, links between Party and people, etc.) is just as disastrous in the international Communist movement as a whole. The same sort of militant superstructures, established in a revolutionary context, are supposed to supply to the organizational needs of a highly industrialized socialist State. This absurdity is productive of the worst bureaucratic perversions. How can the same handful of men propose to direct everything at once—State bodies, organizations of young people, of workers and of peasants, cultural activity, the army, etc., etc.—with none of the intermediate authorities having the least autonomy in working out its own line of action? Whether or not it gives rise to contradictions with this tendency or that, or to confrontations that cannot be resolved simply by arbitration from above.

Never has the internationalist ideal fallen so low! The reaction of the pro-Chinese movements has been to preach a return to Stalinist orthodoxy, as revised and corrected by Mao Tse-tung, but in fact it is hard to see how they will resolve these fundamental problems. At the end of the last century, a militant was someone formed by the struggle, who could break with the dominant ideology and could tolerate the absurdity of daily life, the humiliations of repression, and even death itself, because there was no doubt in his mind that every blow to capitalism was a step on the way to a socialist society. The only context in which we find such revolutionaries today is that of guerrilla warfare, of which Che Guevara has left us such an extraordinary account in his *Testamento politico*.

The political or syndical style of the Communist organizations of today tends to be totally humorless. The bureaucrat experiences politics and syndicalism in the short term; he is often felt to be an outsider at work, even though his comrades recognize the merits of what he is doing, and rely on him—at his request—as one would rely on a public service. There are exceptions, a great many indeed, who are genuine militants of the people in those organizations, but the party machine mistrusts them, keeping them on a tight rein, and ends up by destroying them or trying to expel them.

It is always the mass of the people who have created new forms of struggle: it was they who "invented" soviets, they who set up *ad hoc* strike committees, they who first thought of occupations in 1936. The Party and the unions have systematically retreated from the creativity of the people; indeed, since the Stalin period, they have not merely retreated but have positively opposed innovation of any kind. One has only to recall the part played by the communists in France at the Liberation, when they used force as well as persuasion to reintegrate into the framework of the State all the new forms of struggle and organization that had emerged. This resulted in works committees without power, and a Social Security that is merely a form of delayed wages to be manipulated by management and the State so as to control the working class and so on.

It may be said that the working class must simply effect a "restitution" of these subjective procedures, that they must become a disciplined army of militants and so on. Yet surely what they are seeking is something different—they want to produce a visible aim for their activities and struggles. To return to the notions I put forward provisionally, I would say that the revolutionary organization has become separated from the signifier of the working class's discourse, and become instead closed in upon itself and antagonistic to any expression of subjectivity on the part of the various sub-wholes and groups, the subject groups spoken of by Marx. Group subjectivity can then express *itself* only by way of phantasy-making, which channels it off into the sphere of the imaginary. To be a worker, to be a young person, automatically means sharing a particular kind of (most inadequate) group phantasy. To be a militant worker, a militant revolutionary, means escaping from that imaginary world and becoming connected to the real texture of an organization, part of the prolongation of an open formalization of the historical process. In effect, the same text for analysis of society and its class contradictions extends into both the text of a theoretical/political system and the texture of the organization. There is thus a double articulation at three levels: that of the spontaneous, creative processes of the masses; that of their organizational expression; and that of the theoretical formulation of their historical and strategic aims.

Not having grasped this double articulation, the workers' movement unknowingly falls into a bourgeois individualist ideology. In reality, a group is not just the sum of a number of individuals: the group does not move immediately from "I" to "you," from the leader to the rank and file, from the party to the masses. A subject group is not embodied in a delegated individual who can claim to speak on its behalf: it is primarily an intention to act, based on a provisional totalization and producing something true in the development of its action. Unlike Althusser, the subject group is not a theoretician producing concepts; it produces signifiers, not signification; it produces the institution and institutionalization, not a party or a line; it modifies the general direction of history, but does not claim to write it; it interprets the situation, and with its truth illuminates all the formulations coexisting simultaneously in the workers' movement. Today, the truth of the NLF in Vietnam and the Democratic Republic of Vietnam illuminates the whole range of possibilities for struggle against imperialism that now exist, and reveals the real meaning of the period of peaceful coexistence that followed the Yalta and Potsdam agreements. Today, too, the struggle of revolutionary organizations in Latin America brings into question all the formulations of the workers' movement and all the sociological theories recognized by the bourgeois mind. Yet one cannot say that Che Guevara, Ho Chi-minh, or the leaders of the NLF are producers of philosophical concepts: it is revolutionary action that becomes speech and interpretation, independent of any formal study and examination of the totality of what is said and done. This does not mean that one has no right to say anything—on the contrary, one can say what one wants all the more freely precisely because what one says is less important than what is being done. *Saying* is not always *doing*!

This brings us to a more general problem: does "saying" mean anything more than the production of its own sense? Surely, what the whole analysis of *Capital* makes clear is precisely that behind every process of production, circulation and consumption there is an order of symbolic production that constitutes the very fabric of every *relationship* of production, circulation and consumption, and of all the structural orders. It is impossible to separate the production of any consumer commodity from the institution that supports that production. The same can be said of teaching, training, research, etc. The State machine and the machine of repression produce *antiproduction*, that is to say signifiers that exist to block and prevent the emergence of any subjective process on the part of the group. I believe we should think of repression, or the existence of the State, or bureaucratization, not as passive or inert, but as dynamic. Just as Freud could talk of the dynamic processes underlying psychic repression, so it must be understood that, like the odyssey of things returning to their "rightful place," bureaucracies, churches, universities and other such bodies develop an entire ideology and set of phantasies of repression in order to counter the processes of social creation in every sphere.

The incapacity of the workers' movement to analyse such institutions' conditions of production, and their function of anti-production, dooms it to remain passive in the face of capitalist initiatives in that sphere. Consider, for instance, the university and the army. It may appear that all that is happening in a university is the transmission of messages, of bourgeois knowledge; but we know that in reality a lot else is also happening, including a whole operation of molding people to fit the key functions of bourgeois society and its regulatory images. In the army, at least the traditional army, not a great deal of what happens is put into words. But the State would hardly spend so much, year after year, on teaching young men just to march up and down; that is only a pretext: the real purpose is to train people, and make them relate to one another, with a view to the clearly stated objective of discipline. Their training is not merely an apprenticeship in military techniques, but the establishment of a mechanism of subordination in their imaginations. Similar examples can be found in so-called primitive societies: to be a full member of the tribe, one has to fulfil certain conditions; one must successfully undergo certain ceremonies of initiation—that is, of social integration by means perhaps of mingling one's blood with a primordial totemic image, and by developing a sense of belonging to the group. And, in fact, underlying the rational account one may give of such group phenomena, phantasy mechanisms of this nature are still at work in capitalist societies.

The workers' movement seems to be peculiarly unfitted to recognize those mechanisms; it relates subjective processes to individual phenomena, and fails to recognize the series of phantasies which actually make up the real fabric of the whole organization and solidity of the masses. To achieve any understanding of social groups, one must get rid of one kind of rationalist-positivist vision of the individual (and of history). One must be capable of grasping the unities underlying historical phenomena, the modes of symbolic communication proper to groups (where there is often no mode of spoken contract), the systems that enable individuals not to lose themselves in interpersonal relationships, and so on. To me it is all reminiscent of a flock of migrating birds: it has its own structure, the shape it makes in the air, its function, its direction—and all determined without benefit of a single central committee meeting, or elaboration of a correct line. Generally speaking, our understanding of group phenomena is very inadequate. Primitive societies are collectively far better ethnologists than the scholars sent out to study them. The gang of young men that forms spontaneously in a section of town does not recruit members or charge a subscription; it is a matter of recognition and internal organization. Organizing such a collective depends not only on the words that are said, but on the formation of images underlying the constitution of any group, and these seem to me something fundamental—the support upon which all their other aims and objects rest. I do not think one can fully grasp the acts, attitudes or inner life of any group without grasping the thematics and functions of its "acting out" of phantasies. Hitherto the workers' movement has functioned only by way of an idealist approach to these problems. There is, for instance, no description of the special characteristics of the working class that established the Paris Commune, no description of its creative imagination. Bourgeois historians offer such meaningless comments as that "the Hungarian workers were courageous," and then pass on to a formal, self-enclosed analysis of the various elements of social groups as though they had no bearing on the problems of the class struggle or organizational strategy, and without reference to the fact that the laws governing the group's formations of images are different in kind from contractual laws—like those relative to setting up a limited company, for instance, or the French Association Law of 1901. You cannot relate the sum of a group's phantasy phenomena to any system of deductions working only with motivations made fully explicit at the rational level. There are some moments in history when repressed motives emerge, a whole phantasy order, that can be translated, among other things, into phenomena of collective identification with a leader—for instance Nazism. The individual "I" asks *where* the image is, the identifying image that makes us all members of "Big Boy's" gang rather than "Jojo's"; Jojo is that dark fellow with the motorcycle, whereas it may be someone—anyone—else who has the characteristics demanded by the phantasy world of this particular group. Similarly, the great leaders of history were people who served as something on which to hang society's phantasies. When Jojo, or Hitler, tells people to "be Jojos" or "be Hitlers," they are not speaking so much as circulating a particular kind of image to be used in the group: "Through that particular Jojo we shall find ourselves." But who actually says this? The whole point is that no one *says* it, because if one were to say it to oneself, it would become something different. At the level of the group's phantasy structure, we no longer find language operating in this way, setting up an "I" and an other through words and a system of significations. There is, to start with, a kind of solidification, a setting into a mass; *this is us*, and other people are different, and usually not worth bothering with—there is no communication possible. There is a territorialization of phantasy, an imagining of the group as a body, that absorbs subjectivity into itself. From this there flow all the phenomena of misunderstanding, racism, regionalism, nationalism and other archaisms that have utterly defeated the understanding of social theorists.

André Malraux once said on television that the nineteenth century was the century of internationalism, whereas the twentieth is the century of nationalism. He might have added without exaggeration that it is also the century of regionalism and particularism. In some big cities in America, going from one street into the next is like changing tribes. Yet there is an ever-increasing universality of scientific signifiers; production becomes more worldwide every day; every advance in scholarship is taken up by researchers everywhere;

it is conceivable that there might one day be a single superinformation-machine that could be used for hundreds of thousands of different researchers. In the scientific field, everything today is shared; the same is true of literature, art and so on. However, this does not mean that we are not witnessing a general drawing inwards in the field, not of the real, but the imaginary, and the imaginary at its most regressive. In fact, the two phenomena are complementary: it is just when there is most universality that we feel the need to return as far as possible to national and regional distinctness. The more capitalism follows its tendency to "de-code" and "de-territorialize," the more does it seek to awaken or re-awaken artificial territorialities and residual encodings, thus moving to counteract its own tendency.

How can we understand these group functions of the imaginary, and all their variations? How can we get away from that persistent couple: machinic universality and archaic particularity? My distinction between the two types of group is not an absolute one. I say that the subject group is articulated like a language and links itself to the sum of historical discourse, whereas the dependent group is structured according to a spatial mode, and has a specifically imaginary mode of representation, that is the medium of the group phantasies; in reality, however, we are dealing not so much with two sorts of group, but two functions, and the two may even coincide. A passive group can suddenly throw up a mode of subjectivity that develops a whole system of tensions, a whole internal dynamic. On the other hand, any subject group will have phases when it gets bogged down at the level of the imaginary: then, if it is to avoid becoming the prisoner of its own phantasies, its active principle must be recovered by way of a system of analytic interpretation. One might perhaps say that the dependent group permanently represents a potential sub-whole of the subject group[10] and, as a counterpoint to the formulations of Lacan, one might add that only a partial, detached institutional object can provide it with a basis.

Take two other examples:

First, the psychiatric hospital. This is a structure totally dependent on the various social systems that support it—the State, Social Security and so on. Group phantasies are built up around finance, mental illness, the psychiatrist, the nurse, etc. In any particular department, however, a separate objective may be established that leads to a profound reordering of that phantasizing. That objective might be a therapeutic club. We may say that that club is the institutional objective (Lacan's *objet petit "a,"* at the institutional level) that makes it possible to start up an analytic process. Clearly the analytical structure, the *analyser*, is not the therapeutic club itself, but something dependent upon that institutional objective, which I have defined elsewhere as an institutional vacuole. It might, for example, be a group of nurses, psychiatrists or patients that forms that analytical, hollow structure where unconscious phenomena can be deciphered, and which for a time brings a subject group into beng within the massive structure of the psychiatric hospital.

Second, the Communist Party. Like its mass organizations (trade unions, youth organizations, women's organizations, etc.) the Party can be wholly manipulated by all the structures of a bourgeois State, and can work as a factor for integration. In a sense one can even say that the development of a modern, capitalist State needs such organizations of workers by workers in order to regulate the relations of production. The crushing of workers' organizations in Spain after 1936 caused a considerable delay to the progress of Spanish capitalism, whereas the various ways of integrating the working class promoted in those countries that had popular fronts in 1936, or national fronts in 1945, enabled the State and the various social organizations introduced by the bourgeoisie to readjust, and to produce new structures and new relations of production favoring the development of the capitalist economy as a whole (salary differentials, wages, bargaining over conditions, etc.). Thus one can see how, in a sense, the subordinate institutional object that the Party or the CGT (the Communist Trade Union Federation) represents as far as the working classes are concerned helps to keep the capitalist structure in good repair.

On the other hand—and to explain this calls for a topological example of some complexity—that same passive institutional object, indirectly controlled by the bourgeoisie, may give rise within itself to the development of new processes of subjectivation. This is undoubtedly the case on the smallest scale, in the Party cell and the union chapel. The fact that the working class, once its revolutionary instincts have been aroused, persists in studying and getting to know itself through this development within a dependent group creates tensions and contradictions which, though not immediately visible to outsiders (not quoted in the press or the official statements of the leaders), still produce a whole range of fragmented but real subjectivation.

A group phantasy is not the same as an individual phantasy, or any sum of individual phantasies, or the phantasy of a particular group.[11] Every individual phantasy leads back to the individual in his desiring solitude. But it can happen that a particular phantasy, originating within an individual or a particular group, becomes a kind of collective currency,[12] put into circulation and providing a basis for group phantasizing. Similarly, as Freud pointed out, we pass from the order of neurotic structure to the stage of group *formation*. The group may, for instance, organize its phantasies around a leader, a successful figure, a doctor, or some such. That chosen individual plays the role of a kind of signifying mirror, upon which the collective phantasy-making is refracted. It may appear that a particular bureaucratic or maladjusted personality is working against the interests of the group, when in fact both his personality and his action are interpreted only in terms of the group. This dialectic cannot be confined to the plane of the imaginary. Indeed, the split between the *totalitarian* ideal of the group and its various *partial* phantasy processes produces cleavages that may put the group in a position to escape from its corporized and spatializing phantasy representation. If the process that seems, at the level of the individual authority, to be over-determined and hedged in by the Oedipus complex is transposed to the level of group phantasizing, it actually introduces the possibility of a revolutionary re-ordering. In effect, identification with the prevailing images of the group is by no means always static, for the badge of membership often has links with narcissistic and death instincts that it is hard to define. Do individual phantasies take shape and change in the group, or is it the other way round? One could equally say that they are not fundamentally part of anything outside the group, and that it is a sheer accident that they have fallen back on that particular "body"—an alienating and laughable fiction, the justification of an individual driven into solitude and anxiety precisely because society misunderstands and represses the real body and its desire. In either case, this embodying of the individual phantasy upon the group, or this latching on of the individual to the group phantasy, transfers onto the group the damaging effect of those partial objects—*objet petit "a"*—described by Lacan as the oral or anal object, the voice, the look and so on, governed by the totality of the phallic function, and constituting a threshold of existential reality that the subject cannot cross. However, group phantasizing has no "safety rail" to compare with those that protect the libidinal instinctual system, and has to depend on temporary and unstable homeostatic equilibria. Words cannot really serve to mediate its desire; they operate on behalf of the law. Groups opt for the sign and the insignia rather than for the signifier. The order of the spoken word tips over into slogans. If, as Lacan says, the representation of the subject results from one signifier relating to another, then group subjectivity is recognizable rather in a splitting, a *Spaltung*, the detachment of a sub-whole that supposedly represents the legitimacy and "totality" of the group.

In other words, this remains a fundamentally precarious process. The tendency is to return to phenomena of imaginary explosion or phallicization rather than to coherent discourse. From this point of view, apart from distinguishing between individual and group phantasy, one can also distinguish different orders of group phantasy: on the one hand, the basic phantasies that depend on the subordinate character of the group and, on the other, the transitional phantasies connected with the internal process of subjectivation corresponding to various reorganizations within the group. We are led to distinguish two possible types of object: established institutions, and transitional objects.[13] With the first, the institution never sets out to face the *problem* of the institutional object, though it is obsessed by it; just as the church has its God and has no wish to change him, so a dominant class has power and does not consider whether it might not be better to give that power to anyone else. With the second, on the other hand, a revolutionary movement is a good example of something that keeps asking whether it is right, whether it should be totally transforming itself, correcting its aim and so on. Of course all the institutional objects in a fixed society continue to evolve regardless, but their evolution is not recognized. One myth is replaced by another, one religion by another, which may result in a ruthless war and end in deadlock. When a monetary or economic-system collapses, bad money drives out good, the gold standard is replaced by base metal, and the economy is convulsed. Similarly when a marriage fails; it was based on a contract of a kind not fundamentally different from a banking contract, and there is no scope for development. The contract can be changed by divorce, but that is only a legal procedure and does not fundamentally solve anything. Indeed the chain is snapped at its weakest link: the children are split in two without any thought of consequences in the sphere of the imaginary. When a revolutionary party changes theories, however, there is no logical reason why it should lead to a tragedy, or a religious war: the regimen of the word still tries to readjust the old formulations to bring them into harmony with the new.

To foster analysis and intervention in group phantasy (including family groups) would imply a consideration of precisely these phenomena of the imaginary. Take another example: generations of miners have worked in a particular mine, and it has become a kind of religion to them; one day, the technocrats suddenly realize that the coal they produce is no longer profitable. This of course takes no account of the effect on the miners: those of a certain age are told that they are to retire early, while others are offered re-training schemes. Similar things happen in Africa, Latin America and Asia, where peoples who have had the same social organization for thousands of years are steamrollered out of existence by the intrusion of a capitalist system interested only in the most efficient ways of producing cotton or rubber. These are extreme examples, but they are the logical extension of a multitude of situations—those of children, of women, of the mad, of homosexuals, of blacks. In disregarding or failing to recognize such problems of group phantasy, we create disasters whose ultimate consequences may be immeasurable.

Analysing the institutional object means channelling the action of the imagination between one structure and another; it is not unlike what happens to an animal in the molting season. To move from one representation of oneself to another, though it may involve crises, at least retains continuity. When an animal loses its coat it remains itself, but in the social order, removing the coat shatters the world of the imaginary and annihilates generations. When the group is split up, when it does not know the scope of its phantasies and has no control of them, it develops a kind of schizophrenic action within itself: the phantasy mechanisms of identification, and of the self, operate all the more freely and independently as the function of the word as a collective utterance is replaced by a structural formation of non-subjective utterances. While the group discourses in a vacuum about its aims and purposes, identifications have the same kind of free rein as they would have in a schizophrenic whose speech is disconnected from bodily representation, and whose phantasy world, freed from reality, can operate on its own to a point of hallucination and delusion. A group will end up by hallucinating with its phantasies in just the same way. If it is to interpret them, it will have to resort to irrational acts, wild gestures, suicidal behavior, play-acting of all kinds, until those phantasies can find some means of becoming present to themselves and manifesting themselves in the order of representation.

I said earlier that the unconscious is in direct contact with history. But only on certain conditions. The fundamental problem in institutional analysis can be expressed like this: is it absurd to think that social groups can overcome the contradiction between a process of *production* that reinforces the mechanisms of group alienation, and a process of *bringing to light* the conscious subject that knows and the unconscious subject, this latter being a process that gradually dispels more and more of the phantasies that cause people to turn to God, to science or to any other supposed source of knowledge? In other words, can the group at once pursue its economic and social objectives while allowing individuals to maintain their own access to desire and some understanding of their own destiny? Or, better still: can the group face the problem of its own death? Can a group with a historic mission envisage the end of that mission—can the State envisage the withering away of the State? Can revolutionary parties envisage the end of their so-called mission to lead the masses?

This leads me to stress the distinction between group phantasy as it relates to dependent groups, and the transitional phantasy of independent subject groups. There is a kind of phantasizing that appears in static societies in the form of myths, and in bureaucratized societies in the form of roles, which produces the most wonderful narratives: "When I'm twenty-five I'll be an officer; then a colonel and later on a general; I'll get a medal when I retire; then I'll die…" But group phantasizing is something more than this, because it includes an additional reference point that is not centered on a particular object, or on the individual's particular place in the social scale: "I've been in the French army for a long time; the French army has always existed, it is eternal, so if I keep my place in the hierarchy, I too shall have something of the eternal. This makes life easier when I'm frightened of dying, or when my wife calls me a fool. After all, I *am* a regimental sergeant major!" The institutional object underlying the phantasy of military rank ("I'm not nobody") serves to unfurl a range of references of a homosexual nature that provides society with a blind and relatively homogeneous body of people who shrink from any self-questioning about life and death, and who are ready to enforce any repression, to torture, to bombard civilian populations with napalm and so on. The continuation in time of the institution at the level of phantasy is thus a kind of implicit support for the denial of the reality of death at the individual level. The capitalist controlling several trusts also draws support from this "sense of eternity." In his position at the top of the hierarchy, he fulfils a kind of priestly function for those below, ritualizing eternity and conjuring away death. He is the servant of God/Capital. Faced with pain and afraid of desire, the individual clings to his job, his role in the family and the other functions that provide alienating phantasy supports. In the dependent group, phantasy masks the central truths of existence, but nonetheless, via the dialectic of signifiers, part objects, and the way these intersect with the sequences of history, it keeps in being the possibility of an emergence of the truth.

Would a group whose phantasy functions were working well produce the transitional phantasies of a subject group? At La Borde, for instance, when a group feels that it is getting somewhere, that it is achieving something, the most thankless tasks take on a quite different meaning, even such tedious jobs as taking up paving stones or working on an assembly-line. At such a moment, people's positions in relation to one another, their individual characteristics, their peculiar style, their way of speaking and so on, all take on a new meaning; you feel that you know people better and take more interest in them. In a psychiatric ward where an analytic process aiming to produce such an effect is successfully established—though it never survives for long—everything inhibiting or threatening in the differentiation of roles can be done away with: everyone becomes "one of us" though that includes the whole particularist folk-memory that that phrase implies. Absurd though such folklorism may seem, it does not prevent the "sense of belonging" from being effective. It is a fact that if a boy is to learn to read or to stop wetting his trousers, he must be recognized as being "at home," being "one of us." If he crosses that threshold and becomes re-territorialized, his problems are no longer posed in terms of phantasy; he becomes himself again in the group, and manages to rid himself of the question that had haunted him: "When shall I get to be *there*, to be part of *that*, to be 'one of them?'" As long as he fails in that, his compulsive pursuit of that goal prevents his doing anything else at all.

This getting to the limits of the imagination seems to me to be the fundamental problem of setting up any management body that is not to be technocratic, any mass participation body for whatever purpose that is not to be unhealthily rationalist. It is not a matter of an independent category: if these phantasizing formations are not explored analytically, they operate as death-dealing impulses. From the point when I set out to enjoy my membership of the Bowls Club, I can say that I am dead, in the sense of the death inherent in the eternity of Bowls Clubs. On the other hand, if a group lets me short-circuit its action with a problematic that is open to revolution, even if that group assures me that revolution will certainly not save my life, or provide any solution to certain sorts of problem, but that its role is, in a sense, precisely to prevent my being in too much of a hurry to run away from that problematic, then, most assuredly, the transitional phantasy formations of that group will enable me to make progress.

The demand for revolution is not essentially or exclusively at the level of consumer goods; it is directed equally to taking account of desire. Revolutionary theory, to the extent that it keeps its demands solely at the level of increasing people's means of consumption, indirectly reinforces an attitude of passivity on the part of the working class. A communist society must be designed not with reference to consumption, but to the desire and the goals of mankind. The philosophic rationalism that dominates all the expressions of the workers' movement like a super-ego fosters the resurgence of the old myths of paradise in another world, and the promise of a narcissistic fusion with the absolute. Communist parties are by way of having scientific "knowledge" of how to create a form of organization that would satisfy the basic needs of all individuals. What a false claim! There can be social planning in terms of organizing production—though there still remain a lot of unanswered questions—but it cannot claim to be able to give *a priori* answers in terms of the desire objectives of individuals and subject groups.

All of which is just to say yet again that the ways to truth are, and will continue to be, an individual matter. I realize that what I am saying here can be interpreted as an appeal to "respect human values" and other nonsense of that kind. Such interpretations are convenient, because they spare one the necessity of seeking further for an answer to the problem. I can hear some people saying, "There's a man who hasn't got over his experience of the Communist Party and of the groupuscule[14] he's been in. But all he had to do was stop going!" Braving ridicule, however, I persist in declaring that what is at issue is quite different. It is, first of all, at the core of the revolutionary struggles themselves—not the war of words, but the real struggle being waged by guerrillas and others. Either we fall into post-Stalinist thinking and come to grief, or we find another way and survive.

There are a lot of other things too—far more serious than wondering whether one can work out some compromise between the bureaucrat of the department and desire. Either the revolutionary workers' movement and the masses will recover their speech via *collective agents of utterance* that will guarantee that they are not caught up again in anti-production relations (as far as a work of analysis can be a guarantee), or matters will go from bad to worse. It is obvious that the bourgeoisie of present-day neo-capitalism are not a neo-bourgeoisie and are not going to become one: they are undoubtedly the stupidest that history has ever produced. They will not find an effective way out. They will keep trying to cobble things together, but always too late and irrelevantly, as with all their great projects to help what their experts coyly describe as the "developing countries."

It is quite simple, then. Unless there is some drastic change, things are undoubtedly going to go very badly indeed, and in proportion as the cracks are a thousand times deeper than those that riddled the structure before 1939, we shall have to undergo fascisms a thousand times more frightful.

— Translated by Rosemary Sheed

13

Causality, Subjectivity and History

1. History and the Signifying Determination

Misconceptions about the subjectivity of history arise from the fact that one tends without noticing it to pose the problem of a subject—whether to affirm or deny that there is one—as the subject that produces utterance of discourse and actions relating to history, rather than envisaging it simply as the subject of utterances as we receive them. That there is a subject of history is not in dispute; it is the subject that is constituted by, and remains the prisoner of repetitive structures, signifying chains wound back around themselves. The working class, for example, as alienated subjectivity, becomes the class of class words—in other words the class of utterances, producing, in a given area of historic utterance, significations for such terms as "class," and "class struggle"—whereas it should bear within it the historic destiny of *abolishing* the division of society into classes. Indeed, in a certain time and place, there is a special way in which the word is spoken, a reinforcement of the stress, so that the word itself takes on a particular class. In the workers' movement the word "class" used currently as an abbreviation for "working class" is pronounced quite differently from, say, a class at school.

Every mode of thought thus has its own initiatory code of metonyms, with particular meanings given to "Party," "the Old Man," or even "44."[1] We might take as a starting point something Lacan said in his first Seminar of 1965–66: "One need only say in passing that, in psychoanalysis, history is a different dimension from that of development, and that it is a mistake to try to identify them. History only takes place against the grain of development—a fact which may be to the advantage of history, as to science, if it wants to escape the ever-present influence of a providential explanation of its movement."[2] Now, what I call history is what Lacan calls development. The history he talks of is a history that does not even trouble to be dialectical, it is history considered at the level of subjectivity at the point where utterance intervenes. Considered thus, the signifier has no history; it is not in time; it belongs to the order of structure in that at a certain level there is nothing more we can say of it; it is an a-historical raw material of meaninglessness constitutive of historic significations: purely the effect of interference or resonance, an accident of circumstance that can only be seen with hindsight to have been the start of a series.

Must one conclude from this that time can be broken up into as many orders of time as there are orders of manifestation, temporalities specific to each level of production relations, of the economy, of history (in the usual sense) and so on? There would be a thousand temporalities to match a thousand areas of history, science and technology, but they would all be regulated by the still, silent heating of an order of pure significance, a crystalline structure standing apart from history and constituting its foundation—a kind of new infrastructure emerging after the bankruptcy of the outworn one we had built on Marxism. We could call this Operation Althusser: they give you as many temporalities as you like, but it is up to you to work out a synchronization. And you never will. It is a trick that enables Althusserians to be Stalinist in politics, Kantian in philosophy, Lacanian in psychoanalysis and so on. And where is the phallus, the "padding" between the different levels? It is Althusser himself, accompanied by his fellows, the priests of pure theory, the ultimate guarantors that concepts are scientific.

There is great elegance in thus shattering history into fragments and handing over one to be dealt with by epistemological specialists! But history itself disappears in the process. To me, history—the history made, articulated and remembered by human beings—is a subject. There is a limit beyond which one cannot go in the "de-realization" of history, for history has a certain residual realism. This impregnable reality is the contingent fact that it is human beings alone that make and recount it, and, whatever may be their rights and wrongs, those human beings are in the real world. What they say may be accepted or rejected, but if you accept it then you must also accept unreservedly the principle of a historical realism that cannot be cut up into slices. Historical materialism certainly does not involve turning time itself into an entity. That is a very different matter. To say that the sum of utterances represents a real historical object does not mean that time is a thing.

Man seems to take it upon himself to play about with temporalization and use it as he wishes; but once he has done so, then he no longer has any choice—he has to live with what he has made. The same is true of capital: it is no longer an optional category from which fringe economies, or planned economies, can opt out. Yet one can hardly say that capital is part of the natural order—or, if it is, it certainly has not always been! But now we are in it as in our element, like the air we breathe. The subject and the signifier operate in the same way. In nature there is no signifier or signified unrelated to the subject; the subject is a signifying intervention that produces utterances, beginning with those denying that there is a subject producing the utterance. It looks like becoming a closed circle. This is the structuralist temptation. Considering that the subject refers only to the other (the mirage of intersubjectivity), whereas the signifier refers only to the signifier (the mirage of a linguistics in its infancy) cut off from all reality, one thus posits a subject with no consistency— a purely symbolic operator—and a signifying time which in fact exists only in logic. The subject is there only to beat time for a signifying division that can never be enacted in reality. Reality and history have become subject to an eternal symbolic order from which they are totally isolated and which essentially nullifies them.

Subjectivity and the signifier have become interchangeable; human praxis no longer has any connection with that pure subjectivity; it is secretly returned to a strict order of causal determination, an order craftily reestablished in the guise of structure.

Lacan, on the other hand, has always stressed the profound dissymmetry characterizing the subject in relation to the signifier. Just as you neutralize a Moebius strip by cutting it lengthwise, so the subject cannot be separated from the signifier without becoming reified. The subject depends on its relationship with residuality, upon the *objet petit "a,"* to secure its status, and therefore can no longer be a pure signifier, and is alienated from the desiring condition by means of part objects that destroy its symmetry by weighing it down with a burden of reality. It is thus prevented from yielding completely to its deadly yearning to be abolished in a pure and ideal structure.

Even the idea of a de-totalization coming from within the structure to breathe life into it is marked by the phantom of totality, totalitarianism. Ultimately, there are two ways of using the signifier. Either one makes it a kind of universal category, like space or time: it is then the cleverness of a new idealism that actually betrays the linguistic discovery of the signifier, which is inseparably linked with the sign in its relation to sense and the social reality. Or else one holds with Lacan that the signifier is the screen through which the effects of the unconscious do not pass, a kind of Wilson cloud chamber[3] in which what cannot ultimately be symmetrized, or taken over, can still be recognized (slips, omissions, failures, dreams, transference, acting out and so on).

So we come back to the idea that the signifier in history intervenes at the point when history comes to a halt. Ultimately, history has nothing to do with the signifier. It is when history tips over into meaninglessness that we face the problem of the subject, that is of a production and representation of the subjective position, from a "supplementary" unfolding of the signifying order. Sequence and repetition certainly bring the signifying chains into action, but they are no longer open chains: they are chains of the signified, reified blocs of the signifier. Repetition is death, it is the signifier frozen rigid, no longer signifying, neurosis caught up relentlessly going round and round in the same circle. The signifier emerges as signifier only from the point when the subject comes on the scene, bringing everything into doubt and producing a new utterance, an operation of the signifier as expression of a meaning, a possible split in a given order, a breach, a revolution, a cry for radical reorientation.

It is an error to postulate signifying chains of a linguistic nature apart from a subjective intervention, to actualize the signifier (or capital) as the objective foundation of the mechanisms of the capitalist world in which we live. The revolutionary breakthrough, by breaching history-as-development, is the supreme moment for the signifier. The relationship between traditional history and the signifier operates in repetition: history is at ease in structure, it makes use of the signifier, exploiting it, takes it over, shuts it in. History completely escapes the signifier and the event. It is then that we talk of a signifier existing without the subject. What an unformulatable idea! It is as though one insisted on describing as music a score that for some reason we can never possibly perform—that remains merely signs on paper. If we burn it, are we burning music? A signifier that does not operate, that can be articulated in no real framework of enunciation, cannot be strictly said to exist as a signifier.

This does not prevent the ideologues from manufacturing history as one might manufacture toothpaste. People need this closing-up of the circuit of personal identity, this pretence at standing on firm ground in artificiality, the impersonal and bad faith. One has to attach oneself to something. This is the equivalent, in social terms, of the desiring subject and the part object. The laws of totalization, of the *Gestalt*, then take over—good and bad forms, bipolar values, retroactive and prospective determinations, desire for eternity as a childish negation of time. The subject is thus made to *have* instead of to *be*.[4] It is made to have by the consecutive Other, by spoken and written control of the word; it becomes alienated in supposedly signifying social chains which in fact only gain their power and their deadly fascination from the sheer effect of structure that they present. If the subject is no longer an act of the signifier, then it no longer is at all; it is then dependent upon the signified, in other words upon what happens in terms of other people, of utterances, of what "they" say. Nothing can be drawn from the signified but the imaginary. It belongs to the *Gestalt*, to the order of reason. Even when one has said to hell with reason, with the signified, with values, a split appears, a secondary development starts up, a phantasy counter-production tends to neutralize its stance. For instance, at the same time as the people were scaling the crumbling steps of the Tsarist edifice, that conglomerate of feudalism, modern industry and the last traces of Asiatic despotism, those same steps were the scene of a movement in the opposite direction: the workers' soviets were dissolving among the vast mass of the peasantry, whose inertia—without the counterweight of a strong bourgeoisie—apparently drew its power to resist from the traditional Slav village communities (*mirs*) that no State power had as yet really penetrated, and the vast mass of the Russian people came to venerate a mummified Lenin and to adore Stalin as a god.

One must choose between revolutionary history as significant breakthrough, and evolutionary history as signified; to keep a foot each side of the fence is the surest way of breaking your neck (cf. Kerensky, the Kadets, the Mensheviks). But the choice is not made once for all; one is continually starting again from scratch.

The signified is always the same thing—repetition, death, tedium. Only by being incessantly cut across at the level of the signifier can it be radically remolded. It is as though one were to change around the letters on a typewriter and so end up with something quite different from what one had intended to type. That is what revolution is—true history. Something has happened. Anyone who came to Russia in 1916 and returned in 1918 would see that the people were not where they had been. That could be seen in the signified. Journalists would write, for instance, that "one no longer sees anyone at the race courses," or "the Winter Palace looks quite different." But that was not the important thing: what had totally changed was the meaning of all the significations. In other words, something had happened to the signifier.

History is not the history of repetition, anti-historic history, the history of kings and queens; it is finding the signifying breakthrough, recognizing the point when the scales were tilted. But that signifying breakthrough is as hard to identify as the underlying meaning of a dream: what precisely was broken? Is it just that a few supposedly signifying chains were taken apart and rearranged in different ways? Since the signifier cannot be localized, and anything done to it involves its whole structure, one may admit that what has changed ought to be apparent from the way people talk—though it may be evident from other things too. Of course people talk differently, and even if they are still saying "Good morning, mate," the mate is not the man he was before the Tsar was killed. He is different because he is no longer bound up in the same relationships of signifying articulation, the same signifying constellations of reference—with the other sex, people of a different age or race, with God, or whatever.

There are periods when everything seems to hang in the balance: the signifying chains of structure lose control, events are written into "reality itself" according to a short-term, inconsistent, absurd semiotic, until a new plane of reference "structured like a language" can be established. That was how the signifying systems of the ancient world were shattered, helplessly at the mercy of the passions of a handful of supreme leaders who were ripe for conversion to the new mysteries of eastern religions. Though from a rational point of view the Roman empire may have given the impression of being able to withstand anything, it was actually a society incapable of spontaneously producing the institutional responses needed to repair cracks that became ever more serious as it expanded to integrate, ever more precariously, more and more foreigners. The gainers from this were the Christians; they became the self-appointed champions of a return to nationalism, but the supposed progressivism of their god of love, their universal man with his masochistic passion—as the temporary obverse of a murderous messianism—represented in reality a gigantic step backwards—back beyond the great empires of Egypt, Mesopotamia and China, those vast machines that managed in one way or another to launch the first civilizations—with the invention of writing, of technical innovations, the division of labor among millions and so on. Later things went from bad to worse, to the Greek, the Roman and finally the Christian empires. With each change, the death instinct made permanent gains. Whatever regression there may have been in terms of techniques and institutions, military techniques always held on to, and systematized, whatever improvements they had achieved—iron swords, the use of cavalry and so on. Every new upsurge of civilization preserved bits of the previous edifice in a more or less dilapidated state, but the military machine embarked on a continuous process of innovations, later to give birth to the mechanization and militarizing of labor in capitalist society.

The marauding Greeks took over writing, a certain vision of the city, a memory of empire as a confederation. The Romans, greedy for Greek and Egyptian exoticism, tended rather to behave like American imperialists wherever they went. Then the Christians, like vultures, fell upon the refuse of the empire to try and secure their own hegemony (to the disgust of a man like Julian the Apostate). But they brought with them the poisonous seeds of all the Arianisms and Anglicanisms of the future, for they were incapable of getting the empire away from its claim to universal power, which could only be fought to the bitter end of total destruction.

To pursue this train of thought, let me now take the example of what is happening today at a critical point in the relationship between the USSR and the USA. As we know—Trotsky pointed it out long ago in *The Revolution Betrayed*—the Russians have always imported their technology from the West; but since Khrushchev's day, they have also taken their economic models from there too. In fact, soviet bureaucratism has never been capable of accepting the developments in subjectivation that the Russian revolution carried within it. Hitherto, it has withstood the launching of any process of institutionalization which—without seriously challenging it— would have been comparable to what made Western capitalism transform itself after the 1929 crisis of State monopoly capitalism. (With, it is true, the invaluable assistance of the social-democrat and communist organizations.)

Obviously it will not be by importing models of desire—as they have been obliged to accept the introduction of jazz and Western fashions—that the Soviet bureaucrats will escape the fundamental impasse they have got themselves into, with their endless Five-Year Plans of which absolutely everyone is sick to death. Not merely are they starting no institutionalizing process by importing prefabricated car factories, but by the same token they are transplanting forms of human relationship quite foreign to socialism, a hierarchization of technological functions proper to a society based on individual profits, a split between research and industry, between intellectual and manual work, an alienating style of mass consumption and so on. These are all things that can be relatively harmless in the context of capitalist corruption—the brothel of the small firm and free enterprise—but, in this massive transplantation, become more dangerous by developing in a bureaucratic context that has no longer got the "regulating mechanisms," the alarm bells available to capitalists in the form of public opinion and the state of the market. Not only are car factories imported, then, but also social neuroses, and in hyperactive form. So monstrous are these transplantations that one can depend on their ultimately becoming carriers of radically revolutionary signifying breakthroughs, where Trotsky envisaged only a simple "political revolution" to sweep away the bureaucratic excrescence from a State he considered still fundamentally healthy and persisted in defining as a "proletarian State."

The signifying breakthrough, then, is not just something to expect from linguistic effects, and short of being ready to fall into a realism of the signifier and avoiding the problems, it must be admitted that it can equally well be played on a tom-tom or written with the feet (in the sense that people who walk out of a meeting are said to be "voting with their feet"). The signifier can also carry its breakthrough into registers structured from one substance or another.[5] The Soviet leaders of today still fail to achieve that signifying breakthrough, for they still import their models from the United States in just the same way as the Tsar thought he could build up a modern industry by borrowing the capital and the engineers from France, despite the incapacity of the Russian bourgeoisie.

Ultimately, one escapes from the structuralist impasse by recognizing that an effect of meaning only has repercussions at the level of the signified in so far as potentialities of subjective action are liberated, once there is a breach in the signifier. A phonological system and a certain type of production relations, both closed in upon themselves, contain potentialities of subjectivation. The machinic breakthrough, waiting, masked by the structure, is the subject in aspic, so to say, time at the ready. So long as the structure does not move, the subject does not appear. One day, there will cease to be any difference between, say *b* and *t*. Or, perhaps, between the father/boss and the apprentice (that apprentice who is yet to undertake his *tour de France* and his masterpiece), the distinction giving way to a homogeneous notion of a certain amount of specialized work. To abolish the difference between *b* and *t* means abolishing that between two significations such as *ball* and *tall*. What is abolished is not the difference between the two words in terms of the form of content, but in terms of the form of expression, between the plosive *b*, and the mute *t*. But if *ball* and *tall* could no longer be distinguished in their verbal or written expression, it could certainly have strange consequences in the world of phantasy. And it is primarily at that unconscious level that history is woven and that revolutions arise.[6]

It goes without saying, I hope, that these suggested examples are not to be taken literally. Economic distinctions of the kind that constitute the fundamental axiomatic of a system of production relations, and have therefore little connection with letters and literature, are nevertheless governed by the same signifying laws, repetitions, deadly structural impasses—and, equally, the same necessary breaks, the same potential revolutions.

Hence it is justifiable to think of causality in the order of the class struggle. Though it refuses to recognize the fact, the revolutionary movement is working out its action on the plane of subjectivity and the signifier, setting about causing other signifying breakthroughs, a subjective transmutation when, in a particular system, the bourgeoisie vainly persist in articulating distinctions of every kind (not just of the *ball* / *tall* variety) even though they no longer operate at the level either of unconscious or of economic production. Thus the terms of the class struggle—the class of class words—may perhaps have their fundamental accent and pronunciation changed, while those who continue to put forward their pronouncements without reference to this new unconscious syntax will be turning away from the subjective revolutionary breakthrough that is coming, reifying the logic of history (a logic of nonsense), and falling despite themselves into structuralism.

The subject, as agent of breakthrough, is in eclipse, and what continues is the Ego; in this sense it is as absurd to talk of the subject of history as of the subject of the ego. Think how a child develops: "Me—I'm this, I'm that." Then comes a sudden change when the problem of the subject arises. The infantile ego was still involved in a system of identification in which the subject, the hidden agent of the situation, had up to then been simply an imaginary phallus (the child being for its mother the fruit, so to say, of the father), a phallus imprisoned in the womb of what we designate as the mother of what we designate as the child, still for some time indifferent to the symbolism of such designations, being too busy getting all its little partial machines working. Everything could have gone on like that if that memorable mother had not responded in a certain way, one day, to a certain wink from a certain butcher down the road. Then, suddenly, everything must be looked at with new eyes! The inscription of this simple event strikes home and produces the matrix of the eventful, of development, of history on a large scale, and all the small, sordid histories as well.

From then on, the problem of the structural remolding of the person of the child was unavoidable—and to raise the question of structure is to evoke the principle of closing-up, of the unleashing and intervention of the death instinct, of the split between the ego and the subject, between reality and pleasure, between praxis and enjoyment, between signifier and signified, between the power of uttering and the impotence of what is uttered. The truth that now comes to light is that the subject and the ego had never really coincided. That fact had never presented any great problem, but it now becomes officially intolerable. It is a dismemberment we can see happening before our very eyes. Under this new regime, everything must change; we must at all costs produce the illusion that the subject and the ego can be stuck together again in the ambiguous status of the individual and the person. A myth of totality—a totalitarian myth.

The schizzy subject will in reality remain in the background, and will be the subject of the unconscious, the hidden key to repressed utterances, the potential breakthrough to signifying chains capable of *anything*—including setting free the pent-up energy in wild animals, lunatics and other captives to ravage the formal gardens of the conscious mind and the social order. This subjectivity need give no account of itself either to law or to history. The subject and death are both outside history—they do not recognizably exist, they are nowhere. When do we die? When we are born? When we are alive? When we die? After we die? When? Once there is a concept of death, then we are always dead—even before we are born, since there can be no thought of existing apart from death. History is the opposite of death. In a sense, both are equally absurd. Making history—or making a scene—is to stop making death; it means using every possible means to dissolve the illusory power of structures to give consistency to meaningless utterances about history and death.

2. The Leninist Breakthrough[7]

In history, in the sense in which we normally use the term, everything operates in the order of determination, and historical materialism, providing one does not fall into the simplifications of the Stalinists, remains the only viable method. But dialectical determinism misses one dimension that plays in counterpoint, so to say, to the very principle of determination. That is the paradox of, for instance, an institution like the French Communist Party, whose politics is totally determined by the state of the economic and social relations of State monopoly capitalism, is the prisoner of Gaullism, is dependent on the foreign policy of the USSR and so on; none of which, however, should conceal the fact that there is still, in France, a revolutionary path that depends partly on how the crisis within the Party develops. Or, to take another example, in Cuba one might have thought ten years ago that anything might happen—the sudden breakthrough of Castroism had changed everything, and for a time opened up a series of unpredictable events. I do not mean to say that there could be a Castro in France, but only to suggest that in the order of counter-determination, a whole range of subjective interventions and revolutionary upheavals is possible. This is not by any means to imply that there are necessary causes, but only that there are possibilities of interruptions in historical causality.[8]

Look at the Bolsheviks' intervention between February and October 1917, which was to prevent the natural development of things; they blocked what would "normally" have taken place following a national debacle on such a scale—some kind of coalition of the left and center, living in hopes of better days and the recovery of power by traditionalist parties. The Bolsheviks interpreted the military, economic, social and political collapse as a victory of the masses—the first victory of the socialist revolution. It was Lenin who had the courage to maintain, at this critical juncture for Russia, the intransigent theory of "revolutionary defeatism." Note, too, that Bolshevik policy during this period depended wholly upon Lenin and his sudden awareness that the socialist revolution had become the immediate objective, given that the weakness of the Russian bourgeoisie made them incapable of consolidating their power. The situation Lenin faced was utterly unexpected. Up to then he had stoutly disagreed with all who had predicted that such a bursting of banks would become inevitable (that is, Trotsky and the school of "permanent revolution"). It remained for Lenin to convince his own party, and in the end it was by a kind of *coup* against his own Central Committee that he managed to enforce the line of what were called the April Theses: the immediate mobilization of the party and people to seize power.

The consequences of this about-turn, and the breach it produced in the Bolshevik party, were considerable. Some extremely important militants, like Zinoviev and Kamenev, did all they could by whatever means to oppose this new assumption of hegemony by the Party. The despairing energy they brought to battle against what seemed to them nothing but a dangerous temptation even suggests that they may have had some kind of historical foreknowledge of the Stalinist era that would follow this seizure of power, of the degeneration of the communist ideal that would ensue in the eyes of the masses, and the resulting damage to the entire Marxist revolutionary movement.

But neither Lenin nor Trotsky was disposed to let such premonitions stop them. For the first time in fifteen years, they found themselves in agreement again: they must hurl themselves into the breach with their heads down, and by a kind of collective voluntarism, force history to record indelibly this proletarian revolutionary breakthrough—despite the weakness of the Russian proletariat, and without thought of the consequences, or even of the possible boomerang effects. The hour of the first socialist revolution *must* strike. Soon after, the breach was closed and the cutting edge of the Bolshevik action blunted; some people were to claim that the historical causality of the balance of forces had never in fact ceased to operate, that this great signifying breakthrough—the Leninist breakthrough—was just a mirage and that history was still, in the last resort, governed by the same laws as nature, or rather the laws postulated by the positivist imagination.

Nevertheless, that breakthrough is still imprinted on our history, as much by the contribution it has made to our theoretical understanding and its actualization of an effective class struggle (that had hitherto been more or less hypothetical), as by its limitations, its dependence on circumstance, the scars and blemishes we have inherited from it—of which we cannot rid ourselves because of our inability to overcome its effects of repetition. The real question is in what fashion we should best look back at such moments of history, to what point it is necessary to analyse all the circumstances that affected them, and, by the same token, how much weight we should give to day-to-day events in our own revolutionary endeavors.

One might think it preferable to remain at a certain level of generality, for instance to restrict our analysis of the "recuperation" of Bolshevism to a consideration of the purely historical causality of the prevailing balance of forces, and to rest content with expounding the classic theory that it was inevitable, given the failure of the German revolution, the betrayal of social democracy in Europe, the weariness of the mass of the people and so on. Or one could consider a more complex approach that would cross the traditional boundaries and try to work out the links connecting the different orders of determination—economic, demographic, sociological, the unconscious, etc. One would then no longer have to choose one plane of significance over another—*either* the human factor *or* the economic, for instance—but could follow in detail the winding trail of the signifier, its crossroads, dead ends, ramifications, repetitions, backward turns. Such a study, in which the work of the historian and the economist would be continually tied in with the production of psychoanalytic biographies, linguistic studies and so forth, would be a kind of crucible from which might emerge a new race of militant analysts who would help Marxism at last to recover from the fatal disease of generality that now paralyses it.

To return to the October revolution, it should be possible to understand in greater depth what were the circumstances and the framework of the Leninist breakthrough, without fear of getting bogged down in what seem at first sight to be unimportant details. What complex network of signifiers put the Bolsheviks in a position to launch those "ten days that shook the world"? What were the obstacles that caused them to stumble, and stand by helplessly before the hideous regression of Stalinism that was to distort the revolution and to paralyse and undermine dozens of revolutionary movements in succeeding decades?

It is no discredit to them to say, first of all, that the Bolsheviks very soon—indeed from the beginning of the revolution—showed themselves unable to assume command of the masses, because they stuck to their fundamental policy and their ethical principles. In the paroxysms of October 1917, the Party machine (still a small underground organization) had to cope with the results of generalized collapse and imperialist encirclement. An embryo State had to be set up—in which they were caught between the demands of "War Communism" and the promise of the withering away of the proletarian State in the future—a revolutionary army had hastily to be mobilized, but for technical reasons (or so it seemed at the time) its high command had to include officers of the old Tsarist army, and it had to return almost wholly to traditional military methods. The same Party apparatus had—or so, again, it seemed at the time—a duty to coordinate strategically, and even to plan tactically, revolutionary struggles all over the world. So, without even getting formal agreement from the party of Rosa Luxemburg, and while European social democracy was far from having resolved the crisis it was undergoing, the Bolsheviks improvised a new international out of a lot of small, disparate groups. The Party was everywhere, and felt responsible for everything. The Bolshevik concept of the relationship between the masses and the vanguard meant that the revolutionary Party—the apparatus, in other words—had to put itself forward in every situation, speak for the people, take command of them and so on.

All this calls for analyses in depth of the various "areas"—organizational, political, theoretical and ethical—of Bolshevism. One could start from the fact—that seems to me undeniable—that the handful of "old Bolsheviks," conscious of their mission and, with few exceptions, not intoxicated with success, nevertheless contributed, for reasons of propaganda and party cohesion, to allowing a *collective* phantasy of omnipotence to develop which at times assumed megalomaniac proportions among the newcomers to the Party. The Party became invested with a kind of messianic vocation, being destined by history to be a universal judge of true and false, of good and bad revolutionaries and so on. The mechanistic notions prevailing among the intelligentsia of the period also played their part: for instance there was that deplorable analogy, which still perverts the workers' movement today, of the "driving belt" as an image of how mass organizations should be mediating between the Party and the masses, to make sure that orders were passed on correctly.

The Leninist Party was no more prepared than any other—especially not at the theoretical level—to respond to and encourage such a wholly new process of institutionalization as the development of the soviets was at first. Later on, whether organizing workers, young people, women or anyone else, they never really got away from the traditional pattern. No lasting institutional innovation could have developed. Once power had been seized, the soviets disappeared.

The end result, even before Lenin died, was to be the elimination and persecution of all opposition (the outlawing of the Left Social Revolutionaries, the anarchists, the workers' opposition, fractions within the Party, etc.). There followed, in the absence of any popular counter-weight, a cancerous growth of political, police, military, economic and every other kind of technocracy. The militarization of the Red Army by Trotsky was to be followed by his plan of militarizing the trade unions and setting up a system of forced labor—all justified by laborious arguments based on quasi-lunatic theories, such as the statement that feudal serf labor had been a "progressive phenomenon."[9] It was to be Stalin who actually put all these wondrous theories into practice—and militarized the Party, the State and the Third International into the bargain. As early as 1921, the commune of Kronstadt was universally repudiated and calumniated.[10]

Thus Trotsky, forced into Leninism by the revolution, yet always in two minds, came to apply with savage rigidity a grotesque Bolshevism, a line that was the precise opposite of the one he had followed as leader of the Petrograd soviet in 1905 and 1917. But in his case, unlike Lenin, when he reversed his line, theory seems to have ceased to have any connection with reality—or at least it only became re-connected to it after the event, the whole function of his literary activity being to create a retroactive compatibility. Trotsky in fact always became the man of impossible situations; he was veritably possessed by "iron discipline," the mechanics of regulation, a belief in his "representativeness" verging on self-dramatization— and this despite the fact that he had previously been among the loudest in denouncing the danger of the political substitutionism inherent in Leninist centralism. His exaggerations were undoubtedly a result of his having come late to Leninism; with the Bolshevik "old guard" spurring him on, he was driven to out-centralize the centralists. But he also had a general tendency to excess in everything. Lenin himself thought it necessary, in his Testament, after praising him unequivocally, to warn of Trotsky's "too far-reaching self-confidence" and his "disposition to be far too much attracted by the purely administrative side of affairs."

Lenin, less of a theorist, certainly less literary and perhaps less directly in touch with the masses than Trotsky, never had any such discrepancy between theory and practice. Changing one's mind or altering one's political line never seem to have presented any real problem to him. His whole being was centered on the objective in view, though he was far from despising diplomacy and compromise;

he did not fundamentally believe that questions of the individual mattered—starting with himself. His whole political history illustrates this, but it was perhaps peculiarly significant in relation to what I shall call the moment of the fundamental Leninist breakthrough, in August 1903, at the end of the Second Congress of the All-Russian Social Democratic Labor Party. Yet, at least in appearance, matters did not develop on any clear political or theoretical basis.

The split, according to Trotsky, came out of a clear blue sky.[11] Everything was going normally, with the traditional bickering among the various tendencies: for the fifty-eight delegates (of whom, incidentally, only three were workers) meeting in London after having had to leave Brussels after a police warning, the main aim was to consolidate the constitution of the Party. The trouble arose over the definition of membership, with a disagreement over the meaning of *two words* in one paragraph of the statutes, and the argument then shifted to the number of members of the *Iskra* editorial committee: for reasons of efficiency—which may well have concealed ulterior political motives—Lenin wanted it to be reduced to three. It was problems of this sort that shattered the precarious equilibrium that had somehow been maintained hitherto among the groups that constituted the Russian Social Democratic Party. Trouble had certainly been smoldering for some time: there had been ill tempered polemics over divergences with the "Economists," who in fact comprised most of the Party's working class militants; and the obsessive fear of certain of the Party's intellectuals of falling into revisionism led them to exaggerate the risk (which could only be imaginary in the actual context of Tsarist Russia) of a split between work on the shop floor and political action.

Then too there was the deplorable dispute that led to the exclusion of the Bond: the rationalism of the leaders prevented their understanding the desire of the Jewish militants to maintain a minimum of organizational identity—though God knows the condition of Jewish workers in Russia at the time was precarious. On this point, the leadership made Trotsky their spokesman, and the violence of his interventions won him the nickname of "Lenin's cudgel." But I cannot here give an adequate account of all the details. Suffice it to say that the chain of events could not be halted: Martov broke with Lenin, then Lenin with Plekhanov, then Plekhanov with Trotsky—all accompanied by intransigent invective and the end of longstanding friendships. Yet it was against this black theater, with this claustrophobic psychodrama, that a new signifying system came into being, a new axiomatic of the revolutionary movement, on which our thinking is still largely dependent today.

What happened at that Congress was repeated *ad infinitum* elsewhere. Statements were hardened into dogma, and taken completely out of the context in which they had been made. As dominant utterances, their function then became that of seeking to control all divergent utterance. A whole professional Bolshevik style and attitudes, a perverted fondness for creating splits on matters of principle—accompanied with a flexibility of tactics that almost at times verged on duplicity—entered the sphere of militant subjectivity. I am convinced that phoneticists, phonologists and semanticists would be able to trace back to this event the crystallization of certain linguistic characteristics, the ways—always the same—in which stereotyped formulae are still hammered out by revolutionaries today, whatever language they are taken from. A new variant of the universal language of revolution—a "special language" indeed!—was born out of this theater of the absurd, giving form to a message divided against itself arid solidity to a doctrine of anti revisionism, anti centrism, etc.

It also created an area of inertia that was seriously to restrict the openness of revolutionary militants trained in that school, justifying them in an uncritical acceptance of slick sounding slogans, and causing most of them to belittle the function of desire—first for themselves, in the process of their own, new style bureaucratization, and then for the masses, towards whom they were to develop a domineering and contemptuous attitude, that hateful "love" of the militant who knows everything *a priori* and systematically refuses to listen to anything other than the Party line. The opium of the militant, a sado masochistic enticement! The desire of the masses certainly includes a will to fight, but also a knowledge that does not necessarily coincide with an over schematic Party line that takes no account of the unexpectedness of events or exceptional rearrangements of power alignments: a joyless line. Not that the masses are in themselves anarchist, but it is for themselves that they want to fight, at their own pace, to suit their own inclination and as they please, though they will put themselves in the hands of a Party apparatus when they are baffled by conflicting alternatives, or simply lose interest altogether.

From this fundamental breach, then, the Leninist machine was launched on its career; history was still to give it a face and a substance, but its fundamental encoding, so to say, was already determined. Basically, the question we come up against is what other machine—if a machine there must be—could replace it, more effectively, and with less damage to the desire of the masses. Of course I am not saying that it is the breach of 1903 *alone* that has persisted through history, from Leninism to Stalinism to Maoism; things have developed and altered with circumstances. I am simply saying that the fundamental signifiers, the cardinal positions, entered history at that moment. This is simply a working hypothesis that must be examined with care, reworked, perhaps even ousted altogether. My intention was to give a brief illustration of one possible line of analysis, and I must stress that this reservation is not just a matter of form: I am not going to do to the myths of the present day revolutionary movement what psychoanalysts, for instance, do to the myths of antiquity—taking them as absolute reference points, and claiming that they are precisely the same as themselves, at every stage and in every area of the phenomenology of the unconscious.

Indeed, what must be made absolutely clear is the fact that, as long as no revolutionary *interpretation* has cast any new light on things, every period remains the prisoner of *historically definable* myths. I began with the "Bolshevik complex," but I could equally have taken the "1936 complex" as my starting point, with its variants of anti-fascism—united national front, popular front, and even the crumbling and hollow myth of the "alliance of all the people" that did such harm to the anti imperialist struggle. This time, if one is to pinpoint a fundamental breakthrough (following on from the earlier one), what happened must be seen in relation to a process that was going on in the heads of the Stalinist bureaucrats when they went through the motions of holding a Seventh Congress of the International in 1935, after Hitler's coming to power and the Reichstag fire. Unable much longer to conceal the bankruptcy of the line followed since 1929, Dimitrov became the spokesman of the official abandonment of the factional errors of the so called "third period" in favor of precisely the opposite policy—a switch that was to carry the entire communist movement into the most appalling opportunism to fit in with the policy of Moscow. Moscow, as we know, was to do another about face with the German Soviet pact, and even ended by negotiating with imperialism the dissolution of what was no longer any more than a make-believe International.

That "popular front complex" also left behind another, idealized, aspect, which one could illustrate either by the emaciated outline of the International Brigade volunteer returning from Spain, the bitterness of defeat causing him to leave unasked the question "Why?" after so great an invisible betrayal; or by the rose colored picture of the "spirit of the Resistance" that was impressed on several generations in the days after the Liberation, still largely bound up with the illusions of pre-war times, with pacifism, with the back-to-the-land mystique, all expressing a systematic *méconnaissance* of the hard reality of the class struggle and imperialist confrontation.

I am not concerned here with the question of whether or not a revolutionary praxis can prevent itself being side-tracked into such collective phantasy formations which in a sense punctuate history, but can also paralyse or positively pervert the masses,[12] This question boils down to deciding what conditions would permit the emergence of independent groups capable of controlling their own phantasizing sufficiently to restrict it to transitional phantasies— phantasies whose historical limitation is recognized—and to prevent the group's becoming bogged down in the phantasies of the dominant group and so itself becoming a dependent group. And I would stress, here, that any attempt at analysis, in this sphere, would have to consider not only the utterances of history as they have reached us, but also the way the authors of such utterances are constituted and how they function.

To return to those few dozen delegates at the Second Congress of the Social Democratic Labor Party: they were clearly quite incapable of facing and admitting the truth, perhaps for the very reason that they were totally surrounded by it. Some day it may be possible to talk of the principal delegate, Lenin, without bringing upon oneself a flood of abuse, and to try to explore a phase of his life that was certainly one of the starting points of that radical break that constitutes Leninism: I mean the crisis in his life when, in the spring of 1887, his elder brother Alexander was executed as the chief culprit in an attempt to assassinate Tsar Alexander III. In his biography of Lenin,[13] Louis Fischer shows how official history has misrepresented the relative positions of the brothers. The Stalinist view is a simple one: on the one hand was the Narodnik terrorist, and on the other the young Marxist who, when his brother died, declared, "We must do it differently—this is not the right path…"

In fact, up to that stage, Volodia—the future Lenin, then only seventeen—had not been following his brother's revolutionary path at all. Indeed, they did not even get on very well. Whereas Volodia was a chess enthusiast and loved to read Turgenev, Alexander was translating Marx into Russian, studying *Capital* and leading a group of militants who belonged both to the revolutionary *Narodnjia Volta* (People's Party) and Plekhanov's Marxist group. A far cry from the Stalinist picture! Alexander, by doggedly refusing to beg the Tsar for clemency, became a legendary figure to Russian revolutionaries. It was only after his death that Volodia became interested in his ideas, and at first he was equally sympathetic to the *narodniks*: In fact, though he later became fiercely opposed to them, Lenin was to be abused by legalistic social democrats for the rest of his life for his taste for terrorism and underground organizations.

This very real change was to turn the future of the brilliant student completely upside down, and one must certainly look back to it to understand the fundamental and intractable difference between Lenin's relationship to reality—whatever his politico theoretical utterances—and that of a man like Trotsky.

Trotsky was worlds away: he too had undergone a shattering change, but it had marked him less obviously, affecting mainly his imaginative capacity. There are good reasons for believing that, throughout his life, the fact of being a Jew led him to seek for a sense of belonging, a legitimation, even at the risk of becoming identified with the dominant image. Even his pseudonym was the name of one of his former gaolers in Odessa prison, written on his forged passport on the spur of the moment when he escaped from Irkutsk in 1902. I should like to hope, without offending the sensitive or reawakening Stalinist racism, that historians will one day give more thought to Isaac Deutscher's question: "In this hazardous escape did the identification with his gaoler perhaps gratify in the fugitive a subconscious craving for safety?"[14]

This might give us better clues to interpreting such apparently aberrant facts as the motive given by Trotsky immediately after the October revolution for refusing Lenin's proposal that he become president of the first government of soviets—namely that he was a *Jew*. It might also be possible to see further than Deutscher's rather hasty interpretation of another incident: he puts down to simple jealousy Trotsky's refusal to become deputy chairman of the Council of People's Commissars as Lenin kept begging him to—from April 1922 until he died—in order to provide a counter weight to Stalin at the head of the party apparatus.[15] Innumerable successive inhibitions led Trotsky, Hamlet-like, to refuse as long as possible to take any real action against Stalin, despite the urgings of Lenin, paralysed on his deathbed. It was only long after Lenin's death that he was to embark on a fierce struggle against the bureaucracy, and by then the situation had become so corrupt that any such attempt could only lead to death.

If it is true that such weighty stakes were potentially at issue in the debates of the 1903 Congress, and that they could be sensed in the way the unconscious chains were developing then, it is easy to see why those taking part suddenly ceased to be rational, dazed by threatening historical truths, and tempted to take refuge in stereotyped modes of defence and prejudices.[16] Apart from Lenin—that is—who seems on the contrary to have emerged from the ordeal stronger, and more determined than ever to get rid of the friendly way of doing things in social democracy. However, immediately after the Congress he wrote to Potresov: "And now I am asking myself: for what reason should we part to become life-long enemies? I am receiving all the events and impressions of the congress, I am aware that often I acted and behaved in terrible irritation, 'madly,' and I am willing to admit this guilt to anybody—if one can call guilt something that was naturally caused by the atmosphere, the reactions, the retorts, the struggle, etc."[17]

However, without questioning the sincerity of this, one may still believe that, at bottom, he had no illusions as to the chances of repairing the damage. As far as he was concerned, one phase was over. Former comrades could, of course, always return to what he considered the majority of the Party, but it would be on the basis of a new, and henceforth unquestioned, centralism. In fact, those militants who had not at first been formally affiliated to the Leninist camp drifted towards the rather vague group that comprised the Mensheviks. A number of them emerged from the ordeal permanently in two minds: Martov, for instance, who had been a front-ranking militant, continued ambivalent through the Zimmerwald Conferences and the revolution, and on up to his death in exile in 1923.

Though it may be said that the fundamental options of Leninism were crystallized from that time forward, the same is not true of the other tendencies. The available alternatives seem always to have been in search of people to adopt them, and moving with a certain fluidity from one adherent to another. The militant scenario of 1903 was still far from having developed into that vast man-eating machine that post-revolutionary Russia was to become, in which a show trial, theater of a very different kind, would inform everyone once and for all what official history would record them as having been—or not been. At this stage, Stalin, who was single-minded if ever a man was, had not yet become the prototype and leader of a sadistic pseudo-Bolshevism. Trotsky was not yet the man whose every statement must be refuted, and who must eventually be murdered—the main effect of lies and calumnies being to neutralize any possibility of the Stalinists' producing their own ideas, dooming them by a paradoxical kind of reaction to repeat word for word, though later, out of context and with distaste, Trotskyist pronouncements on the economy, international politics and so on. Karnenev and Zinoviev were not yet the centrists and ultimate traitors who had from the first merely been biding their time. And, be it also said, Lenin himself was far from being that intransigent figure representing a rigid centralism presented to us by simplistic historians. Truth to say, in 1903 centralism was in the air; it was even fashionable in social democracy—the venerable Plekhanov himself was a centralist, and the young Trotsky used his success as an orator to become even more of a centralist than Lenin.

I mention all this here, summarily enough, merely in order to illustrate my view that a split of the kind that officially divided Russian social democracy in 1912 into two irreconcilable parties (with all that it entailed for the unfolding of the revolution) could have been counter determined long before, *nachträglich*, by deferred action (to use Freud's term), and in areas quite different from those traditionally focused on by those who plan history. This is especially the case in the detail I have barely touched on of what I call "militant representation," which is itself simply the manifestation of unconscious signifiers, potential utterances and creative crises relating to substances as yet insignificant, and producing subjective effects simultaneously affecting the whole of the historical sequence under consideration.

It is as though history, to recover its extension in time, can only depend on contingent support, in the form of those breakthroughs more or less unconsciously actualized by agencies of collective utterance, that is to say subject groups—which at the present time are militant revolutionary groups. Such statements will no doubt be deprecated as reducing historical causality to trivia; and in a sense this is quite true. To what extent are the mass of people prepared to sacrifice themselves for things that "really matter," to shoulder their fundamental historical tasks? Under what conditions would they consider uniting as one man to form a vast war machine like the one that swept all before it in 1917? Surely the first condition (without which the death instinct would take over collectively) should be an assurance that the "trivia" that are for them the salt of life, the source of their desire, would not be forgotten in the process? One has only to recall the vast and interminable drinking spree that followed the popular seizure of power in Petrograd—and the shocked horror of the Bolshevik leaders it was disastrous, certainly, but it could also be said that people have sometimes earned a holiday.

Desire, subjectivity, at this level of collective crystallization, is something that necessarily remains very close to the masses and can only be related extremely indirectly to fundamental historical goals still programmatic and abstract at the time of being formulated. Analysis, as a revolutionary undertaking, contributes to forming a link between two disconnected orders, between what happens and what people say, or rather, what does not happen and is not said openly in the official or unofficial headquarters of the revolution—things which to a large extent, alas, condition the possibilities of popular expression, combined with their fatal capacity for self-repression when it comes to innovation, spontaneity and desire. We might say, briefly, as a reference point, that the object of such analysis would be to identify and interpret the coefficients of transversality relative to the various social spheres under consideration.

3. Integration of the Working Class and Analytical Perspective[18]

After 1936 there began a transformation in French political society, which led to working-class organizations being integrated into the capitalist system.

At first, it was a matter of situations arising out of events, of dramatic crises, but the workers' movement was gradually integrated into the legal order of things, despite the protests—admittedly, increasingly timid of its spokesmen. The "spirit of the class struggle" was to weaken still further among communist militants in a context of supposedly peaceful coexistence among differing regimes and, implicitly, classes. In practice (despite the declarations of principle produced at annual congresses) it was understood that movements to improve wages and conditions would shy away from any political opening that might present a serious threat to capitalism. In 1936, and again in 1945, when the balance of forces made it possible to envisage going much further, the communist leaders let themselves be guided by formulae for working-class integration which successfully plastered over the cracks in capitalism, and indeed reinforced it.

Khrushchevism marked a new stage, and the *de facto* social democratization of the Communist Parties became a rightist ideology. It could not be said in so many words that the Communist Parties had become the good and faithful servants of capitalism, but with a view to the national interest and popular unity (including small capitalists) it was realized that communist ministers would be the best people to administer a capitalism of the "left," without seeking to make any really fundamental changes. And so it proved, as the national economy, the French army and the Union Française were reconstructed under the Tripartism of the Liberation. The fact that the French Party is now trying—long after the Italian—to adopt a more liberal image, accepting the idea that a pluralism of parties could establish socialism and so on, is, of course, *purely* coincidental! It becomes more liberal in its promises for "after the revolution," as it becomes less determined to have a revolution.

What we are seeing, then, is a process leading not merely to the decay of all working class political life, but consequently, if it is still true that the class struggle is its mainspring, of political life in general. When we seem to be having a political debate, in other words a debate that might lead to questioning the established political power, we are in fact merely organizing a pseudo-participation, a "consultation" of "consumers," to persuade them to be concerned with such problems as the standard of living, the normalization of economic processes, national and regional standardization, investment, the movement of manpower, consumption, etc.—all of which is in fact manipulated by technocrats and pressure groups.

The bourgeoisie can favor this de-politicization all the more since the most important centers of economic decision do not coincide with existing national structures but with other imperialist and oligarchic bodies altogether, distinct even from such "maxi markets" as the EEC. Those international, cosmopolitan intersections of capitalism actively foster depoliticization—in the sense of traditional national politics—because their economic strategy, based on keeping profits high, disregards national barriers: their "openings" to Eastern Europe and the Third World are calculated in the long term in the hope of absorbing them as well. What we are seeing is a general evolution of all industrial societies towards removing altogether the need for a political society.

Bourgeois political society was indispensable when it came to coping with one stage of the class struggle, but since the working classes are tending to neutralize themselves via their organizations, we are now witnessing the fading-out of any prospect of a revolutionary takeover by the masses. And when modernists fight for a leftist government, it is not merely that they do not fear the possibility of communist participation, but that they actually hope for it: they know quite well that there is no longer any risk of the French Communist Party getting out of control, and that the communists would be far more effective in containing any possible mass movement that might arise than the riot police.

Everyone knows this, and it may seem pointless to mention it when talking of the validity or otherwise of trying to analyse political groups. However, it seems to me that this must be our starting point: we must understand that the "treason" of the French Communist Party is no more than a desperate attempt on the part of a traditional body to keep itself going in the context of radically altered production relations. This change should have involved a radical transformation of the methods, the line and the aims of the great old days of the Popular Front. All of which, needless to say, lacks credibility and interests no one, apart from those whose profession is electoral pimping. It is just a lot of surface activity and has no real bearing on politics, but it is guaranteed to be effective with the trade unions, whose leaders are now the real agents of working-class integration.

Under these circumstances, the French Communist Party is peculiarly badly placed to combat the myths of the consumer society, for it has no sort of alternative to offer. By comparison, the leftist groupuscules undoubtedly represent an attempt to keep alive the basic themes of an independent, working-class revolutionary policy. Unfortunately, all we see of them is their failure. We as individuals who have worked our way from the Communist Party to our present groups should at least have discovered the total inadequacy of both theory and praxis everywhere—characterized by the fact that the problems that exercise us have generally been around for at least as long as the forty years the Israelites spent in the wilderness.

When the French Communist Party come to analyse a situation "objectively," their immediate response is to justify the most banal opportunism, the abandonment of those fundamental concepts of Marxism that would link the struggles now taking place with a true, overall perspective. When the left groupuscules defend a revolutionary program, they always misunderstand what is actually happening, for their vision is totally distorted by their ideology.

In spite of everything, therefore, the Communist Party and its organizations are still the only ones with some slight grasp on social reality. They represent an apparatus whose mission seems to be to gain control of the latent reformism of the working class. But unlike Lenin, who analysed the nature of that reformism, the Party is busily adjusting itself to it, and ever taking the lead at every step, as is evident from its policy for its cadres. Can one reasonably consider that apparatus as an "analyst" of the working class's unconscious? Can one, correspondingly, consider that the left groupuscules are at present the only ones to embody the working class's historic mission as midwife to the class struggle of a new society in which classes are abolished?

I would suggest, rather, that this split between two modes of social subjectivity—reformist working-class subjectivity, more or less canalized in the French Communist Party, and revolutionary subjectivity, more or less embodied in the left groupuscules—could be the point from which to consider the question of an analytical undertaking, of putting bodies whose work is analytical in contact with socio-professional and political groups. Experience of the Left Opposition and the FGERI has made us better able to appreciate the difficulties and risks such a project involves. There is especially the risk of absorbing the myths of the modernists more than the Communist Party or the Unified Socialist Party ever could: the entry onto the scene of the famous "new working-class," the peaceful occupation of the "real centers of decisionmaking," the promotion of "inter-disciplinary research"—to which we add, to indicate our originality, "based, if possible, on mass study." It all sounds fine, and generally works pretty well. But where does it get us? We could, like a political groupuscule, calculate that at some point we shall decide on a sudden change of direction, on defining clear political bases for the FGERI, and trying to take over all or part of that movement within a revolutionary perspective.

Anything could happen, of course, but as long as we have one foot in reformism, in the wake of the PCF, and the other in a dogmatism barely distinguishable from that of the left groups, it would seem that our successes in the FGERI are unlikely to advance the formation of a revolutionary vanguard or to get the workers' movement out of its present quicksands. For years now we have continued to exist as a group, without any valid reason in terms of the ordinary logic of a classic revolutionary. What the hell are we doing? We argue, we do this and that. We should have given up long ago and, as individuals, each according to our own desires, have joined the various traditional left groups, or gone back to the Communist Party, or vegetated in the PSU, doping our minds with banalities or resigning ourselves to the impossibility of doing anything.

Open possibilities would thus be closed again: "The whole thing was too complicated—this isn't the time—the workers wouldn't have understood us," and all that. It may be that there is no way out for us from this maddening contradiction: having somehow or other to sustain this kind of analytic pretension—these analytic operators—that proposes, right among the masses and without ceasing to pose the fundamental political problem, to overcome the disastrous split between the political and the syndical. What this means for us is attempting to establish a bridgehead between an analysis at the level of the masses and a revolutionary praxis for overthrowing capitalism.

From the point of view of the working class, young people and students, the reality is that they are always made to see themselves in reference to production, merchandise, results, diplomas and so on. (In this respect, we know that the kind of critique undertaken by the FGERI is possible and useful.) From another point of view, they can only turn to fossilized organizations that claim to represent them, but in fact merely act *for* them. This is the sociological manifestation of the preservation by inertia of institutional objects void of all substance, the sheer repetition of a bureaucratic routine and a meaningless web of words.

Just like the managerial system or the State system, these empty institutional objects are also instruments of alienation of the working class, helping to hold it back from its historic mission and its revolutionary reality. These objects will not be made to disappear by any magic wand, any revolutionary program: they represent the essential cogs and wheels of anti-production relations. People may try to evade them by all manner of means—setting up Trotskyist enclaves, a policy of entrism—but it will make no difference. On the contrary, the repeated failure of such attempts only provides them with further justification: "However corrupt the Church may be, nothing else works…" Stalinist and social democratic organizations are seen, by those subject to them, as a kind of lamentable necessity, and therefore the first thing we have to be convinced of is that the destruction of such edifices and the transformation of leftist groupuscules involves the deployment of new conceptual references, the production of new forms of organization not even hinted at in the regular assortment currently on offer on the Marxist-Leninist market.

It is the revolutionary vanguard's failure to understand the unconscious processes that emerge as socio-economic determinisms that has left the working class defenceless in the face of capitalism's modern mechanisms of alienation. The bureaucratic organizations that claim to represent the working class take root in the very fabric of that social unconscious. As long as that vanguard remains helpless, disorientated, with no understanding of those structures of social neurosis of which bureaucratism is only a symptom, then there is no chance of those structures miraculously disintegrating. Khrushchev-style "liberalism," far from beings a step forward, far from finally weakening the internal bureaucracy, it seems actually bound to reinforce it under the benevolent, indeed the playboy image, of the young leaders now being brought to the fore.

Capitalism carries this bureaucratic cancer within it precisely in so far as it is unable to overcome its underlying institutional contradictions. Where once it needed a radical-socialist republic, it now needs to control the means of production, especially the movement of labor. So long as the organizations of the working class are not only entrapped into the politics of participation, but can see no clear way out of the morass, and are making no start on any process of revolutionary institution along the lines of dual power, then there is little to be hoped for from future struggles.

Bolshevism represented a certain potential of intervention against social democratic bureaucratism, but things are different today: the problem now is how we can possibly blow away the participationist fumes that are gradually stupefying the working class. That they are in the main effective at the level of the imaginary only aggravates the danger. Despite its theoretical inadequacy, Leninism managed to put its finger on the mechanism whereby the working class, left to itself, tends to slide into trade-unionism, in other words into the primacy of demand over desire. The Leninist solution of a political break, of establishing a separate institutional object, a machine of consciousness and action composed wholly of professional revolutionaries, was, as history has shown, the right one in a catastrophic situation like that in Russia in 1917. But it could not give the working class the means to seize power in highly developed capitalist regimes—in regimes, that is, where power was not concentrated into an identifiable oligarchy (the "two hundred families") but held in the meshes of an infinitely complex network of production relations covering every element of the world economy and even the smallest of our everyday actions.

However, Leninism has left us a line of thought to explore what I have called, for want of a better term, "group castration," the "Leninist breakthrough,"[19] in other words the effect of the emergence of subject groups on ordinary human relationships. What happens when as solid a machine as Lenin's Party goes into action? None of the usual rules apply. To paraphrase Archimedes, Lenin asked to be given a party, and he would lift Russia. But for us, today, what sort of revolutionary machine could blow up all the citadels of bureaucratism and get the revolution started? We shall not find out by blindly groping about. The theoretical problem of analysis remains as great as ever. We must have the means to demonstrate theoretically, and interpret satisfactorily, the mechanisms whereby wage-earners simply become the tools of the exploiters, the forces that account for the continuity of the French Communist Party, the CGT, etc., so that workers go on trusting them despite the repulsion they inspire. Apart from this, the revolutionary vanguard must itself experience the repetitive mechanisms to which the working class is subjected.

The syndical and integrationist mentality is rooted deeply in people's minds. Questions are expected to be asked as a matter of urgency, even of scandal: the boss, or the minister, is expected to "accept his responsibilities." But the legitimacy of his power is never really questioned. How can analytical politics break through all this, and consolidate itself by finding points of support in other areas? "People must meet and discuss freely, placing themselves as far as possible outside what is going on, no longer playing along with the system…" Well, that does not really get us much further. Yet surely this decentering, this change of style, is precisely what constitutes the essence of the breakaway of politics, its divergence from demand? Of an other politics, a politics of otherness, a revolutionary politics?

The work so far done in the FGERI must not be overestimated. In the main, it has affected only sectors little marked by Stalinism, sectors, too, relatively free of capitalist interference (education, urban studies, health and such). I say "relatively," because things are changing, and because the respective status of the middle and working classes is also changing—not in the direction of a "new working class," but towards a working class being fitted into a new situation and tending to absorb the whole of the tertiary sector.

Think for instance of psychiatry, a sector in which we have had direct experience of the failure of the trade unions to define any consistent program of demands on behalf of psychiatric nurses. As we all know, their profession is undergoing profound modifications because of the development both of medical techniques and of institutional innovations. From the warders of the past, nurses are now tending to become highly qualified technicians who may well be called on in future to take over a large part of the role traditionally allotted to the psychiatrist (district policy, home care, etc.). But the unions do not want to know. All that matters to them is to defend established gains. They are not interested in reviewing the system of three eight-hour shifts that paralyses the organization of life in the hospital; instead, they will fight to the last to defend a nonsensical hierarchy rejected by the majority of the staff. Some of the national union leaders were nurses in their youth but are now totally out of touch, and these too the majority reject. One attempt to achieve something—organizing staff associations—has made it clear that at this level the bureaucrats are not likely to get much response, even where they do not resort to the sort of abuse and threats of expulsion from the CGT that one so often hears: "You are Gaullists, you are acting against the unions, you have no right to go over the heads of the unions…"

Yet all that the psychiatric staff were asking was the right to meet and discuss their work, forgetting grading and qualifications, and involving district supervisors, administrators, psychiatrists, house doctors, ancillary staff and so on. Within a few weeks, more than fifteen hospitals had such associations, and were beginning to form federations: there were national meetings, inter-hospital visits, exchanges and unprecedentedly open discussion of what really went on in various departments. The CGT federation made considerable efforts to destroy this movement, and they succeeded. But they could not kill the idea.

The analytic effects of such an enterprise cannot be disputed (though one would have to go into considerable detail to demonstrate them exactly), but it had certain in-built limitations because of its isolation, and because it lacked the coordination that would have made it possible (a) to make clear its political and theoretical impact at a certain level and (b) to establish a better balance of forces to defend it. Neutralizing your local bureaucracy is one thing, but to neutralize the whole bureaucratic system is quite another. One obviously could not get very far on the basis of experiments of this kind, or even of more sustained efforts like the work that has been going on for several years among the comrades in the Hispano group.[20] It would take the complex interaction of a great many such efforts to get us over this barrier that we keep coming up against. But it must be stressed that the analytical study and action groups that we do manage more or less successfully to establish in various sectors may well fill us with illusions, unless there can be more groups of the Hispano type, that is to say groups working in key sectors of production.

I think one should still be a Leninist, at least in the specific sense of believing that we cannot really look to the spontaneity and creativity of the masses to establish analytical groups in any lasting way—though "Leninist" is perhaps an odd word to use when one remembers that the object at this moment is to foster not a highly centralized party, but some means whereby the masses can gain control of their own lives.

Ultimately, what analysis means here is detecting the traces of contamination from capitalist fall out in all the crannies where they may lie concealed. Revolutionary politics should be something that redirects people's demands, their "natural" understanding of things, and does so out of the simplest situations; revolution creates trouble out of events that common sense would say were quite unimportant—out of the problems of the housewife and the kitchen cupboard, of the everyday humiliations meted out by a domineering hierarchy. Only by slow steps—though there are sudden startling leaps—can one work back from such situations to the key signifiers of capitalist power. And that transition is also a transformation, for moving into politics marks a breakthrough: the political concept is not just a straightforward extension of people's ordinary demands.

The analysis of those demands has the effect of an acid that strips away the inessentials to sharpen the cutting edge, so that the social subjectivity becomes open to desire, and at the same time continues to reintroduce the peculiar, the unpredictable, even the nonsensical, into the coherence of political discourse. From this point of view, the analysis is never-ending, which is what makes it different from any self-enclosed program. Not "permanent revolution," perhaps, but "permanent analysis"! The political concept is continually being re-examined by the analytical operation, and continually having to be worked out again from scratch; the work of analysis takes it back again and again to its beginnings, while always withholding total agreement. Nothing is more dangerous than to throw oneself into promoting the idea that the scientific accuracy of a political concept can be ensured by the appropriate philosophical processes. There can be no such thing as absolute certainty in this sphere.[21] Political-theoretical concepts, however apparently well organized, cannot in themselves guarantee a consistent revolutionary praxis. Morbid rationalism, masquerading as a scientific rereading of Marx, can lead to the most enormous political mystifications and mistakes. Furthermore, the death instinct inherent in such efforts ensures them a certain success among the many militants who have not yet recovered from the fall of the Stalinist idols and dogmas. It is not preaching opportunism to want to see a theory in its proper context, that is to say in the symbolic order rather than in terms of immediate practical effectiveness. Whether we like it or not, political knowledge will always be on the verge of the analytical vacuoles. On the other hand, that analytical vacuole is, and must be, surrounded on all sides by revolutionary praxis. Analysis, in the social field, is conceivable only in so far as its declarations result from effecting a political utterance and breakthrough.

Only a group committed to revolutionary praxis can function as an analytical vacuole, alongside the processes of society, without any mission of leadership, without any pretension other than that of taking truth along paths from which people generally strive firmly to exclude it. Only an analytic undertaking that takes shape against the background of revolutionary praxis can claim to be genuinely exploring the unconscious—for the good reason that the unconscious is none other than the reality that is to come, the transfinite field of the potentialities contained in signifying chains that are opened, or ready to be opened and articulated, by a real uttering and effecting agent.

This amounts to saying that signifying breakthroughs, even the most "intimate," even those in our so called "private life," can turn out to be decisive points in historical causality. Will the revolution that is coming elaborate its principles from something said by Lautréamont, Kafka or Joyce? Isn't the current thrust of both the imperialist and the so-called socialist regimes being directed towards such institutions and archaisms as those related to the family, for instance, and consumerism? We can see why capitalism wears profit next to its skin like a shirt of Nessus, but how can we accept its also clothing the offspring of the October revolution?

These potentially revolutionary blocks and splits operate simultaneously, at all stages of the phenomenology of the subject and of history. Internationally, the worldwide balance is damaged by irreparable contradictions in that existing social regimes have demonstrated their inability to foster any system of international relations that would enable them to express or handle by diplomacy the signifying breakthroughs, the particular stopping points, of contemporary history. Such points, for instance, as the following: the Long March that was to lead to the coming to power (against Stalin's advice) of the Stalinists in China; Titoism, the result of the Yugoslav Resistance's coming to power, against the Yalta agreements (also signed by Stalin); the first war of liberation in Vietnam, whose quasi-accidental launching the communist leaders did everything to prevent; the struggle of the FLN in Algeria, which, despite its precarious beginnings, was to lead in the end to the collapse of French colonialism (at least in its traditional form); the stranger-than-fiction escapades of the Cuban revolutionaries, which planted a chronic abscess in the heart of the Pentagon's strategic system. Another accident, or rather perhaps artifice, was the transplanting of an Israeli colony that was finally to constitute a factor for revolutionizing the Arab world (though there was a time when Max Nordau almost[22] got the Zionists to accept the idea that the "new homeland" of the Jews should be established in Uganda!).

The Stalinist and social-democratic associates of imperialism are less and less able to *represent* oppressed peoples or the exploited masses, or to negotiate on their behalf. Yet still there is no decisive way of stopping the infernal machine of "substitutionism." The process whereby the revolutionary masses will recover the direct control of their own fate has barely begun, and until that happens we shall have to go on being prepared for vast bloodbaths, like Vietnam and Indonesia, bearing witness to the desperate impasse of the international revolutionary movement—as the Paris Commune did in an earlier age. Hymning the praises of the heroic people of Vietnam must not make us forget the truth: there was something sacrificial in that holocaust; its appalingness is matched by the criminal policies of the leadership of the international workers' movement, which left the Vietnamese people to struggle alone in our day, as it left those of the Spanish Republic in the past.

One may urge at least that the lesson be drawn, that the truth be faced at whatever cost: the fact is that we have got to start again from square one, that our whole orientation must be different, that we must put behind us an epoch of the strategy and theory of the communist movement that is finished.

4. Vietnam 1967[23]

In Vietnam, American imperialism has tried to prove that it is always able to enforce its law and its methods when and where it might wish. It has mobilized its huge economic and human resources to do this, it has been willing to compromise its so-called prestige as a great nation/protective elder brother of the free world. The international *status quo*, precariously maintained since the Second World War, has thus been overthrown. The Vietnamese people have thrown themselves body and soul into the struggle against aggression. Their heroism and skill are unprecedented. They are fighting for survival, national independence, unity and sovereignty, and they are aware that their cause is also that of oppressed classes and subject nations everywhere. French public opinion is not on the whole much concerned. Yet the interests of the Vietnamese people are fundamentally the same as those of workers, of intellectuals, of everyone who is threatened by the possible rein-forcement of the various types of repression used in even the most up-to-date capitalist societies. I hardly need remind you that the defence of truth is at the root of every fight for emancipation: the most subtle and effective forms of alienation are those that we take for granted, those we do not even notice unless we stop to think about it, those that are part of the fabric of our everyday life.

Thus a kind of collective "avoiding action" has led to what I can only call a systematic misunderstanding of the real nature of the tragedy now taking place in Vietnam. Up to a point, perhaps, the more clearsighted among us have not totally failed to see it, but it seems to me that there is a very important problem to be elucidated. The fact is that the savagery of the American aggression against a Third World people should not be seen as simply the stray manifes-tation of a "historical accident." The whole nightmare needs to be interpreted in a worldwide perspective. It inaugurates a new phase of history. In other words, I do not think that it is just as citizens or militants of a particular organization that we have to decide where we stand in relation to what is going on, but also in so far as we have specific research to do in different areas of the human sciences.

The Vietnam war has been accompanied by a reinforcement of the dominant race ideology in the United States, with its puritanism and its myths of destroying the "bad object"—that is, whatever is different, whatever tries to or manages to elude the American Way of Life. The worst acts of barbarism committed daily by the American forces, the puppet troops of Saigon and their allies are methodically repressed from the consciousness of a public opinion manufactured by "information machines." It reminds one of fascism. Hitlerism, of course, developed in a quite different historical context, but that should not prevent our reflecting on the moral degeneration now afflicting the most powerful nation in the world—apart from the vocal minorities who are fighting against it, though without yet achieving any solid results. Freud, following Marx, has shown us how to understand the function of this repression and ideological defence.

The psychoanalytic interpretation, by insisting on disregarding the fact that our objects of love or hate, our most intimately related models of identification, are directly bound up with historical processes, automatically excludes vitally important unconscious determinisms from its field of examination. At the level of unconscious activity, truth is a single whole: distinctions between one's private life and the various areas of social life become irrelevant. Consequently, the effectiveness of value systems does not depend on the conscious knowledge one has gained from education, information or culture. That is why violence has been able to win its "rights" throughout history, to formulate its gospels and even its international jurisprudence. Fascism produced one unprecedented and overwhelming form of this, and American aggression in Vietnam today presents another. We tend not to see quite what an *extraordinary* thing is happening, to reassure ourselves that it will all come right in the end, that common sense will emerge triumphant when the American nation pulls itself together. In point of fact, this sort of thinking seems to proceed from one of those defence mechanisms I referred to that exist to ensure the peaceful slumber of society. Should one ascribe this refusal to give serious consideration to any historical view offering a glimpse of the unknown or the disturbing, this tendency to refer every new event to a phantasy system of historical memory, to what Freud described as the death instinct? The clear consciences of rationalists and progressives are loath to approach this dimension of the problem. The most militant of us are peculiarly liable to an *a priori* optimism where the development of industrial societies is concerned.

A cursory survey of recent history, however, offers innumerable indications of the incapacity of the present style of international relations to find stability. Can there be any stability as long as the countries of the Third World are in such a desperate economic impasse? The recently almost universal myth of "peaceful coexistence"—remember the spirit of Bandung?—has become meaningless: the only coexistence there is now is the *de facto* coexistence of the dominant industrial powers, who only give thought to the fate of the poor nations in relation to their strategic and economic value, their neo-colonialist allegiance. Capitalist production relations have undergone no decisive change in essentials, and the socialist States have proved themselves unable to enforce any international law other than the law of the jungle. The leading State of world imperialism is devoting its efforts to altering the balance of forces to its own advantage, and setting up an international police force. In this, too, the post war period is definitely over, symbolically represented as it was by international bodies whose role as arbitrators was supposed to secure peace forever more. Another system of value is in the process of replacing that one, and is still seeking to establish its legitimacy: think of the incredible idea of the "right of pursuit" that now seems taken for granted, which can justify any form of aggression. In such changed circumstances, the traditional battle-cries of the anti-imperialist struggle are useless; the analyses and strategies offered by the traditional left remain mirror images of those of imperialism, in as much as imperialism has taken up a great deal of its opponents' ideological baggage. Both parties appear to be playing the game by the same rules, because both lack the leverage to effect a genuine transformation of production relations on a worldwide scale. In his last message, Che Guevara spoke of the tragic isolation of Vietnam. But surely what is just as tragic is the isolation of the oppressed classes within wealthy societies? We must also look squarely at the secret and paradoxical despair of revolutionaries in the West,[24] and at their sense of powerlessness against the tightening economic vice that obliges the workers to accept their fate without flinching, and even perhaps to enjoy its sickening banality in a banal kind of way. In contrast to that, the heroic isolation of the people of Vietnam, their creativity, the wealth of social relations they have created out of their struggle, and the inventiveness of the bodies established by the FLN, all seem like a sheer hymn of hope.

— *Translated by Rosemary Sheed*

14

Counter-Revolution is a Science You Can Learn

The specific action of the March 22 Movement cannot be reduced to direct confrontation with state power or the return to forms of violence. It was not the drop that caused the cup to overflow, the catalyst, etc. No matter what a certain number of sociologizing minds might think, "consumer society" has done nothing to reduce the potential violence of current society. It has simply been concentrated, parceled, integrated.

The specific action of March 22 foiled the channeling methods of state institutions, unions and the party *politically*.

"Normally," when cops block the entrance of a building like the Sorbonne, you negotiate, draw back, protest, go through the motions. "Normally," there are people in place to play along with these negotiations: representatives of the UNEF, unions, elected figures, etc. Here, the mechanism did not work. In his text, Coudray seems to think that the majority of workers—except for a young avant-garde—are fundamentally complicit in syndicalist bureaucracy. In fact, they do not have any alternate solution within reach. Occupation of the factories followed the illegal occupation of the Sorbonne and other public edifices.

The refusal of many workers to accept the Séguy protocol agreement reflects the lack of authorized interlocutors in the student movement.

Today, the fanatics of the "period of ascent" and "period of decline" have declared a general retreat and are starting to count their winnings; this explains the calls for renewed disciple, organization, long term perspectives… In fact, the protest movement is absolutely not in decline. It is seeking new means and new weapons. The groupuscules claiming to "capitalize on the avant-garde" are behaving like the guard dogs of syndicalist bureaucracy. They want to channel the movement into an organizational framework that has already failed. We are already seeing the reemergence of the reactionary ideology of the pyramid structure, the CC [Central Committee], PB [Politburo], secretariat, avant-garde party, mass organizations as "conduits," etc.

An original form of revolutionary organization is now searching for itself in the struggle and in the efforts to outmaneuver the "seasoned specialists" of revolutionary organization, the ones who claim to have ideological capital and absolute knowledge from which the masses are supposed to expect great things. If these fossilized militants take over the action committees, when they have shown themselves incapable of understanding the development of the struggle and on several occasions, have tried to act against it, it would be *disorganization* and, in the end, a retreat.

March 22 should not only reject the blackmail of so-called "centralist democratic" integration of grassroots committees, but it must also defend the right of these committees to remain independent of any structure that claims to oversee them.

Federating grassroots committees would only make sense at a much later stage, when it is time to establish a structure for taking power at a regional or national level. Today, grassroots committees are carrying out their actions like a guerilla; too much unification would sterilize them. An altogether different structure of coordination would leave open the possibility of a full extension of the committees and especially freedom of expression, creativity from the base, which is the essential weapon of the revolutionary movement.

15

Self-Management and Narcissism

Self-management, like any order word, can be combined with anything. From Lapassade to de Gaulle, from the CFDT [French Democratic Confederation of Labor] to anarchists. To speak of self-management itself, without any context, is a myth. It becomes a type of moral principle, the commitment that the self of a group or company will be managed from and by itself. The effectiveness of this order word depends on its self-seduction. Determining the corresponding institutional object in each situation is a criterion that should allow clarification of this question.

The self-management of a school or a university is limited by its objective dependence on the state, the means of financing, the political commitment of its users, etc. If it is not articulated with a coherent revolutionary perspective, it can only be an order word for transitory action that risks being passably confusing. The self-management of a factory or workshop also risks being reclaimed by psycho-sociological reformist ideology that sees the "interrelational" domain as something to be dealt with using group techniques, for example, *training groups* of technicians, managers, owners, etc. (For workers, these techniques are too "expensive.")

Hierarchy is "contested" in the imagination. In reality, not only does no one touch it, it is given a modernist foundation and dressed up in Rogerian or some other morality. The impetus behind self-management in a company involves effective control of production and programs: investments, organization of labor, business relationships, etc. A group of workers that "places itself under self-management" in a factory would have to resolve countless problems with the outside. It would only be lasting and viable if the outside was also organized under self-management. A single post office would not survive long under self-management; in fact, all of the parts of production are interconnected like telephone exchanges. Experience with self-management during strikes, reestablishing the production sectors in a factory *to respond to the needs of strikers*, the organization of supplies and self-defense are very important, indicative experiences. They show the possibility of moving beyond the confrontational level of struggle. They show a way to organize revolutionary society during a *transitional period*. But it is obvious that they cannot give clear and satisfying answers to the types of relationships of production, the types of structures adapted to a society that has expropriated the economic and political power of the bourgeoisie in a very developed economy.

Control by the workers raises fundamental political problems as soon as it touches institutional objects that call the economic infrastructure into question. A self-managed lecture hall is probably an excellent pedagogical solution. A branch of industry under direct control by the workers immediately raises a plethora of economic, political and social problems on a national and international scale. If workers do not take charge of these problems in a way that moves beyond the bureaucratic framework of current parties and unions, pure economic self-management may turn into a myth and lead to demoralizing stalemates.

Talk of political self-management may also be an all-purpose, deceptive formula, since politics fundamentally accommodates one group with other groups in a global perspective, whether it is explicit or not. Self-management as a political order word is not an end in itself. The problem is defining the type of relationships, the forms to promote and the type of power to institute at every level of organization. The self-management order word can become a distraction if it significantly takes the place of differentiated responses to the different levels and sectors according to their real complexity.

Changing state power, changing the management of a branch of industry, organizing a lecture hall, and challenging bureaucratic syndicalism are entirely different things that must be considered separately. The concern is that the order word of self-management, which has just appeared in the protests against bureaucratic structures in the universities, will be appropriated by reformist ideologues and politicians. There is no "general philosophy" of self-management that would allow it to apply everywhere and to every situation, especially to those situations that come from the establishment of dual power, the institution of revolutionary democratic control, the perspective of labor power, and the creation of systems of coordination and regulation between the various sectors of the struggle.

If no theoretical clarification of the scope and limits of self-management comes in time, this "order word" will be compromised by reformist associations and rejected by workers in favor of other formula that follow "democratic centralist" lines, formula that are more easily appropriated by the wide-ranging dogmatism of the communist movement.

— June 8, 1968.

16

Excerpts from Discussions: Late June 1968

Part 1

F: ... If you admit that the masses can be said to be "structured like a language," you could also say that the conscious expressions of the organizations are structured like a neurosis! In any case, the notion of masses is idiotic and needs to be tossed out.

FF: The striking thing about the night of the first barricades, May 10, was that the barricade strategy, the defensive strategy, was not rational at all. You could even say that if there was anything irrational to try, they did it immediately. There was an element of fantasy, but one that was shared by all of the people there. I mean this whole mythic tradition of the French proletariat since the Commune: barricades, the red flag, the black flag, the *International...* You could tell that it was not a minority of anarchists or Trotskyists taking up the standard of traditional themes of the working class but an immediate and brutal "mass capture." Two hours earlier, no one was thinking about it, nothing was planned, and then all of a sudden the "crowd" was structured, not in a classic organizational manner, but purely on the basis of fantasy.

Here we find the idea that a hierarchical organization is incapable of expressing the rationality of economic processes. You outline "subjective units," to use the expression from *Nine Theses*, which are articulated with each other in a relationship of language. They should not be interpreted as a type of symbolic rationality that is now repressed and only appears on the surface. I think that the function of subjective units is precisely to express irrationality, to allow the expression of fantasy elements that are as irrational as the one that appeared on the night of the barricades. It seems that fantasy, not on an individual level but on a historical level, is the only expression of the rationality of unconscious processes, including economic ones.

P: I don't like the expression "irrationality" because, when seen from another angle, the barricade phase, with all of its institutional aspects, was part of an extraordinarily rational process, in the sense of the rationality of the unconscious. It may have been irrational in relation to certain insurrectional methods, but when you look at the way it was articulated with a method of revelation, self-teaching, self-training to recognize instances of repression in all their forms, then you can say that a Maoist-type attack method with small commando groups—small street guerilla groups—would probably have meant the end of the movement. It would have completely blocked off the possibilities of a fantasy-type progression: the masses were in a position to be attacked and not to be attackers. It is very important that this phase was respected. Geismar, in his speech while the barricades were being built, had some brilliant insights. He said: "We are building barricades, but that is all; obviously, if they are attacked, we will have to defend them." He created an eminently dialectical fantasy situation. Finally, the progress of a certain demand, of a certain political consciousness among the protesters was subordinate to the revelation of a certain level of repression by the state. The barricades represented a strategic solution, a possible mode of interpretation, the possibility of revealing this repressive aspect. An offensive strategy would have been premature and would have closed down the movement. I think there is something rational there and not irrational; it is rationality of another order.

F: True, I do not think that we should be trapped in an alternative between rationality, on the one hand, and fantasy as irrational expression, on the other. Completely rational things can come from fantasies. Wild things can come from rational constructions! The contribution of Freudianism is to show that there is also super-rationality in fantasies, parapraxis, slips, dreams and symptoms; analysis finds the reasons for them when traditional reasoning would be unable to account for them. On the level of the masses, however, this kind of decryption can only take place with the accumulation of things that would only play out with individuals and small groups. Transgression occurs with pre-established signifying chains that constitute the entire system.

Beyond a certain point, individuals and small groups are almost manipulated by history. Historical signifiers work for themselves while being supported by them. If you look at the statements by Cohn-Bendit and Geismar during the night of May 10, you might think that they were doing everything they could to avoid the outbreak of violence—in particular with Cohn-Bendit's delaying tactics with the rector to warn him of the dangers of the possible degradation of the situation. The logic of the situation bypassed these hesitations. The same Cohn-Bendit's attitude at the Bastille, as a prisoner of the official head of the great procession and trying to prevent the bureaucrats from dispersing the protest, had an altogether different result.

In the first case, the transgression came from the base, with the frustration of students, with the power of the barricade myth. In the other, a majority of protesters respected the agreement the leaders passed with the CP [Communist Party] and blocked the transgression. In the end, the power of the myth of the "big party," of the "party of the working class," of great labor confederations... In the first case, Cohn-Bendit and Geismar were tentative spokespeople—the ones who spoke into the microphone. In the second case, they were the mandated representatives of their organizations who had concluded agreements, who were supposed to be responsible for leading operations…

At the beginning of the March 22 Movement, during its brief existence as a producer of transitional fantasies, its various spokespeople were truly accountable;—at the same time, no one could have truly claimed to "represent" March 22. No one was really appointed to transgress or not transgress the common law. It was not an economy of individuals and persons that influenced decisions but a collective acknowledgement that emerged despite the weight of people. It was impossible, during this phase to be "more leftist" than anyone else! No one could "overdo" it because every initiative was allowed and, in any case, no one was obliged to follow them "in the name of" an internal discipline, no one was in a position to have to choose the middle road to maintain group cohesion. What was exceptional about March 22 was not that it was a group that could speak in the mode of free association, but that it was able to constitute itself as the "analyzer" of a considerable mass of students and young workers.

Another transgression—the result of duplicity, in this case—is the fact that, during this first period, Cohn-Bendit and Geismar let the authorities believe that they were the spokespeople of the movement. They may never have wanted it, but things evolved so that even if it had been the case, problems could no longer be posed in these terms. Whoever decided to go negotiate with a rector would have simply been ridiculous. Even the simulacra of representativeness fell apart when Cohn-Bendit disappeared from circulation. All of the regulatory mechanisms fell apart. Groupuscules rushed in to fill the void left by March 22's inability to confront the situation on a national scale. The FCP took advantage of this situation to launch a campaign against the leftists, the irresponsible and "Geismar's gangs."

March 22 itself was turned into a groupuscule. Its free internal expression and creativity faded, maybe because of a sudden awareness of its "historical responsibilities." I think that what happened is something that I proposed long ago using the term "transversality": a certain opening or closing of the collective acceptance of superego investments, a modification of the typical oedipal data of the castration complex, something that returns collective power to the group to the detriment of individual inhibitions, decreasing the fear of being hit by batons or asphyxiated, because of a transgression at the level of unconscious signifying chains. This same system of transgression affected—relatively—the notion of property with the occupations, the bourgeois notion of personhood with the arrests and the systematic use of the familiar pronoun "tu," the respect of venerable objects like the Sorbonne, the CGT, etc.

Other layers were contaminated from a nodal point of transgression—both in the social order and in other regions of subjectivity. The primitive scene of this transgression probably played out in Nanterre, when a few people told the professors: "Shut up, you're pissing us off, let someone else speak, " or when they told Juquin to get out, or when they publicly mocked their minister, when they invaded the administrative offices... Making waves came before the first paving stones... The abandon of this technique of subversion, the loss of humor and renewed control of the groupuscules marked the decline of the real power of March 22. Remember the seriousness that terrorized the leaders of the March 22 general assembly when they were transferred to Paris—the only humor that was still allowed consisted of facial expressions. The groupuscules, which hardly existed in Nanterre before May, reappeared there, or were unconsciously guided there by their former militants.

One of my friends—particularly gutsy on the barricades—despaired of persuading students to elect Fouchet as president of the UNEF [National Union of Students of France] for "services rendered to the Revolutionary Cause"... Nothing serious about that! Yet he was full of ideas about organizing parades with floats, street fairs, etc.

No question of that with the famous UNEF enforcement services—another monumental scam! By itself, the UNEF would never have been able to gather more than 10 militants for something like that; it must have been a collection of cops and cretins! UNEF authorized cops, an internalization of cops, the fear of injuring, of being misunderstood, the disavowal of the Katangais… and, deep down, the respect of laws and private property—except, for symbolic purposes, consumer goods like automobiles and occupying *public places*. We should not forget that in 1936 there was a break in the signifiers of property with the occupation of factories, whereas the opposite took place in 1968: workers occupied the factories to protect them from the outside. The order word of an active strike, the use of factories to strengthen the potential struggles of the strikers and revolutionaries, was countered very effectively by the syndicalist sages. Just look at the bureaucrats of the IPN and RTS[1] defending their "work tools" against a minority favorable to leftist intruders…

Once university signifiers were paralyzed, it was up to the reformists and revisionists to continue neutralizing the other contaminated chains… the result was not long in coming. Yet why is it that this active strike and self-management that they were calling for in the factories never took shape in the Sorbonne or other schools? Instead, there was a pathetic and depressing folklore show that did nothing to bring together the students and the workers who ventured into these areas! Transgression, then re-inhibition…

P: This transgression is so nodal that it does not only concern "social discourse" but also the type of organization of all of the groupuscules. In my opinion, it started with the history of intermixing in the university residence halls. It seems that the first transgression, the original transgression, took place in the dormitories. If it didn't work elsewhere, in Antony, Nantes or Nice, it was because either the Party or the groupuscules were strong. They were ready to see this type of protest as a threat to their own organizations. It was generalized transgression. The groupuscular disorganization in Nanterre allowed the phenomenon to appear with enough freedom that at a certain point, it represented a real transgression. The guys at the windows of the girls' dorms were the first occupation. The signifier "occupation" was contemporary to a transgression of a sexual nature, which was the point of departure for a language. The transgression was so focused on organizations, any organization, that it was incarnated in a place where there was no organization.

MR: I wonder why it all broke out in France, and not in Berlin or England, where there were some serious fights. I think the Party was an additional factor of transgression. In France, it represented a much greater obstacle.

J-PM: Last year, in Rome, the Communist Party reacted immediately to the student demonstrations. Not like the FCP but by giving the communist youth the order to integrate anyone who showed up, to enter into dialog with them and bring them back. It stopped the movement completely.

F: If we had had Leroy and the pro-Italian contingent at the head of the French Party, we would probably still have a Mendès-Mitterrand government and the youth would have been brought into a super UJRF,[2] etc. I think the re-appropriation had two stages: the demonstration at Denfert-Rochereau (May 13) and the Gaullist demonstration. It was the same march! As soon as the Party could prove that it was able to siphon off this stuff, it was over: the Party was confirmed in its mission as a "viable interlocutor" in the figure of Séguy. The fantastic, sickening stupidity was performed by the JCR [Revolutionary Communist Youth], which also placed itself at the service of order and discipline. Everyone was inhibited before the majesty of reunification. A few paving stones in the Prefecture could have made this great religious festival turn sour! The March 22 Movement was despondent. No one took the initiative. Overwhelmed, even locally, this demonstration of a million people could have turned into a disaster for the Party and, maybe, toppled the regime. Instead, everyone fell for it: "Not so loud! The Working Class, with a capital W and C, will follow us… Go back to being good and polite!"

In a certain number of companies, of course, the movement developed on a revolutionary foundation, but everywhere where the CGT and the Party were in control, they only defused the conflicts! The negotiations of the leftists to enter the factories, "please, Mister Delegate," the symbolic processions in front of Citroen and Renault, it was all a sickening mystification. It was as if the students were negotiating with the cops! And everyone, from the FER [Federation of Revolutionary Students] to the UJCML [Union of Young Marxist-Leninist Communists] started to declare with the authority of "old connoisseurs": It isn't happening in the Latin Quarter; it's happening in the working class. As if they were ashamed of this detour of history, as if it should never have happened with the students! Yet, it could *also* have taken place elsewhere precisely because it started with the students! These stupid groupuscules saw it as shameful to think that the workers would have had to follow a movement started by students, or petit bourgeois, etc. An infraction of class morality!

P: It was already typical before the barricades, at the time of the Saint-Denis demonstration. For the UJCML, not going would have been committing a petit bourgeois act leading away from revolution. They went to Saint-Denis, where there was nothing, no strike…

F: In Flins, I picked up three very young hitchhikers. We started talking: What do you do? We're students. Studying what? They hesitate. Well… at the Sorbonne. They were very young workers, maybe apprentices. They weren't bluffing by calling themselves students, it was only by calling themselves students that they could find the dignity to go brawl.

L: In Flins, now, if you ask kids "What do you want to be when you grow up?," they say, "We want to be students."

F: The notion of mass was called into question and now it is the question of class. In the end, if we are not talking about sociological classes, the working class was essentially embodied, represented by the people fighting in the Latin Quarter. The working class rebuilt itself progressively through this fight. Before, there were factories, unions, a working class shaped by petit-bourgeois ideology, manipulated by organizations. The working class, if taken as something other than sociological, statistical, electoral data is not something that is embodied as a permanent class consciousness.

L: The phenomena of transgression occurred spontaneously: there were people that stole paper for us from companies, which was unthinkable for the CGT.

P: At the beginning of the Bolshevik Party, there was an institutionalization of theft. Stalin was very specifically responsible for organizing commando units...

F: We're joking around, but in the themes of the labor movement a hundred years ago, the right to relax, individual attacks, "appropriation," violence, etc., were givens for the consciousness of the working class. There was no shame; on the contrary, only discussions about the most efficient methods. The legalist perspective was really consolidated in 1936. Already in the 2nd International, there was a systematic critique of individual attacks, in particular by terrorist groups in Russia. But it mostly came from the reformists, who were deeply disturbed by the attacks. Individual attacks were later condemned by the Stalinists, even though they continued to use them against the "Leftists" of the time, in the Spanish Civil War, during the Resistance, etc.

Part 2

F: The meaning normally attributed to the general strike of May 13 probably needs to be interpreted in the opposite way: it is the deployment of a system of resistance in the face of the unconscious rift opened by the first conflicts, the search for a fantastical normalization—a general strike is something that has already occurred; we know how it ends—in the absence of an institutional normalization of the crisis. After revolutionary transgression, the search for a minimum of normalization. Yet there was significant hemorrhaging; not only were deans like Grappin and the CRS brought in to counterbalance it, but the whole machine of the state and de Gaulle himself!

This signifying hemorrhage was absolutely unexpected; no revolutionary movement was ready to face it. This may be why the old myths of the French Revolution and the Communes were quickly dusted off... In 1936, a strike with occupation had represented a real transgression and was also appropriated by the Popular Front government. In May, they made sure not to go that far. Everything was muted, when the CGT obtained that the directors held hostage were released compassionately, and loud, when the workers became accomplices, it must be said, of their bureaucracy, by accepting that the factory not be opened to outside militants, students and others.

The strike movement finally contributed to extinguishing the revolutionary movement by channeling it into ritualized scenarios. After that, the revolutionary forces became lethargic. They were happy when Cohn-Bendit marched with Séguy!

Deep down, phenomena like Flins and Sochaux were the most significant: there, there was a direct clash with the government in a completely original way. One can imagine a follow-up to this type of confrontation, and even the development of entirely new forms of struggle from it. If the general strike had not broken out so quickly, like a fire break, maybe other revolutionary bastions like Flins or Sochaux could have developed further and taken on the importance of the revolutionary struggles of the Latin Quarter. It would have then been possible to move beyond the façade of revolutionary fraternity, with the respect for the "tool," the isolation of the factory from the outside, etc.

In Flins and Sochaux, the CGT and the cops were in a panic: they were both denouncing the "uncontrollable elements." They had to be stopped no matter what, especially to prevent these bad examples from spreading. The turmoil in the Latin Quarter was already troublesome enough that they did not want it to spread into other important sectors of the working class. The prejudice in favor of syndical unity worked against the development of wild forms of struggle and the essential question was to figure out how a revolutionary organization could foster its means of self-defense, not only against the police but first and foremost against itself, against its own internalization of the repression. It once again raised the question of action committees that were not specifically syndical or political but both at the same time and capable of serving as a place to house militants.

J: I think that in Flins things were not as clear as you are saying. They did not have the initiative. They were not participating in determining political objectives. They were more like the armed wing of the working class, basically the Katangais of the workers.

F: The question may not be to know if there were common objectives or whether students in Flins were seen as Katangais. Like you,

I am very much in favor of having completely heterodoxical, contaminated elements, elements that disjoint the system. It is very important that they were tolerated, and especially that they came to the struggle. Even if the action in Flins was only carried out by Katangais, it wouldn't have changed anything. In the imaginary system of castes that people live in and with its infinite differentiation, a movement of insurrection, a student revolutionary movement remains in castes in the imagination, even when viewed with a sympathetic eye. The strike creates a situation which implicitly makes the workers say: "If there has to be a revolution, we're the ones who will do it, not you, the students. The proof is that we had a general strike and occupied factories…"

Flins is very different. It was a sort of *melting pot*[3] of the local population that took part, the local authorities and institutions that were powerless to solve problems and workers who only had traditional organizations until then. An *event* occurred there: while the possibility of a significant dialog was rejected everywhere else, here there was an encounter on the very terrain of labor struggle. This was the difference with the barricades: workers went to the barricades *of* the students, which is important but relatively minor, because they seemed like individuals acting on the students' terrain, while the students acting on the terrain of Flins changed the situation completely. I think this is what plays directly into the signifying order: not the size of the struggle or its results, but the fact that something broke—like the transformation of a primitive religion—something else opened up.

For this type of phenomenon to occur again, the groupuscules have to break the ideology that keeps them from reaching the imaginary dimension of the struggle. The Lambertists in Saint-Nazaire would surely have been against this movement. You can hear them from here: "Students are not to go… Student cells must not mix with workers," etc.

J: At the time of the "Bolshevization" of the Party, in 1928–1930, the cells were split up in a completely different way: an intellectual, for example, was sent to a cell of railway workers; no one was sent anywhere that resembled them. Now, each factory workshop is sealed off from the others, each factory is closed off from the other factories, all factories from the countryside, and so on indefinitely…

There is also the vertical plane: hierarchization. Everything started with what the young workers heard and remembered about what happened at the University: the fact that students and professors were together, that Grappin was being insulted, that authority was being rejected… Where does it start for the working class? It starts with people who cannot speak, the youth and the non-union affiliated, those that are neither suffocated or crystallized. Everything that happened was a phenomenon of language, a problem of speaking.

F: If they had other means of making themselves heard, they should have denounced the general strike and said: "We don't give a damn about your strike under these conditions; this is not at all what we want to do. Not only do we have to put up the red flag, lock up the boss, and occupy the factory, but we also have to keep it running, use it like a bastion to occupy the area, bring the families in, organize life there, self-defense, etc." That would have been interesting: developing a prototype for labor struggle.

FF: At HS [Hispano-Suiza], some friends asked us to come take part in a show of force of M-L [Marxist-Leninists] in front of the factory. We quickly noticed that a surprising number of workers, even some that our friends didn't know, were against the CGT apparatus. The people who were there in front of the factory asked if we could talk "institutionally," in other words, *inside* the factory. A compromise was made on an annex of the factory, the office of the shop committee. We went in; the meeting was run by the president of the shop committee, there were thirty students and a few people we didn't know. They started talking so violently and intensely that made *the apparatchiks* panic. The next day, the same thing happened, but the apparatchiks were the ones going full steam; they practically monopolized the floor, and they made it so that what seemed to be a chance for the workers to speak in a dialog between worker representatives—in other words, them, the apparatchiks—and student representatives. The M-L and a few friends from March 22 went along with this recognition of representation, so much so that at the end the apparatchiks could say: "It's over. We had a good discussion; we let everyone speak." It was a decisive moment. We all felt that we had to establish, to impose continuation in a place where the workers themselves were calling the apparatus into question in a violent way. But it was over. The apparatchiks said: "We have to take a step back to attack again." And we were back to the same as before: students outside the factory, etc. We tried everything, peasants came to speak with the workers; we thought that it would trigger something initiatory… It was frightening. Transgression was there, it just had to be triggered for the mechanism to start working…

J: What allows it to be inscribed in reality? Discussing things for days like the M-L doesn't serve any purpose; it is just a parody of transgression.

One thing that the M-L have a very hard time understanding, and the JCR does not: What is the position of March 22? One day, they offered us "a coordination of mass movements." But we are not a mass movement. Then "a coordination of avant-gardes"? No, we are not an avant-garde. What are you then? We are not in those two categories. Finally, they proposed the concept of "spontaneous avant-garde." It's good that they proposed it; they are trying to define us, it's important for their evolution. But the concept still needs to be found: *what allows speech* or *what instigates acts of transgression*. The cops, in fact, understood. After a friend was interrogated, it turned out that, for them, March 22 was the most dangerous.

F: We developed a category like that: the analytical group interpreting the situation, at a given moment; in any form; *acting out*,[4] provocation… If the HS friends had functioned like an analytical group and not like an opposition avant-garde group, they would have analyzed their own fear, their own terror in the face of transgression first.

Part 3

P: When we wrote the *Nine Theses*, we tended to situate ourselves in relation to two essential problems: denouncing the false problem of Sino-Soviet confrontation and refuting the strategy of peaceful coexistence and the Chinese strategy. A second group of theses dealt with the more general problem of oppositions within the Party and groups controlled by the Party. And the chapter that would now be the most interesting, the one on revolutionary organization, is precisely the one that was the most "slipshod." It would be worth rewriting the *Nine Theses* to place the accent on this aspect.

F: I think that we would definitely have to resituate a certain number of ideas for all of the problems we raised: crisis of the international communist movement, problems of the Third World, the Vietnam War, and connect them to the problems of May in France. This would help avoid the seesaw where everyone rushes to analyze themes of self-management and other themes, just like during the time of the Algerian War when everyone rushed to analyze the Third World, etc.

The overall concept of the "theses" was based on a relatively pessimistic vision of revolutionary possibilities in developed nations, despite some overtures. We criticized the traditionalist conception of the Party and the modernists. The third particular political analysis concerned groupuscules on the far left, and there was also a questioning of the Chinese line that have not yet initiated the Cultural Revolution. In short, to come back to the perspective that we had at the time—which is the characteristic of the theses, and their limit—we showed the impasse that all political and syndical organizations were in, without getting caught in a modernist analysis. Yet we had only touched on the idea that a series of fundamental contradictions remained in French society and the different European capitalist countries; we only briefly evoked the notion of a *generalized crisis*, economic crisis being only an aspect of a crisis that could take many other shapes. Moreover, we said that because of the fictive character of the attempt to constitute large markets, the crises would get worse. We analyzed the Common Market as a false solution from an economic point of view, because it goes without saying that the future of the European economy—on economic and technological levels—not only depends on the constitution of a large market but on the constitution of extremely powerful units of production.

In short, we were a little timid concerning short-term revolutionary perspectives, and continued to think, without saying it explicitly, that guerilla opposed to the organizations of the communist movement was a prerequisite… Maybe I am exaggerating, but it is better to exaggerate in critique.

After abandoning the plan of a working class that was pure, hardcore and aware, drawing all of the other layers behind it mechanically, we may have to come to the following formula: the economy is, in the end, the driving force of subjectivity. Rifts on an economic level will lead immediately, not by gradual, successive steps or protests and awareness, to questioning the perspective of struggle, the perspective of a radically different existence. There is an articulation here between Freudianism and Marxism that needs to be grasped. When people are numbed by the so-called consumer society, neurotic on a social level, the traditional reasoning is to think that they are in fact dull-witted and accomplices of the system because they take advantage of it and an increase in the level of their lifestyle has a direct effect on their level of consciousness. In reality, however, as alienation and integration increase, by means of the invasion of certain types of consumer objects, the contradiction grows and assaults unconscious subjectivity. Not as an individual subject this time, but as a group subject that, through a collective ideal and group fantasies, calls for an institutional subjectivity as the only possible solution.

What comes to consciousness is stupidity, TV, betting, reformism. Behind this layer of over-investment in repression, participation and denial, however, there is another possibility, at the level of key signifiers. It is not a potential that asks for more, for even more consumption (all of which is part of the mechanisms of resistance). It is, on the contrary, a "power," a potential to question institutional plans on the level of the family, of group relations, of branches of industry, on the national level, etc.

For a symptomatological point of view, one of the very interesting aspects of the May movement is that while, since 1936, both official ideology and the labor movement have systematically trained people in the context of a defense of nationality, internationalist signifiers reemerge naturally, without causing any problems. It shows that unconscious schemas and their institutional referents have reemerged in a complete cut. Some people typed up the words of the *International* to bring with them—proof that they didn't learn it in their groupuscules! To put it another way, if we take this idea: we can hypothesize that, in terms of the unconscious, the people who are closest to cuts in the economic field are in the best position to give the correct interpretation of the "institutional revolution," with all of the mythical aspects it comports, including the massive protest against what Medam called "revolution for production."[5]

The movement is significantly lacking in terms of finding something that could become a viable institutional formula. It is clear to see what is at stake with action committees as the hypothetical "mass organization" of a hypothetical avant-garde organization: how could these committees continue to exist while being centralized, etc.? At the current stage, it is an utter shambles. If we approach the problem at the same level that some do, psychosociologically (how to arrange it so that it communicates...), then we'll just be turning in circles. In fact, the institutional formula is an extension of a possible solution on the most developed economic scale. In other terms, how could automobiles and traffic, for example, function in Europe according to the logic of the development of productive forces while respecting as much as possible the interests and desires of the parties in presence?

Let's make a utopian hypothesis: the functioning of this sector of production would be ensured thanks to the existence of a sort of communist party of the automobile, at least in Europe, which, as such, would enter into talks and disputes with another communist party of metalworking. The total integration of union and party. In other words, from a European socialist perspective articulated with socialist groups in Third World countries, there would be negotiations with, for example, a cotton party, another mass international party. At that point, one could imagine that adjusting the various demands, the various local institutional aspects would extend to the implementation of regional, national and international policies at every level, and lead to a regulation of different relationships of investment, standards, pricing, distribution, salaries, training, etc.

Currently, regulation is essentially performed by adjustment mechanisms connected to capital and state policies. It is blind to the social subjectivities concerned. Only subjectivization on the level of branches of industry, for example, articulated with large markets would be able to attain a level of planning that would be more effective in its social aims and more profitable, including in economic terms.

As long as power continues to evade the only class that has the vocation to propose an institutional model, a subjective counterpart to productive forces, the existing institutional models will continue to be imposed archaically. For this reason, the concept of the model of organization and the axiom of the organization of the struggle of the working class are not to be found in an intrinsic study of the working class, but based on the potential capacity of a revolutionary working class to respond to the unconscious demand for an institutional revolution, such that a return to the embryonic organization that it takes on in immediate class struggles allows it to reveal and clarify more long term perspectives.

In the March 22 Movement, I was surprised by the sudden enthusiasm for trips to the countryside and delivering supplies to factories: instinctively, with my groupuscular past, I thought of ergotherapy or the Boy Scouts. But why not? *Something else* had to be put in place that gave an immediate illustration of something else. No matter how ridiculous: what is important is to offer a model of action that aims globally and approximately at the mass of workers at a company, and which is an illustration, an almost unconscious *signifying prefiguration* of what could be the type of relationship between another peasantry and another working class. Finally, another peasantry and another working class! None of it was formulated by the members of March 22, but in the end, I believe this signifying chain was in the unconscious of the main actors of this exchange.

17

Students, the Mad and "Delinquents"

The institutional earthquakes of May [1968] in France did not spare the world of psychiatry. They have in fact left some lasting effects: for example, in some sectors the whole hierarchy has been brought into question, "colleges" of psychiatry have been set up,[1] and the teaching of psychology has been separated from that of neurology. Unfortunately, it would seem that the events were experienced as a serious trauma, rather than being assimilated and integrated into theory and practice.

The school of "institutional psychotherapy" should have been better placed to understand them, since its main characteristic is precisely a determination never to isolate the study of mental illness from its social and institutional context, and, by the same token, to analyse institutions on the basis of interpreting the real, symbolic and imaginary effects of society upon individuals. We must admit, however, that though members of this school did not stand completely aside from events, they were only marginally involved in them. This I believe to have been the consequence of a certain immaturity in terms of theory, and a fixation upon such archaisms of the medical profession as "neutrality" and the avoidance of anything political.

Starting from the crisis in the universities, the institutional revolution of May soon presented problems that affected society as a whole: people who had considered such problems only as they touched on their particular hospital or their particular psychiatric district were taken completely unawares.[2] Though the proponents of institutional psychiatry found themselves powerless to act, their approach to problems over the past decade was such as to make them potentially on the wavelength of the extraordinary social phenomena we have witnessed. From 1962 to 1966 a certain number of them had been working, at the request of the national student organizations, on the mental-health problems peculiar to student life. Over the course of many talks with student representatives, certain more general questions arose about students' situations—the absence of university institutions, the absurdity of teaching methods, plans for setting up university work groups, education clubs, running university centers for psychotherapeutic help and so on.[3]

The school of institutional psychotherapy, which at that time received very little attention from the world of psychiatry, found a considerable response from the student leaders of the period. We came to feel that the student world was suffering from a kind of social segregation not unlike what had long been the experience of the world of psychiatry. We had a sense of having reached the intersection of what one might call "residual situations" incapable of being integrated by the technocratic State machine.

Unlike traditional psychoanalysts and psychiatrists, our view is that there is a profound interaction between individual psychopathological problems and the social, political and work context. There were, consequently, two ways of looking at the problems we faced in relation to the student movement: either they were marginal phenomena, mere aberrations, or they were symptoms heralding a far larger crisis in society, as some students instinctively felt they were. Other militants later came to the leadership of the student movement who were less concerned with these problems, and the institutional psychotherapy school gradually moved away from their problems. But they are well worth another look now.

At the time, I stressed the role of group phantasies, as possibly indicating the specific entry-point of the different generations into society, and their connections with each other, The phantasy of the *poilus* of the First World War, for instance, created a kind of echo in the Bolsheviks in 1917, the phantasies of the new popular front age of 1936 and the Spanish Civil War Nazism, and similarly later on, with the Liberation, the Cold War and soon. I think we should recognize the phantasy echo of the May barricades from the fact that the generation who put them up were the same generation that forgot French atrocities in Algeria while militantly condemning, with pious unanimity, American aggression in Vietnam.

The social contradictions to which the masses are subject do not strike them as a set of theoretical problems: they are experienced in the order of the imaginary and seen as massively simple alternatives, whereby social death instincts or visions of progress (the "cities of the future," the "happy tomorrows") become present by way of group phantasizing.

As soon as the Algerian war was over, it became evident that a great many students were in search of some new focus for militancy, some mobilizing vision that would get them out of the university ghetto, if only in imagination. The leftist tendencies that took over the leadership of the UNEF (the national students' union) from 1963 to 1966 had tried to induce the student movement to take some responsibility for the problems peculiar to students. The problem of student power arose in relation both to university structures and to teaching methods. The students were urged to an awareness of their special situation, their role in society, and the irresponsibilities as regards production, the class struggle and so on. (Don't forget that the first occupation of the Sorbonne was attempted back in February 1964.)

The government was then setting out systematically to sabotage any move in that direction (refusing all dialogue with the UNEF, whose financial support was withdrawn and given instead to the FNEF[4]). The workers' movement, too, was either manipulating or simply ignoring the student movement (the French Communist Party disbanded its student organization, and the PSU took control of the UNEF national headquarters). The leftists in the UNEF became dispersed, the organization gradually lost its point, and it was left to a few groups of the extreme left to ensure the continuance of a minimum of political activity in this sphere.

This situation resulted in two things: any real plans for transforming university life were abandoned, and the old failure to understand the specific problems of students once again prevailed: political theorizing always dealt with society as a whole and international relations—with the natural concomitants of dogmatic formalism and a sectarian and bureaucratic type of organization. Ultimately, however, this still enabled a few students to be politically educated, to broaden their view of the world and not become bogged down in the *status quo*. Nevertheless, the militants and professors who had tried to develop a new kind of psycho-sociological understanding of the student situation no longer had any influence.

The new conversion to militancy only began with the organization of mass campaigns against American aggression in Vietnam and of solidarity with the anti-imperialist revolutionary movements in Asia, Latin America and Africa. This time, a completely new kind of mobilization developed, involving a continuing militant commitment—especially among the Vietnam committees. But an international problem, in which France was not directly implicated, could never affect more than a tiny vanguard. The campaign against American aggression, in the nature of the case, was only of metaphorical importance; only very distantly did it hint at an answer to the agonizing problems with which the mass of students were wrestling from day to day as they groped their way blindly through the absurd world in which they lived.

The situation in Nanterre at the beginning of 1968 was the result, and the symbol, of this general failure both of government policy and of the student unions. The architecture of the place set the stage—one has only to visit it to feel anxiety oozing from the buildings. The campus is a perfect image of the student world cut off from the rest of society, from the whole world of ordinary work—and the contrast is all the more vivid since the university stands at the very center of one of the oldest communist municipalities.

It became the scene of a subjective, unique and radical crisis, embodied in a series of actions that were to serve as a model. The young people of May went on from there to get their imaginations working along the lines of what I would call "transitional phantasies," phantasies that were to find their way back to reality through a plan of activity which—it must be recognized—was to involve far more than chucking paving stones about. What the militants of the 22 March movement did at Nanterre became adopted by "analysts" as an "interpretation" of the "transference"—the "analysts" being such student activists as Dany Cohn-Bendit, who was advised by the Minister of Education, when questioned about the sexual problems of students, to have a cold bath.

Starting at Nanterre, a signifying chain developed; an ever-mounting escalation led to questioning every element in French society, and indeed there were international repercussions as well. The two forms of dominant power—State power and the power of workers' organizations—felt their very foundations to be in danger, and there was a new understanding of the latent crisis threatening industrial society as a whole. For a time those in power remained helpless as though hypnotized: the surprise had been total. Never again will they be taken unawares, for since then the bourgeoisie has taken the measure of such phenomena, and has been busily producing systems of repression and antibodies of all kinds. In phenomenological terms, what happened was characteristic of revolutionary upsurges: something happens that would have been unimaginable only the day before; imagination is set free and is called upon to take power. Was it a brief madness? How does one explain this coming to light of long-buried ideas? This is the point at which the notion of the transitional phantasy comes into operation. It authorizes a mode of representation for what is essentially non-representable: a radical change, the possibility of a different state of affairs, something absolutely other, a newborn and as yet uncertain revolutionary commitment. The Bolshevik phantasy system repressed all suggestions of "anarchism": barricades, fraternity, generosity, individual liberation, rejection of all hierarchy and constraint, collective exaltation, permanent poetry, daydreaming. All this had seemed dead and buried, just part of a kind of regression or collective infantilism. "Poor kids: they were misunderstood and unloved, and they've tried to compensate with a kind of psychodrama"—nothing to worry about really, just a bit of psychological self-help, probably in the end the surest way of making them better integrated into society. (All of which is not unlike the "understanding" professed by technocrats like Edgar Faure.)

Psychoanalytic methodology might lead us to look at things differently. Could it be that this return to pre-Bolshevik repression is a sign that the mechanisms of defence produced by society as a whole are no longer adequate to deal with its own deepest drives?

For a long time now, there has been a kind of complicity between social democracy and communist organizations on the one hand, and the State power on the other. It was obvious that the Gaullist government and the employers could never have regained control of the situation had it not been for the help of the trade-union federations; if the railway strike had gone on long enough, or there had been a real, all-out electricity strike, then the forces of repression would have been totally paralysed, and there would have had to be a decisive revolutionary confrontation. All the institutional mechanisms that have kept French society going since, say, 1934 (to take a date representing a major turning point for the French Communist Party) had proved to be inadequate. Militant revolutionaries had only the most imperfect systems of doctrine with which to interpret this crack in the structure. It is true that some left groupuscules had worked out an analysis, but it was only very sketchy, and reached only a minority of militants. This being the case, the shortcomings of the institutional system were essentially felt and expressed in a mode of phantasy, and dealt with accordingly. A vast mass, mainly of young people, but also of workers, teachers and intellectuals, used their own forms of expression—symbolic actions, serious struggles, allusion to themes from the past, holding a kind of festival to demonstrate against the consumer society, with even the occasional sacrificial destruction of cars or other things. The archaic nature of some forms of struggle and organization was due to the fact that all people could turn to for material of signification for the new situations were statements and images from the past.

The development of the forces of production has tended more and more to enforce a specific model for the image that individual producers and consumers have of themselves. In other words, that image has become an essential part of the economic machine itself. Hence the legitimation of one's "existence" depends less upon institutions like the family, the job, the social group, the church, the nation, and more upon one's place in the economic structure. The vital part played by consumption in regulating production means that a stereotyped image of every type of individual must be established as a "norm" to work from. But, contrariwise, those same forces of production need more "human factors." The worker in today's society is measured not so much in terms of man-hours as by the quality of the work he does and his position in the structure of the production system. What matters, in short, is the production of the signifier, which is in turn inseparable from the production units of subjectivity, in other words of *institutions*. The contradiction lies in the fact that the forces of production tend on the one hand to reduce individuals to stereotyped models, while on the other demanding the production of ever more complex units of subjectivity (with work organization, job training, technological innovations, re-training schemes, research and all the rest).

In the days when it was the institution that legitimated existence—the corporations, the hierarchy, religion and so on—institutions came before production. Nor were institutions then related to production in the same way as they are today; in general they inherited their structure from pre-capitalist production relations, some even still retaining traces of the feudal era. (It was these latter, I may point out, that were under special attack in May: the professions of architecture, law, medicine and so on.) Those legitimating institutions tended to exist in their own right, as the foundations of the established order; to be part of that order was valuable in itself, for the order was the basis of specific unconscious desires that could be expressed by a vow, or by certain emblems, such as a pulpit or a particular form of dress. The industrial revolution, on the other hand, tends to give the production machine precedence over the institution: the machine has become the mainstay of the institution's action. The industrial revolution has tended to expropriate institutions, taking from them their metaphysical substance. But the development of productive machines and economic structures of reference are not things directly grasped by our conscious minds. The various social classes continue to go about their business in a kind of phantasy state of nature; they are forever in search of a phantasy stability. The consequence is that they become more and more out of phase with the changes taking place in the forces of production. The traditional representation of "the nation" or "the working class" depends today solely on the politicians, militants and organizations who, with their quasi-clerical authority, continue to represent the phantasy that corresponds to it. The deputy who professes his "sincere" dedication to the public interest makes us smile. But so does the militant who tries to prove the legitimacy of what he is *doing* now by his having been in the Resistance, or by his fidelity to his own particular image of the working class. Absurd though it may be, the "militant theater" put on by the managers of the various political shopkeepers nonetheless represents the inevitable, constricting, official world of representation. Luckily there are still a few residual areas—like the student world and psychiatry—that have resisted the general integration. These two, however, occupy a rather special position in relation to signifying production.

The production of signifiers in the universities is becoming more and more detached from society; this is particularly noticeable in literature and art. The products of genuine research are not very saleable, because they question the social order. The essence of mass consumption is to turn away from the truth, to avoid actually having to face an active agent, or desire, or eccentricity. In the end, students and academics reach the same position in relation to signifying production as mental patients. Neurosis and madness, as a basis of truth, are subject to permanent suppression. Because Freud discovered the function of symptoms in revealing the truth, he had to defend his work against massive attempts to take it over. The aim was, and still is, to contain madness, to define it in such a way that it poses no threat to the clear conscience of the man in the street. It seems to me that this is a problem that must be faced by all revolutionary militants who are in any way concerned with madness, neurosis, delinquency or indeed with young people, children or creativity: how to grasp the purport of deviant symptoms as a means of interpreting the social arena as a whole. Thus it is not a matter of passively allowing the uniqueness of the intellectual or the mad person to be reduced to the order of generality, but rather of setting out to interpret the modern world from the uniqueness of their subjective positions. Paradoxically, the less response the institutions of contemporary capitalist society give when the suffering of the desiring subject is laid bare, the more artificial vitality they are re-injecting into their own most archaic bases. The national problem, regionalism, racism and the cult of the family are all getting fresh and massive promotion from large-scale propaganda methods, yet this remains precarious since it does not really reach the level of the unconscious. We can see, for instance, that the *de facto* internationalism of the forces of production makes nonsense of the patriotic politics of someone like de Gaulle. Along with the rediscovery of the attractions of the family, the region and the nation, there is also the cult of the individual. Knowing who is actually the agent of doing what is done does not necessarily mean stressing the role of the individual: the search for the agent in the social hydra may not lead us to an individual subject at all. In a city, for example, detached single-family houses are not the only alternative to vast, faceless, concrete housing jungles. Instead of seeing people as a mass of disconnected egos, we can recognize signifying connections among unconscious subjects and *group-subjects* capable of effecting a breakthrough in the processes of identification.

In this sense the beginnings of the 22 March movement may be looked upon as the prototype of a group-subject: everything revolved around it without its becoming part of any overall movement or being taken over by any other political group. Those involved set out to interpret the situation, not in terms of some program laid down at successive congresses, but gradually, as the situation itself unfolded in time. The attitude of the State power and the police really told them what they should then say about it by issuing statements that said the precise opposite. They refused to present their movement as the embodiment of the situation, but simply as a something upon which the masses could effect a transference of their inhibitions. With their vanguard action to provide a model, they opened a new path, lifted prohibitions, and opened the way to a new understanding and a new logical formulation outside any framework of dogmatism.

This was certainly the first time any political movement had gone too far in integrating psychoanalytic factors. The limitations of that integration were undoubtedly the result of the limitations of psychoanalytic theory itself, or at least of that theory as they understood it. The cult of spontaneity, the naturalism of the movement, probably indicated a massive resurgence of anxiety at facing the unknown; it was certainly this that enabled the Communist Party, left groupuscles and the movement itself to define the whole thing more reassuringly in terms of anarchist conformism. Everything conspired to close the question that had been opened. Yet there can be no doubt that the future of the workers movement depends on its ability to absorb a certain amount of recognizably Freudian theory. There is no use in denouncing the bureaucratism of traditional organizations if one can do no more than attribute the causes of it to particular mistakes in strategy or tactics, or to particular crises in the history of the workers' movement. There is a whole logic of signification behind the pyramidal organization whereby the mass organization, the grass-roots militants, the Party, the Central Committee, the Political Bureau and the Secretariat are all stuck in a series of fixed gradations that leaves no room for any authentic self-expression by the masses or by individuals. A desire economy of a homosexual nature pervades militant organizations in general, preventing their having any real access to the Other—be that Other a young person, a woman, a different race, a different nation. The pyramidal organization of our political groups is simply an echo of the dominant social organization.

The answer certainly does not lie in psycho-sociological blueprints: group alienation as such is probably not capable of being resolved from within—group psychoanalysis can never "cure" a group. But the setting-up of action committees does seem to have opened up the possibility of a kind of analytical activity actually among the masses, not an analysis conducted by a self-appointed vanguard standing apart from them, but as something close to, and permanently interacting with, their own self-expression. The student militants who went to Flins were able to join in the struggle of the workers and the local people without being resented as a foreign body. The group's analytical activity was not directed to adjusting individuals to the group, but to ensuring that the group, as an opaque structure, would not become a substitute for the mass movement's study of the problems of signification: it broke off the signifying chain in order to open up other potentialities. The activity of the militant group is not aiming to provide ready-made rational answers to the questions they think people should be asking, but on the contrary, to deepen the level of their questioning, and to make clear the uniqueness of each phase of the historical process. It is precisely because the movement of 22 March managed to preserve its particular message intact for so long that it could make itself heard in so many different situations and countries. (Events in Czechoslovakia, for instance, were almost certainly precipitated by fears of a similar development there.)

In psychiatry, the dilemma is often presented in terms either of making changes inside the hospital or of giving priority to community programs. Perhaps we should be recognizing a symmetry between the one phantasy of a revolution within the bin, and another that would justify "revolution in one country." On the other hand, there is a considerable Anglo-Saxon school of social psychiatry, or "anti-psychiatry," now proposing that we should be trying in some sense to re-absorb psychiatric illness into society at large, thus equating mental alienation with social. We keep coming back to the same place: madness is felt to be something shocking, something whose every manifestation we should disown and suppress. Psychiatrists, and all those involved in psychiatric work, could certainly still do a lot to change, humanize and open their institutions. But it may be that their real responsibility lies elsewhere. The fact of being involved in this particular "residual" situation puts them in a position to offer a radical critique of the status and methodology of the human sciences, of political economy and of all the institutional reference points that add up to a systematic disregard of the subjective attitudes of all types of all those who escape social control—of "Katangais" the world over—who are, in this sense, prototypes of the true revolutionary militant as well as of the "new man" of the future socialist society. Psychiatry and the human sciences seem as though they must, by definition, be outside the political domain; perhaps, one day, a different psychiatry related to a different politics—politics of the type that seemed to be emerging in May may provide a link between the two.

— Translated by Rosemary Sheed

18

Machine and Structure

The distinction I am proposing between machine and structure is based solely on the way we use the words; we may consider that we are merely dealing with a "written device" of the kind one has to invent for dealing with a mathematical problem, or with an axiom that may have to be reconsidered at a particular stage of development, or again with the kind of machine we shall be talking about here.

I want therefore to make it clear that I am putting into parentheses the fact that, in reality, a machine is inseparable from its structural articulations and, conversely, that each contingent structure is dominated (and this is what I want to demonstrate) by a system of machines, or at the very least by one logic machine. It seems to me vital to start by establishing the distinction in order to make it easier to identify the peculiar positions of subjectivity in relation to events and to history.[1]

We may say of structure that it positions its elements by way of a system of references that relates each one to the others, in such a way that it can itself be related as an element to other structures.

The agent of action, whose definition here does not extend beyond this principle of reciprocal determination, is included in the structure. The structural process of de-totalized totalization encloses the subject, and will not let go as long as it is in a position to recuperate it within another structural determination.

The machine, on the other hand, remains essentially remote from the agent of action. The subject is always somewhere else. Temporalization penetrates the machine on all sides and can be related to it only after the fashion of an event. The emergence of the machine marks a date, a change, different from a structural representation.

The history of technology is dated by the existence at each stage of a particular type of machine; the history of the sciences is now reaching a point, in all its branches, where every scientific theory can be taken as a machine rather than a structure, which relates it to the order of ideology. Every machine is the negation, the destroyer by incorporation (almost to the point of excretion), of the machine it replaces. And it is potentially in a similar relationship to the machine that will take its place.

Yesterday's machine, today's and tomorrow's, are not related in their structural determinations: only by a process of historical analysis, by reference to a signifying chain extrinsic to the machine, by what we might call historical structuralism, can we gain any overall grasp of the effects of continuity, retro-action and interlinking that it's capable of representing.

For the machine, the subject of history is elsewhere, in the structure. In fact, the subject of the structure, considered in its relationship of alienation to a system of de-totalized totalization, should rather be seen in relation to a phenomenon of "being an ego"—the ego here being in contrast with the subject of the unconscious as it corresponds to the principle stated by Lacan: a signifier represents it for another signifier. The unconscious subject as such will be on the same side as the machine, or better perhaps, *alongside* the machine. There is no break in the machine itself: the breach is on either side of it.

The individual's relation to the machine has been described by sociologists following Friedmann as one of fundamental alienation.

This is undoubtedly true if one considers the individual as a structure for totalization of the imaginary. But the dialectic of the master crafts- man and the apprentice, the old pictures of the different trades flourishing in different parts of the country, all this has become meaningless in the face of modern mechanized industry that requires its skilled workers to start from scratch again with every new techno- logical advance. But does not this starting from scratch mark precisely that essential breakthrough that characterizes the unconscious subject?

Initiation into a trade and becoming accepted as a skilled worker no longer takes place by way of institutions, or at least not those envisaged in such statements as "the skill has precedence over the machine." With industrial capitalism, the spasmodic evolution of machinery keeps cutting across the existing hierarchy of skills.

In this sense, the worker's alienation to the machine excludes him from any kind of structural equilibrium, and puts him in a position where he is as close as possible to a radical system of realignment, we might say of castration, where he loses all tran- quillity, all "self-confirming" security, all the justification of a "sense of belonging" to a skilled trade. Such professional bodies as still exist, like doctors, pharmacists, or lawyers, are simply survivals from the days of pre-capitalist production relations.

This change is of course intolerable; institutional production therefore sets out to conceal what is happening by setting up sys- tems of equivalents, of imitations. Their ideological basis is to be found not solely in fascist-type, paternalistic slogans about work, the family and patriotism, but also within the various versions of socialism (even including the most apparently liberal ones, like the Cuban), with their oppressive myth of the model worker, and their exaltation of the machine whose cult has much the same function as that of the hero in antiquity.

As compared with the work done by machines, the work of human beings is nothing. This working at "nothing," in the special sense in which people do it today, which tends more and more to be merely a response to a machine—pressing a red or black button to produce an effect programmed somewhere else—human work, in other words, is only the residue that has not yet been integrated into the work of the machine.

Operations performed by workers, technicians and scientists will be absorbed, incorporated into the workings of tomorrow's machine; to do something over and over no longer offers the security of ritual. It is no longer possible to identify the *repetition* of human actions ("the noble task of the sower") with the repetition of the natural cycle as the foundation of the moral order. Repetition no longer establishes a man as someone who can do that particular job. Human work today is merely a residual sub-whole of the work of the machine. This residual human activity is no more than a partial procedure that accompanies the central procedure produced by the order of the machine. The machine has now come to the heart of desire, and this residual human work represents no more than the point of the machine's imprint on the imaginary world of the individual (cf. Lacan's function of the "a").

Every new discovery—in the sphere of scientific research, for example—moves across the structural field of theory like a war machine, upsetting and rearranging everything so as to change it radically. Even the researcher is at the mercy of this process. His discoveries extend far beyond himself, bringing in their train whole new branches of researchers, and totally redesigning the tree of scientific and technological implications. Even when a discovery is called by its author's name, the result, far from "personalizing" him, tends to be to turn his proper name into a common noun! The question is whether this effacing of the individual is something that will spread to other forms of production as well.

Though it is true that this unconscious subjectivity, as a split which is overcome in a signifying chain, is being transferred away from individuals and human groups towards the world of machines, it still remains just as un-representable at the specifically machinic level. It is a signifier detached from the unconscious structural chain that will act as *representative* to represent the machine.

The essence of the machine is precisely this function of detaching a signifier as arepresentative, as a "differentiator," as a causal break, different in kind from the structurally established order of things. It is this operation that binds the machine both to the desiring subject and to its status as the basis of the various structural orders corresponding to it. The machine, as a repetition of the particular, is a mode—perhaps indeed the only possible mode—of univocal representation of the various forms of subjectivity in the order of generality on the individual or the collective plane.

In trying to see things the other way round, *starting* from the general, one would be deluding oneself with the idea that it is possible to base oneself on some structural space that existed before the breakthrough by the machine. This "pure," "basic" signifying chain, a kind of lost Eden of desire, the "good old days" before mechanization, might then be seen as a meta-language, an absolute reference point that one could always produce in place of any chance event or specific indication.

This would lead to wrongly locating the truth of the break, the truth of the subject, on the level of representation, information, communication, social codes and every other form of structural determination.

The voice, as speech machine, is the basis and determinant of the structural order of language, and not the other way round. The individual, in his bodiliness, accepts the consequences of the interaction of signifying chains of all kinds which cut across and tear him apart. The human being is caught where the machine and the structure meet.

Human groups have no such projection screen available to them. The modes of interpretation and indication open to them are successive and contradictory, approximative and metaphorical, and are based upon different structural orders, for instance on myths or exchanges. Every change produced by the intrusion of a machine phenomenon will thus be accompanied in them with the establishment of what one may call a system of anti-production, the representative mode specific to structure.

I need hardly say that anti-production belongs to the order of the machine: the keynote here is its characteristic of being a subjective change, which is the distinctive trait of every order of production. What we need therefore is a means of finding our way without moving as though by magic from one plane to another. We must, for instance, relate to the same system of production both what goes on in the world of industry, on the shop floor or in the manager's office, and what is happening in scientific research, and indeed in the world of literature and even of dreams.

Anti-production will be, among other things, what has been described under the term "production relations." Anti-production will tend to effect a kind of re-tilting of the balance of phantasy, not necessarily in the direction of inertia and conservatism, since it can also lead to generalizing within a given social area a new dominant mode of production, accumulation, circulation and distribution relations, or of any other superstructural manifestation of a new type of economic machine. Its mode of imaginary expression is then that of the transitional phantasy.

Let us then look at the other end of the chain, the level of dream production. We may identify anti-production with working out the manifest content of a dream, in contrast to the latent productions linked with the impulse machine that constitute part objects. The *objet petit "a,"* described by Lacan as the root of desire, the umbilicus of the dream, also breaks into the structural equilibrium of the individual like some infernal machine. The subject finds it is being rejected by itself. In proportion with the change wrought by *objet machine petit "a"* in the structural field of representation, successive forms of otherness take their places for it, each fashioned to fit a particular stage of the process. Individual phantasizing corresponds to this mode of structural signposting by means of a specific language linked with the ever-repeated urgings of the "machinations" of desire.

The existence of this *objet-machine petit "a,"* irreducible, unable to be absorbed into the references of the structure, this "self for itself" that relates to the elements of the structure only by means of splitting and metonymy, means that the representation of oneself by means of the "stencils" of language leads to a dead end, to a breaking point, and the need for a renewed "otherness." The object of desire decenters the individual outside himself, on the boundaries of the other; it represents the impossibility of any complete refuge of the self inside oneself, but equally the impossibility of a radical passage to the other. Individual phantasy *represents* this impossible merging of different levels; it is this that makes it different from group phantasizing, for a group has no such "hitching posts" of desire on its surface, no such reminders of the order of specific truths as the body's erogenous zones, and their capacity for touching and being touched by other people.

Group phantasy superimposes the different levels, changes them round, substitutes one for another. It can only turn round and round upon itself. This circular movement leads it to mark out certain areas as dead ends, as banned, as impassable vacuoles, a whole no-man's land of meaning. Caught up within the group, one phantasy reflects another like interchangeable currency, but a currency with no recognizable standard, no ground of consistency whereby it can be related, even partially, to anything other than a topology of the most purely general kind. The group—as a structure—phantasizes events by means of a perpetual and non-responsible coming and going between the general and the particular. A leader, a scapegoat, a schism, a threatening phantasy from another group—any of these is equated with the group subjectivity. Each event or crisis can be replaced by another event or crisis, inaugurating a further sequence that bears, in turn, the imprint of equivalence and identity. Today's truth can be related to yesterday's, for it is always possible to re-write history. The experience of psychoanalysis, the starting up of the psychoanalytic machine, makes it clear that it is impossible for the desiring subject to preserve such a system of homology and re-writing: the only function of the transference in this case is to reveal the repetition that is taking place, to operate like a machine—that is in a way the precise opposite of a group effect.

The group's instinctual system, because it is unable to be linked up to the desiring machine—*objets petit "a"* returning to the surface of the phantasy body—is doomed to multiply its phantasy identifications. Each of these is structured in itself, but is still equivocal in its relationship to the others. The fact that they lack the differentiating factor Gilles Deleuze talks of dooms them to a perpetual process of merging into one another. Any change is precluded, and can be seen only *between* structural levels. Essentially, no break is any longer accepted. That the structures have no specific identifying marks means that they become "translatable" into one another, thus developing a kind of indefinite logical continuum that is peculiarly satisfying to obsessionals. The identification of the similar and the discovery of difference at group level function according to a second-degree phantasy logic. It is, for example, the phantasy representation of the other group that will act as the locating machine. In a sense, it is an excess of logic that leads it to an impasse.

This relationship of the structures sets going a mad machine, madder than the maddest of lunatics, the tangential representation of a sado-masochistic logic in which everything is equivalent to everything else, in which truth is always something apart. Political responsibility is king, and the order of the general is radically cut off from the order of the ethical. The ultimate end of group phantasy is death—ultimate death, destruction in its own right, the radical abolition of any real identifying marks, a state of things in which not merely has the problem of truth disappeared forever but has never existed even as a problem.

This group structure represents the subject for another structure as the basis of a subjectivity that is clogged up, opaque, turned into the ego. Whereas, for the individual, it was the object of unconscious desire that functioned as a system of change or machine, in a group it is either the sub-wholes that happen to come into being temporarily within the group or another group that will assume that function. This area of structural equivalence will thus have the fundamental function of concealing or abolishing the entry of any particular object represented *either* on the screen of the human subject by unconscious desire, *or* on the more general screen of unconscious signifying chains by the change effected by the closed system of machines. The structural order of the group, of consciousness, of communication, is thus surrounded on all sides by these systems of machines which it will never be able to control, either by grasping the *objets petit "a"* as the unconscious desire machine, or the phenomena of breaking apart related to other types of machines. The essence of the machine, as a factor for breaking apart, as the a-topical foundation of that order of the general, is that one cannot ultimately distinguish the unconscious subject of desire from the order of the machine itself. On one side or other of all structural determinations, the subject of economics, of history and of science all encounter that same *objet petit "a"* as the foundation of desire.

An example of a structure functioning as subject for another structure is the fact that the black community in the United States represents an identification imposed by the white order. To the modernist consciousness this is a confused, absurd, meaningless state of things. An unconscious problematic challenges the rejection of a more radical "otherness" that would be combined with, say, a rejection of economic "otherness." The assassination of Kennedy was an event that "represented" the impossibility of registering the economic and social otherness of the Third World, as witnessed by the failure of the Alliance for Progress, the endeavor to destroy Vietnam and so on. One can only note here the points of intersection and continuity between the economy of desire and that of politics.

At a particular point in history desire becomes localized in the totality of structures; I suggest that for this we use the general term "machine": it could be a new weapon, a new production technique, a new set of religious dogmas, or such major new discoveries as the Indies, relativity, or the moon. To cope with this, a structural anti-production develops until it reaches its own saturation point, while the revolutionary breakthrough also develops, in counterpoint to this, another discontinuous area of anti-production that tends to re-absorb the intolerable subjective breach, all of which means that it persists in eluding the antecedent order. We may say of revolution, of the revolutionary period, that this is when the machine represents social subjectivity for the structure—as opposed to the phase of oppression and stagnation, when the superstructures are imposed as impossible representations of machine effects. The common denominator of writings of this kind in history would be the opening up of a pure signifying space where the machine would represent the subject for another machine. But one can no longer then continue to say of history, as the site of the unconscious that it is "structured like a language" except in that there is no possible written form of such a language.

It is, in fact, impossible to systematize the real discourse of history, the circumstance that causes a particular phase or a particular signifier to be represented by a particular event or social group, by the emergence of an individual or a discovery, or whatever. In this sense, we must consider, *a priori*, that the primitive stages of history are where truth is primarily to be sought; history does not advance in a continuous movement: its structural phenomena develop according to their own peculiar sequences, expressing and indicating signifying tensions that remain unconscious up to the point where they breakthrough. That point marks a recognizable break in the three dimensions of exclusion, perseverance and threat. Historical archaisms express a reinforcing rather than a weakening of the structural effect.

That André Malraux could say that the twentieth century is the century of nationalism, in contrast to the nineteenth, which was that of internationalism, was because internationalism, lacking a structural expression that matched the economic and social machineries at work within it, withdrew into nationalism, and then further, into regionalism and the various sorts of particularism that are developing today, even within the supposedly international communist movement.

The problem of revolutionary organization is the problem of setting up an institutional machine whose distinctive features would be a theory and practice that ensured its not having to depend on the various social structures—above all the State structure, which appears to be the keystone of the dominant production relations, even though it no longer corresponds to the means of production. What entraps and deceives us is that it looks today as though nothing can be articulated outside that structure. The revolutionary socialist intention to seize control of political power in the State, which it sees as the instrumental basis of class domination, and the institutional guarantee of private ownership of the means of production, has been caught in just that trap. It has itself become a trap in its turn, for that intention, though meaning so much in terms of social consciousness, no longer corresponds to the reality of economic or social forces. The institutionalization of "world markets" and the prospect of creating super-States increases the allure of the trap; so does the modern reformist program of achieving an ever-greater "popular" control of the economic and social sub-wholes. The subjective consistency of society, as it operates at every level of the economy, society, culture and so on, is invisible today, and the institutions that express it are equivocal in the extreme. This was evident during the revolution of May 1968 in France, when the nearest approximation to a proper organization of the struggle was the hesitant, late and violently opposed experiment of forming action committees.

The revolutionary program, as the machine for institutional subversion, should demonstrate proper subjective potential and, at every stage of the struggle, should make sure that it is fortified against any attempt to "structuralize" that potential.

But no such permanent grasp of machine effects upon the structures could really be achieved on the basis of only one "theoretical practice." It presupposes the development of a specific analytical praxis at every level of organization of the struggle.

Such a prospect would in turn make it possible to locate the responsibility of those who are in any way in a position genuinely to utter theoretical discourse at the point at which it imprints the class struggle at the very center of unconscious desire.

— *Translated by Rosemary Sheed*

19

Reflections on Teaching as
the Reverse of Analysis

1. Argument

The teaching of psychoanalysis would be to bring to awareness that
we are, in any case, always extra in terms of the exercise of truth.
Always too early or too late,[1] the "knowledge" of the analyst, like a
gadget of pleasure—which "works very well" these days—cuts
across any interpretation, masses, short-circuits, intersubjectivizes
the transfer.

I say "bring to awareness" to distinguish it from "being aware."
Because, of course, in practice, analysts are quickly brought into the
loop by neurotics themselves. For me, it is even one of the aspects
that separates training from teaching. Well or poorly taught, an analyst is quickly trained to be prudent; he or she even learns to keep
quiet, and for a long time! In terms of interpretation, he or she just
has to stay still. It usually tends to work out by itself! It is in his or
her interest to be as little involved as possible to avoid the risk of dis-
sent that, these days, could lead God knows where! (Remember the
poor analyst dragged by tape recorder all the way to the pages of the
Temps modernes.)

For training, then, everything is simple; you manage as best you
can. For teaching, as long as there is Lacan, the future is bright.
Since none of the constant attempts to silence him since his career
began have discouraged him, some are saying that he must be

immortal... And we are settling into a collective feeling of eternity that everyone uses in his or her own way.

It must be said that the few "statements" by various "wings" of Lacan have hardly been conclusive. How does one explain, under these conditions, that Lacan always seems to be so attached to these strange things that he introduced under the name of "cartels"?[2]

As far as I know, no report has been made on the way they function. Maybe there is none? What was involved here precisely? A singular panacea, a maieutics of the "one extra"... In order to see more clearly, I propose to indicate the different ways the "one extra" functions in training and teaching (performance and competence). From one "one extra" to another, if it does not make two, it may make "a."

When there are two of us, in appearance, the analyst + the analysand, the "one extra" should probably been counted as one less. The analyst tends to be reduced to the unenviable position of embodying the object "a" and finds little relief in the memory of his or her masters or in recalling his or her knowledge.

Yet when we are four or more ([3 + 1] + 1), everything changes.

Knowledge of a frank and honest truth reasserts itself, willingly or not. You are "among colleagues" and then object "a" really circulates! With a little practice, you can always send it discreetly back into the eyes—or other parts—of your neighbor!

In the fog of my memories, I seem to recollect that cartels were meant to avoid this very thing. A propadeutics of the "one extra." The cartel's work would then be the topological reverse of analytical work, a basic deciphering—a "new archivism."

No transference in the cartel, definitely not lateral, and hierarchical even less! As soon as there is a hint of transference in the compartment, they flatten it, like the Chinese rail workers during the Four Pests campaign.

Fundamentally, the prototype of the cartel is the archaeological origin of Lacan's seminar before Sainte-Anne,[3] when he was alone or close to it. A guy like Descartes, breaking with the claptrap to stick to the text. In this case, Freud's text. For the cartel, however, it could just as well be a theoretical text, a clinical study, a "control"…

In short, the teaching of psychoanalysis is something that Lacan did by himself (alone with 300 people in the room), but, even today, he has been lacking in groups.[4] A school composed of cartels and only cartels… of work. Was that the idea? Work does not mean analytical work or, if you will, an analysis in reverse. No more manners, "as for me," or imagination of all stripes, a one way return, always a return to the text, to the letter of things.

We can dream of what a congress of this School would be where an account of this type of activity would be given.

Let's make this distinction even more clear. Alongside analysis, desire, the object "a" on the thread of a discourse that is ready to slip from one articulation to another: morphemic, imaginary, phonemic, symbolic…

On the cartel side: a reading machine that doesn't want anything to do with knowledge as pleasure of the other which—perversion to the nth degree—proposes to catch said knowledge, not by the tail, but by the letter in its very substance. But what weight can we mere apostles carry against the solitary, fanatic perversion of Lacan for transfinite references, rare books, or even, I think, typeface, justification and, who knows?, the smell of ink.

Just two of us would be like Bouvard and Pécuchet. Three of us would be Oedipus, which is no good, as everyone knows!

With four, then, is the cartel and beyond that, the School. An entire program. Teaching would be the perversion of the letter *against the backdrop of a school,* mediated by cartels.

On the one hand, analysis, the mad dash of the object "a," the phantom confrontation with the "one extra," the production of another subjectivity. On the other, the differentiating work of the "one extra," a desubjectivization of relationships, a depersonalization of analysts, in the sense that one speaks of a strong personality, a strong ego, etc.

This "disimagifying" of teaching, which implies constant vigilance to have to break with the mirages of the profession (the analyst's couch of which we described the attraction in a congress), would open it to other horizons. What about castes and classes today, their fantastic entanglement, the new ways and means of appropriating surplus labor… and more! In what direction can the path of taking today's psychoanalytic speech and writing literally take us?

Long ago, in May 1968, a social interrogation deftly avoided by psychoanalysts aimed clumsily, confusedly but nonetheless aimed to bring the contribution of Freudianism to social revolution. Is it still pertinent to mention here that many people on the far-far-left are wracking their brains on the old question of how to build a Revolutionary Party? How can a group avoid focalizing at will the perversion of knowledge—militants, leaders—subjugating or crushing the "truth without knowledge" of the masses?

How can the "one extra" of the party or the organization avoid blocking all institutional production and any true speech "at the base"?

"Open your mouths," [*Que les bouches s'ouvrent*]: this plea heard during our last meeting—maybe I am the only one who heard it this way—echoes the one Maurice Thorez made in 1936, I believe, to a closed, muzzled, fascinated, perverted party that was only living by delegation and the deeds and acts of its leaders. Some accents, some bad faith, some maneuvers in the School remind me of Stalinism. Do these things have to be said?

Deep down, don't the School and revolutionary movements revolve around the same problem?

Saying that teaching psychoanalysis should be different from university teaching is still not saying anything about what it should be in the School and—why not?—in the University or anywhere else!

What conditions should be met so that a body like the School can function for its members and for the outside as a machine of analytical deciphering, without any false assimilation with the psychoanalytical relationship? Yet doesn't this question have a more general scope? Doesn't it concern any attempt to decipher social segments that is not simply sociological, no matter which one, from conjugal families to oligopolies, from "primitive" ethnic groups to the state?

Correlatively, wouldn't one come to think that a third institutional articulation should necessarily be deployed to authorize the correct discovery of the various modes of fantasy?

Is it conceivable to develop a teaching that, to return to the letter—what Oury called "positive teaching"—to refuse all "paradigmatic perversion," would establish a scene "on the level of the significant" where group fantasies could come play and be reduced from wherever they come, such as the fantasy I mentioned about "Stalinism" in the School…

What guarantees should the School provide to avoid closing in on itself, only offering itself to others as a rumored subject of psychoanalytical knowledge, the incarnation of a supreme pleasure, while, in reality, it is only the place where everyone is secretly reveling in the pleasure of being in a "cutting-edge group" behind a Master? A pleasure that is not very demanding in material terms: a meeting every once in a while, disparate "reading Lacan" groups, no newsletter.

By not establishing a structure that is radically different from a corporate group, a club or even a lobbying group, the School keeps itself from any teaching other than Lacan's, *which is not the teaching of the School*; develops a pedagogy of mimeticism; distributes analytical tricks; revives, from the Lacanian ranks—and this seems particularly serious—the ailing model of a transposition of the true analytical relationship with an interpretation of groups, institutions, and even society…

The question of teaching would finally be reduced to the defini-tion of the conditions of signifying production beyond the seminar of Lacan, beyond the pleasure of being in his wake, to the establish-ment, articulation and control of the cartels in the School.

2. Comments

Hoping above all to start a discussion, instead of returning to my introductory text, I would prefer to start with what [Jacques] Nas-sif suggested and try to articulate it with my comments. First, in a few words and apologizing for the poor treatment I will put his texts through, here is what I remember: if I understand correctly, *analytical discourse*—which "produces" object "a" "from scratch"—is articulated with the *discourse of science* through the mediation of the *discourse of the analyst,* on the condition of thwarting the specific operation of *university discourse* that consists of hypostasizing a subject beneath knowledge.

The psychoanalyst, to carry out his or her work of truth on the undecidable knowledge of proper nouns, would find support in the discourse of psychoanalysis. This discourse is constituted in such a way that this knowledge can never be "capitalized in favor of the archive" and the "author function" but on the contrary it can be constituted like the other side of the constitutive cut of science, since it is perpetually divided between what must shift from it to reality as the "impossible of a given discourse," and this author func-tion ejected into the symbolic order, undergoing a "derealization": proper noun in the third person, name of nouns…

Having to "account for all cuts," to "know all metaphors," the psychoanalytical institution—institution of all other institutions—does not have to privilege any concept, according to Nassif. The work of treatment would only be a screening of everything related to fantasy, and the work of Freudian theory would be a screening of the discourse of sciences "made so that the question of desire is never asked or that the psychological knowledge that it refers to allows it to be avoided" (*Lettres de l'Ecole*, March 1970, p.17)

The specific function of this *discourse of analysis*, built as it is on *psychoanalytical discourse* producing a "counter-discourse," an "other discourse," could therefore be compared to a sphinx posted at the gate of the garden of science, in charge of watching the risks of ideological contamination by means of a kind of anti-proper noun Geiger counter, a pure index of events, refusing to know anything more of them than their repetition.

It would mean a lot of extra work for psychoanalysts! Yet I think there would still be a few "to play the game" proposed by Nassif, especially on the condition that they are guaranteed that no one will bother them with worldly things, except of course for this business of proper nouns... I am less certain than Nassif that "there is nothing new except in and through science." I am afraid that this may be a mirage of imperialism and the all-powerful hold of science on reality, another radical procedure to avoid desire, which, under the traits of the object "a," nevertheless remains the fundamental root of all scientific machinations. This promotion of a pure theoretical machine from analytical praxis, "scene and instrument" of the extraction of events and of their resolution in pure repetition, seems to me to have the inconvenience of relieving analysts from their political responsibilities. Nassif, I think, senses this danger when he refuses to take the last step that would lead him to declaring directly that there is no analytical knowledge.

This reserve—which may only be the result of a misunderstanding over difficult texts—does not seem to condemn what he develops. His work to "deflate" the proper noun—in other words, Oedipus—should, however, be developed. It is not only correct to say that psychoanalysis has something to do, for example, with the object of logic or mathematics, but its concrete relationship with the full set of contemporary political issues should be indicated as well. The only complaint I would make to Nassif is that he seems to have the tendency to reduce the order of history to the order of science, a tendency that, with Althusser for example, is reinforced by further reductions of science to theory, and theory itself to literary activity, which is not without its appeal!

Let us return to the battery of concepts Nassif proposes: you will remember that he threatened us with the strict loss of the merits of scientificity and collapse into the abyss of ideology in the case where a *domain* ceases to be *definable* in a field of *knowledge* by means of the *structure* of the discourse that *produces* said knowledge.

The same would be true in cases where one of the four terms of this circle—domain, knowledge, discourse or object—goes missing, or one of the three relationships that constitute it—definition, structure or production—and to which Nassif was careful not to add a fourth: the *affiliation* of the object produced to knowledge, precisely for fear of seeing his formula close in a circle. Yet an essential part of the object of knowledge—its historical reality—escapes him.

Taking into consideration the reality of the involvement of psychoanalysis in political discourse would lead us to imagine, alongside the discourse *of* the analyst in his or her daily performance on the level, for example, of transference and interpretation, another discourse that also defines a distinct domain: the counter-performance that is institutional discourse *on* psychoanalysis and which echoes, all of the way into the heart of analytical praxis, the immense and interminable chatter *on* psychoanalysis, on received ideas on the subject on Radio-Luxembourg just as well as in different accreditation companies. Polarized between these antagonistic domains, analytical *training* is only the result of these performances vectorized in the opposite direction, while *teaching*, which has to deliver certificates of competence, according to one procedure or another, peacefully continues to sacrifice an essential part of the psychoanalytical field on the altar of the dominant deities of medical and psychological thought.

The question for us is to know under what *effective conditions* psychoanalytical discourse could disengage itself from both the inextricable institutional network in which it is imprisoned and the various myths that tend to subject its production to a composite ideal of conformity with the dominant social models in terms of morality, religion, politics, science, etc.

What type of effects and counter-effects should we expect during the structuring of a school for the new domain that is thus defined? We cannot expect that the response will come from the "discourse without archives" that has now moved into a referential position in relation to other discourses, and which can only roll with the punches without being able to make them work in terms of truth, just as Nassif noted quite correctly.

Couldn't Lacan himself make this "discourse without words" speak? By the way, everyone in the School hopes that he will tell us more about it one day. Couldn't he serve us a spoon-fed truth, accompanied by precise directives on these questions of teaching? The way things are, unfortunately, even man-made science cannot supplement collective involvement or common political projects in this domain. It is most probably up to the School to shoulder the formidable responsibility of transforming this institutional "templum," to use Nassif's expression, on which, as a sign and with the mediation of a certain number of structural operators, the assumption of a repeated cut could be inscribed in place of the traditional separation between teaching and formation, making them suture each other in a reciprocal extension, so that teaching becomes the topological reverse of analytical work. The functioning of analysis on the mode of an "axiom schema"[5] and as a pure repetition of a "discourse without archive" could not protect it from grasping all scientific, political, institutional, etc., domains. On the contrary, it would be led to a work of expulsion within these different domains, expulsion of all of the forms of "one says" *on* psychoanalysis, of every compulsion to university archivism, of all medico-social finalism, of all "revisionism" bogging down the cutting function of the object "a," in no matter what order the incidence of desire manifests itself in its call for truth.

The least we can say is that the School still has a long way to go on this road! To measure the remaining distance, I propose to examine the current situation in light of a further axiom that could be formulated as follows: *Lacan's teaching is not the teaching of the School.*

The School cannot content itself to knowledge *on* teaching, *on* Lacan's writing. Lacan's teaching is one thing; what the teaching of the School should be is another. On these questions, and although it cannot replace the work of the School itself, Lacan has given some indications on the theme of cartels that we may have covered (or passed over) too quickly. They are taken for granted, yet the members of the School are still far from having a common gauge of what the function of a cartel may be as a mode of structuring the psychoanalytical field. We often hear formulas that propose the cartels as an intermediary step to "gain access" to the difficulties of Lacan's teaching(!). It led me to turn to my neighbor to say that it was like distributing a vaccine, an attenuated strain of Lacanianism. There are also "Lacan reading groups," but until someone proves me wrong, I continue to see them as a dilution of his writing and seminars. They either produce simplified or popularized Lacan, a sort of fermentation of formulas without real respect of their texture; or they tend towards the ultimate ideal of Bouvard and Pécuchet: copies, pure and simple.

What is true for Lacan's texts is *a fortiori* true of all other forms of teaching, the reading of theoretical texts, "controls," etc. How can another mode of production be developed in this domain that would constitute a "reexamination" of the text, which I would place in the register of a "new archivism"? Reexamination or "coming right out and saying it" concerning the extension of analysis to group phenomena, in particular inside the cartels, with the goal of neutralizing these famous "lateral transfers" and any kind of "extra-textual" use of the object "a." On this subject, wouldn't it be better to distinguish the way the object "a" functions in psychoanalytical practice and in teaching? In the first case, the analyst is potentially in the position to be this object "a" him- or herself; the function of the "one extra" acting more like a "one less" in the so-called dual relationship, tangential to narcissistic abolition. In the second case, the "a" acts as "differentiation" in identifications and roles, always threatened with seeing its effect weighed down by this social game, this play of intersubjective places that infinitely increases mutual indulgence, secret hierarchies, alienating fascination, etc.

I am convinced that this effect of group imagination on teaching requires the establishment of an analytical practice that is specific in its techniques and constitutes, strictly speaking, the *reverse* of the analysts work on the couch. The reverse of psychoanalysis, because, in this case, it is no longer question of a process that, after a series of transformations, ends by grasping the object "a" on the level of what psychoanalytical literature has localized around partial objects, erogenous zones and the entire realm of corporality that is popular with analysts of children and psychotics. It is instead the extension of its effect, through group fantasies, to all segments of the social field, including the solitary perversion of the letter that I mentioned in my introductory argument.

Promoting this "new archivism" within the cartels relates to what Oury called the narrative; its objective is to recapture the writing of analytical literature as the event or advent of a repeated cut, the effect of recurrence of the discourse of Anna O., for example, on the discourse of Freud, or the discourse of Aimée on Lacan, but also the repetition of events that have marked the history of the psychoanalytic movement, the reiteration of schisms, exclusions, ruptures, starting with the very first steps by Freud. A deliberate confrontation with the "impossible reality" manifested by these breaks, repeated as an echo both in the history of Lacanianism and the recent history of the Freudian School should represent an essential anchor for any teaching.

Recapturing the text in its meaning as a repeated cut without relating it to the subject of the utterance, without personalizing it, blocking the proliferation of what I called paradigmatic perversion… There is a problem that I cannot develop here, but that seems particularly acute in one wing of Lacanianism: the spiritualist ambiguity that sees the letter as being able to be inscribed on the body, the "erogenous body," and the body itself is seen as a univocal linguistic substance. The essence of the letter, however, is not to be inscribed on the body, but to inscribe the functioning of the object "a" on other supports, other chains that are much more "deterritorialized" than the all too famous "body map"…

The work of the analysand[6] is this recapturing, this fantastical reduction of the functioning of the object "a" in the heart of the psychoanalytical relationship, which is, however, in question for the field of teaching. This work is also an extension beyond and below the imagination in its relationship to the body and to the person. It is certainly the failure of the School to function as a reading machine, an analytical machine on the level of teaching and training that allowed the emergence and the persistence in the School of a certain number of ideological currents that have nothing to do with Freudianism.

Will the School function one day like a relay-structure between the discourse of the psychoanalysand and the various domains in which the object "a" is implicated? Or should it be considered, in the end, in the same way as the other psychoanalytical dens, as a further obstacle to the development of Freudian-Lacanianism, secreting a more virulent species of "misunderstanding disease" against it for the very reason that it comes so close to the truth? Will this fine flour mentioned by Nassif stop being transformed in the mills of special enterprises into the moldy dough from which psychoanalysts made their daily bread until the unfortunately exceptional intervention of Lacan? Let us say that, for the School, the demonstration that this question has not already been shifted into the realm of the undecidable… has yet to come.

In the meantime, two working objectives should be determined: on the one hand, the development of the *theory of fantasy* from psychoanalytical practice and, on the other, the *theory of group fantasy* from the ideological discourses of the different strata of the socius to which analysis has access, and from the conquest, discovery, and invention of praxis on the level of institutions that might refuse the "archivism of knowledge" at any level where it appears, be it the University, hospitals, the labor movement, etc.

To come back to Nassif's texts, I think that the distinction he proposes between the discourse of psychoanalytical praxis and the discourse of theory is of no real interest unless it gives us the means to situate the responsibility of the psychoanalytical movement more precisely in relation to the various domains in which it would have to intervene. On the condition, of course, that it begins by changing itself from head to toe. If not, then I am afraid it is only an epistemological presupposition with the sole function of according the exclusive privilege of critical intervention in all social domains to Marxism. I find, in particular, that Nassif is too quick to reduce the "terrain of psychoanalytical discourse" to psychiatry, and when he states that Freudianism did not carry out an epistemological break with medical ideology! For him, it is justified by the fact that fantasy, which carries a principle of rupture within itself, relieves the domain that it constitutes from having to throw out the dominant ideology through any other means than the repeated cuts that form the essence of analytical practice. With each treatment, psychoanalytical discourse would start from scratch, as if nothing had happened before, and each analyst would be reduced each time to become Charcot, then Jackson, Berheim, etc. Each time, a pure theory would be deployed again, one where the authors' names would be mere contingent indices; a pure theory of repetition, impervious to contingency and historical icons, which make psychoanalysands today—very informed *about* psychoanalysis—different than the ones with Freud and Breuer. By the force of history, the practice of treatment has been radically changed, with the work of the analyst sometimes reduced to being no more than a stubborn struggle to counterbalance an anti-analytical process that tends to develop on its own.

Nassif seems to have no problems with the fact that revolution could be credited with having two theoretical heads: Marxism accounting for the discourse of science and psychoanalysis accounting for "impossible reality." This reassuring marriage seems to be founded on a topology of collapsing domains—let Nassif choose the image that suits him—like Chinese boxes or Russian dolls.

I would find it clearer, but also more disturbing, to recognize all at once that: 1) Freudianism has remained impregnated with the *dominant ideology*, and lends itself to integrationist use by capitalism and the denial that has developed around it in so-called socialist countries (it authorizes this contamination more by the questions it avoids than by its the explicit positions); 2) it also represents a *new theory*, it brings new concepts that imply a radical epistemological break that concerns not only the discourse of science, but also all theory and practice of social institutions, beginning with Marxism—the next-to-last true theory to date. Marxism is gestating another break which should, in the end, give the labor movement weapons that will help it extricate itself from the bureaucratic muddle in which it continues to bury itself, precisely because of its deficiencies on the question of desire.

Under these conditions, it does not seem appropriate to prepare a theoretical balm to soothe the worries that have troubled part of the psychoanalytical field since May 1968. Let me be clear: saying that psychoanalytical discourse should situate itself as an extension of revolutionary discourse does not mean, at present, that it is capable of compensating miraculously for the inability and the refusal of the labor movement to take desire into consideration on the level of class struggle. This is shown by its uncontrollable tendency towards internal bureaucracy and its misunderstanding of the real aspirations of the masses, by its repressive interventions against so-called wild forms of struggle, etc. What is asked of psychoanalysts is to avoid involvement simply by chance, or "voting for the left," and to make it so that the domain of psychoanalytical discourse is no longer an obstacle to the necessary involvement of other discourses. They are also asked to contribute to the creation of a theory of desire that allows the production of the object "a" to bring its full structuring effect to all domains where desire is implicated. In practice, this would mean promoting analytical groups as a counterpoint or adjacent to various institutions, analyzing the imagination of castes, analyzing the instance of the letter in bureaucratism at every level, relationships between the phenomena of bureaucracy and the death drive, etc. Everything that could now be advanced in these different directions would be like helping hands, ones that would be grasped quicker than you might think.

I also think that we should be wary of a restrictive definition of the inside and outside of analysis as the limits of the School's area of intervention. The cartels, in particular, should remain open to all domains, while waiting for real work on desire. Along with their duty to archive, read and reread, the cartels would gain from contact with the practice of institutional analysis, or, in other words, political analysis.

20

Where Does Group Psychotherapy Begin?

Group activities aren't necessarily the best option! Or the group could get turned into a religion! Group life can have harmful effects: when people use the other as a pretext to quietly turn inward and let things happen. Groups can regress. It is the division of labor in reverse. And working in a group is a big deal.

Well, all this to say: we should be vigilant and avoid falling prey to groupist traps. God knows that there are a few of those right now, especially in our field. Still, we use groups all the time at La Borde!

Are we fighting evil with evil? Individuals are not clear about themselves; they can't find themselves, pull themselves together, or figure themselves out. They are looking for something bigger than they are, a reference point, something to go by. You know, instead of letting them bleat at the moon, you may as well give them plenty of group. And it definitely works; most people love it. They keep asking for more. And they don't want to leave. They come back. And they talk about it everywhere.

No need to panic, though! After all, it's the least we can do for them.

Give people food, education, manners, vitamins, vaccinations, time off… group time, it's only natural. It's one of the necessities of the modern world. As Oury often says on this topic, if this is what we call psychotherapy, then you have to admit that any baker around the corner does a better job than us, and without all the fuss, the conferences and reviews…

So, I'll stop here! Nothing more to say?

I thought we could introduce a new notion to clear things up: the notion of *subjective consistency*.

With two people, psychotherapy doesn't work that well. It works sometimes, but only in specific cases; people's heads have to be screwed on a certain way. Freud used to say that a certain level—he should have added a certain standing—had to be reached before you could be psychoanalyzed. At La Borde, of course, there are never just two people; there are always others around; it's almost as if they eavesdrop outside the door! With a thousand people, it doesn't work all that great either: like a thousand people in the waiting area at Saint-Lazare station.

If it's a revolution, it works well. But those are rare…and they don't last long.

There has to be an intermediate number, an appropriate range; that's my aim with this notion of consistency.

A family is not necessarily a bad number; but there are other reasons why a family doesn't work: family members aren't a group of people who can speak with each other.

It's a jumble where people can't find their way. Speaking happens in a family, but no one can be sure where it's coming from: everyone speaks for everyone else, and in the end it might just be the voice of ancestors still hanging around. No, it's not healthy! In any case, it's rarely psychotherapeutic!

We've tried everything at La Borde. But, until now, it was always a little too big: the four groups,[1] or definitely too small: individual care. With the "basic therapy units" (BTUs) we have tried to adjust our aim, to form some artificial families.[2] It's no longer a matter of individual schedules, decisions about entry or leaving, places at the table, medication, etc. without consulting the BTU first. The person of the BTU supplants its individual members. And far from eliminating the individuals in question, it seems to energize them. Why would that be psychotherapeutic?

Well, because of what I was just saying: it's a surface of reference, and with that surface in place, it's harder to duck out. When people stop falling for the groupism trap, they become wary of its harmful effects. For example, suppose you're in a crowd defending a barricade against the cops. If you don't know the people around you very well, you can always slip away. It's not important. But everything changes if you're with your BTU. It can have all sorts of consequences: people will talk…It's pretty rough! You can get stuck. Caught like a rat in a trap. Words stop slipping away. Promises made, bets held, deals done.

Again, we see how a family is different. In a family, someone says something, then someone says the opposite. There's an argument, and it makes no difference:

—You said that… And then…, etc.

—You're not going to call me a liar…

—Oh, yes I am!

—Well, I've had enough. I'm not eating my soup, etc.

We know the rest!

All alone, an individual has trouble focusing his or her words. They go everywhere and nowhere. Sometimes they take off; they speak on their own. It's the principle of the famous "inner discourse."

When it works, classical psychoanalysis, the kind with the couch, it works. The guy talking is trapped by the other. Only there are a lot of cases where it doesn't work because he has nothing to say or because he doesn't want to say anything.

In the BTU, we take turns being psychoanalysts. And then, sometimes, the psychoanalyst can be the thing you're planning to do, the person you meet: going skiing, going to the bakery… Words circulate in a field of reference, a finite but open field that has, you might say, a certain subjective consistency.

21

Raymond and the Hispano Group

The Hispano factory "Youth Group" and some of the political militants who led it certainly had exceptional success promoting an activist lifestyle among workers, one that broke sharply and consciously with the so-called "mass" action practices of Stalinists and social-democrats.

The post-war Trotskyists had some areas of support in companies. But those militants were isolated and under surveillance. The sectarian nature of the circumstances also made any in-depth campaigning impossible. They were always on the defensive, accomplished polemicists whose physical courage was often admirable at a time when there was a real wall of fear and hate, almost paranoia, separating the Stalinists of the French Communist Party (FCP) and the General Confederation of Labor (CGT) from the Trotskyist "slippery vipers."

At the time, I was actively involved in the youth hostel movement, which gradually brought me closer to the International Communist Party (ICP) (the Trotskyist party from before the great schism of 1951). But my involvement remained mostly ambivalent: on the one hand, I was fascinated by the small, smoky inner circles, and the discussions of global strategies ("Here we're nothing, but our comrades are almost in power in Ceylon and in Bolivia..."). Then another schism was announced and hope faded again... On the other hand, there were our "youth hostel buddies," the really active groups from La Garenne, Courbevoie, Suresnes, Puteaux. The young local militants from the Union of French Republican Youth (UJRF) and the French Communist Party coexisted in peace and were even on friendly terms. And for good reason: they knew each other from school, in the hostels, we were all mixed together, and there were some pretty cute girls in our group, unlike the UJRF!

Each year, fifty or more of us would go on trips to the country, and hitchhike around Europe. The long nights, the friendships of a day, the absolute confidence… It was really something! After many extraordinary adventures on the roads of Liberation, Raymond was especially allergic to the washers he punched out all day long at the Hispano-Suiza plants. Even on the work floor, he kept the scent of blooming broom flowers from weekend camping… Dozens of young people from work bonded with him, and right away Hispano's Youth Group was off to an amazing start.

At first, the local FCP chapter saw no harm in it. The management at the factory was a different story: from the first camping car trip to the country, organized in August outside of any institutional framework, they understood that they had to reconcile with the "agitator" (by offering him a quick promotion) or get rid of him as fast as possible (by making life unbearable at work). Granted, Raymond did have second thoughts when it came to the "apparatus," but he had no choice: he agreed to become a permanent member of the company committee to focus on recreational opportunities for the factory's young workers.

We often discussed the complex struggles for influence within the party to preserve the Youth Group's autonomy and overflowing dynamism. The General Confederation of Labor was involved in finances and meeting rooms, and the Party wanted to create a UJRF group to regain control of operations… Some old militants privately supported the experiment. Unable to carry it out, the Party apparatus abandoned it. Raymond was forced to rejoin the rank and file.

He found his "bike" and his buddies from work. Some time later, he became an official personnel representative. The story would have normally stopped there, but things were just getting started!

In high school, and later as a Trotskyist student, I sometimes had trouble accepting Raymond's prudent tactics... Why was he so cautious? I only gradually came to understand the nature of the extraordinary resistance, the egotism, and the "me-ism" that were invested in the local Party apparatus and the CGT, resistance that would have to be outmaneuvered and foiled. I had several opportunities to talk directly with these "bigwigs." There was one particular workshop in Baillet where I gave participants an opinion survey of sorts in the form of a game. The results revealed new organizational demands and aspirations that were the polar opposite of the CGT's platform and practices (particularly on the question of non-hierarchical wage increases).

On some occasions, I more or less directly disagreed with Raymond: particularly in 1950, when the Trotskyists clamored to send "brigades" to Yugoslavia. We were going to investigate and tell "the truth about Yugoslavia," which the Stalinists had started calling "fascist" overnight. (One militant from the Courbevoie section of the PCF, a veteran of the International Brigades, told me, "Go take a look. You'll see; the Americans have installed bases there, I'll give you a map of their layout. You'll tell us what you've seen when you come back. We trust you. If you were a Trotskyist, it wouldn't be the same. There wouldn't be any discussion, we'd just bust your jaw!") I had just received my card from the Trotskyist party after a long probationary period and after testing from the Revolutionary Youth Movement (MJR). I remember that there had been a big brouhaha because I had convinced the son of the communist ex-mayor of La Garenne to go to Yugoslavia. The Party's militants started giving me funny looks: "You'll be denounced in the local press." Naturally, I had brought my propaganda for the "brigades" to the Youth Group at Hispano. Soon after I had gone through, Raymond prudently removed the posters from the local... In hindsight, I think he was right. Did there have to be a showdown over this? His break with the apparatus had to be public, but the showdown came with a protest in the street by factory workers. The young workers imposed it on the bureaucrats to protest the war in Algeria and also against emergency powers. Truth be told, we were practicing a politics of "entryism" before the term existed. It is up to the Trotskyist theorists of "*sui generis* entryism" to say whether they were inspired by the results of our actions.

With the International Community Party's schism, all my hopes collapsed. The Pablo-Frank-Privas group, which was favorable to entryism in the FCP, was isolated. Entryism became a fiction, and the best militants began following Lambert Bleibtreu, including my best friends from the MJR. With a heavy heart, I voted for the Pablo group. At the time, I was in charge of the Trotskyist movement in the youth hostels (in the CLAJPA)[1]. Suddenly, I dropped everything! I left in the middle of the Youth Hostel National Congress. I went and talked for hundreds of hours with Jean Oury, who was the director of the Saumery clinic in the Loir-and-Cher department. We went through everything: politics, psychoanalysis, psychiatry, literature... From there, I would leave my family, and change the focus of my studies. *In practice*, it was then that Raymond and I started to organize an autonomous political group, an "entryist" group, if you will.

There were three elements in the group:

—veterans of the local youth hostel movement,

—the core members of the Hispano Youth Group.

—students from the Sorbonne: primarily members of the "philosophy cell" of the French Communist Party (which Lucien Sebag would later join).

In 1951, we started organizing original projects in several sectors, in the Party, with the "Franco-Chinese Friendship Association"

(Raymond was one of the first French people to visit China in 1953), and in organizations like "Tourism and Work," etc. Students and young militant workers would be able to mix together. But the bureaucrats from the 6th *arrondissement* section and those from Hispano and the local cells (for example, the leaders, at the time, of the Courbevoie Youth Home) were on the lookout: something like this would have to be stopped. We were overwhelmed by the number of new students and new workers joining us. With many reservations, we slowly grew closer to the Franck-ICP group (*La Vérité des travailleurs* [*The Workers' Truth*]). This was the moment when Michèle Mestre and Corvin were undertaking their mini-schism to found *Le Communiste*. We got roped into doing "training workshops," then finally we all joined the International Communist Party. We were taken in! It meant I had yet another probationary period! The worker comrades in our group were carefully isolated from the students in separate cells. (Soon afterwards, Dany's brother Gaby Cohn-Bendit and Lucien Sebag joined the ICP—*Workers' Truth*, while the Krivine brothers joined for a much longer haul.

Earlier, we had felt crushed by the responsibilities of our autonomous group. Now we were free and a little distraught. Along with some student comrades—including Lucien Sebag—and taking care not to alert the leadership of the ICP, which we regarded with suspicion, we founded an internal dissident organ within the French Communist Party: *Tribune de discussion* [*Discussion Forum*]. Only *Unir* [*Unite*] existed back then, but that newsletter was quite unjustly maligned and generally disparaged. *It* was a complete success! Dozens of intellectuals from the Party joined the *Tribune* (including Henri Lefebvre), Sartre threw in his support....The *Tribune* was popular: people were convinced that it was led by militant workers—this may have been a further influence of the Hispano group's existence!

1956: the year when things came to a head. The 20th Congress, the Algerian War, and the FCP vote for emergency powers, the Suez expedition, Budapest, the fire at the headquarters of *L'Humanité*, the retreat…

Other dissidents awoke. They founded *L'Etincelle* [*The Spark*] (with Gérard Spitzer). With help from the Trotskyists, a dark confusion descended: communist opposition eventually fell to pieces. The ICP took with it the original version of *La Voie communiste* [*The Communist Way*], which claimed in its sub-title to "continue" *L'Etincelle-Tribune de discussion* [*The Spark-Discussion Forum*] (n.1, January 1958), the product of a fleeting merger of the first two newsletters. *La Voie communiste* was there to contend with the *Voies nouvelles*, which was mainly run by militants from the "Sorbonne-Literature" cell of the Party. There was also a *Tribune du communisme*, which was supposed to join the Unified Socialist Party that was then under construction.

Clearly, everything was a mess! Raymond, the comrades from our group and I decided to leave the ICP. We'd had more than enough! When May 13, 1958 came, the ICP mobilization geared toward organizing the "resistance" was an implausible masquerade. We wanted to save all we could of the dissident element, so we made our return in force by editing *La Voie communiste* and we openly set about eliminating the Trotskyists who were rampant there. Some leaders of the ICP secretly encouraged us, but very few followed us in the schism. (My articles in *La Voie communiste* were signed Claude Arrieux.)

I do not know if all the comrades from the Hispano group were quite aware that *La Voie communiste would never have been in a position to gain its independence* without their support and, of course, without the precedent their group had set. For a long time, we had been nostalgic about restarting an open and non-sectarian group; we had never been able to adapt to the Trotskyists' maniacal centralism.

Moreover, if most of the Trotskyist students followed us (aside from the Krivine brothers), at least for a time, with this new *Voie communiste*, it was in part due to their high opinion of the Hispano-Suiza militant group.

There may have been some mythical efficiency involved. It happens! Some of the militants leading the Montreuil section of the FCP would also join us, a group of libertarian communists, Gérard Spitzer and dozens of anti-colonialist militants whose trust we had gained after our public split with the Trotskyists.

It was an epic adventure to publish those 49 issues of *La Voie communiste* (November 1959–February 1965)! It was the only Marxist movement with any audience that supported the Algerian National Liberation Front's struggle without prejudice or reticence. (The Manifesto of the 121 was repudiated by the majority of the Unified Socialist Party, which people forget, including Claude Bourdet but was published by *La Voie*, which was quickly seized by the police.) With *La Voie communiste*, "support" lost its delirious, romantic character and became linked to the struggles of the French revolutionary vanguard. Our Hispano comrades weren't the last to join in this fight! Papers seized on an ongoing basis, secret distribution, several years of prison for two directors in a row, spectacular escapes organized...

Raymond was laid off from Hispano in 1958 (along with a lot of others); the General Confederation of Labor had closely monitored him, and denounced him as a Trotskyist. Activism in the factory was no longer possible for Raymond, who then became a staff member at *La Voie communiste*. He worked incredibly hard, always with the same calm and the same rigor.

Aside from the general assemblies, the militant groups were all on their own. There was, in fact, fairly little contact with friends from Hispano (called the "Simca Group" to cover their tracks, which would lead to some comic misunderstandings!). This group, however, was basically committed to the FCP and the General Confederation of Labor—and was secretly distributing several dozen copies of *La Voie communiste* in the factory.

At the end of the Algerian War, it was mayhem: the wilayah hassles, the founding of Boudiaf's Revolutionary Socialist Party… isolation. Three quarters of the militants from *La Voie* became Ben Bellists, singing the praises of revolution-via-self-management in the manner of the "Pablists," or they scattered into the woods. We were on our own. It was hell!

Raymond and I had distanced ourselves from the activist core that maintained editorial control of the journal, which was starting to entertain quite a few illusions about the possibilities opened by the Chinese Communist Party's new orientation ("The 25-Point Declaration"). This led to the foundation in late 1963 of the short-lived *Association populaire franco-chinoise* [Peoples' Franco-Chinese Association], quickly disavowed by Chinese leaders.

For my part, I was particularly close to the militants from the National Union of Students of France (UNEF). and the Communist Students Union (UEC) which was going through the early stages of the crisis that would break it apart.

Emptied of its substance and devoid of perspective, *La Voie communiste* eventually closed its doors.

A more open, wider movement was formed under the umbrella of the *Opposition de gauche* [Left Opposition], uniting militants from the UEC, *La Voie communiste*, UNEF, etc. In addition to collaborating with students, the "OG" took part in the fight against the Vietnam War, working most notably with the *Mouvement du milliard* [One-Billion Movement]. It also supported struggles in Latin America with the founding of the Latin American Revolution Solidarity Organization (OSARLA), an initiative by a former militant from *La Voie communiste*, Michèle Firk, who died in combat in Guatemala.

At the same time, the Federation of Study and Institutional Research Groups (FGERI) was founded along with its revue *Recherches*.

After a political clarification, the Hispano group decided to continue its efforts by collaborating with this new Left Opposition. Together, they discussed a collective political reassessment: their *Nine Theses of the Left Opposition* were published in a pamphlet in early 1966.[2]

In addition, the Hispano comrades led the Study and Work Group on the Worker Movement (GETMO) in the framework of the FGERI.

In fact, it was the first time that all of these militant workers, teachers, students, and healthcare workers could engage in a real dialogue together, even though they had known each other for a long time. Before this new orientation, however, it was as if they weren't allowed to speak about anything other than politics! A new imaginary barrier was broken, and, in a way, this break prefigured what would happen in May 1968.

The fact that the members of the UEC National Bureau, for example, could work in constant liaison with a group like the Hispano group was certainly a determining factor in their evolution.

It is true that May 1968 overwhelmed us all, even though all the militants from this movement were in step with the March 22 Movement and the action committees (as early as February 1968, contact was made by students at Nanterre). The arrival of Hispano group militants at the General Assembly of the March 22 Movement in early May may have also contributed to moving things forward. Again,

I know that this is something that is related to the psychological realm. Yet why not?

After all, hadn't we been carrying out a psychoanalytic attempt at demystification over many years: to explore, break, and overcome the tics and mannerisms of traditional revolutionary militancy as much as possible. Raymond and some other worker militants from the Hispano group were passionate about psychoanalysis and psychiatry. Each time they discovered this, the "serious militants" who came from the outside were stunned. Before being judged on his ideas or his program, a militant was gauged by his or her seriousness, based on criteria that were, strictly speaking, psychoanalytical. Discussions of the political orientation or psychosexual problems of the group were equally important. Militants with this training had a talent for annoying and disorienting interlocutors from traditional political and union apparatuses. They also had a gift for connecting with young militants who weren't yet deformed.

I think the Hispano group owed its success to the fact that it deliberately broke with the usual texture of militant relationships. The fact that this break happened *in a major metallurgical business* also made it important. This group was like a bone that no one could swallow. Our private expression for it is "analytical group." A group that positions itself against the "normal" order of things. A "parapraxis-group" that allows the deep desires of young workers to be expressed: the desire to put an end to formalism, dogmatism, and bureaucratic ways of doing things; to put an end to boring meetings that only serve as a stage for the narcissistic displays of bureaucrats; the desire to finally speak about real—and therefore revolutionary—things at all costs—which make people uncomfortable and makes them want things to change…

Maybe one day, history—history with the ability to address the unconscious—will put the work of the Hispano group in its rightful place.

22

The Masochist Maoists or the Impossible May

Rereading their self-criticism about a post-May '68 book, *Toward Civil War*, two leaders of the *Gauche prolétarienne* [Proletarian Left] may realize that their words unfortunately slipped on an "s."

After a summary, three-line, Zhdanov-style execution of their Freudian-Guevarist transgressions—residue of a petit-bourgeois past—they celebrate the redemptive virtue of the Mao-broom that swept all this dust away as follows: "What really swept it away was the acknowledgment via the Proletarian Left of Maoism's universality minus [*sans*] its reality in France, as well as the edifying work of the Proletarian Left in its mass struggle."[1]

Dear Comrade-Proofreader of *L'Idiot*, please note that you read an "s" instead of a "d."

Having given up all recourse to the Freudian theory of parapraxis, slips or typos, it is up to these authors to propose their own theory to account for this phenomenon. They did not miss this typo, since they inserted a mimeographed sheet to correct the "s," which incidentally attracted even more attention to it. It would be a good time to apply the formula from page 31 of this same pamphlet: "If there is conscious or unconscious resistance, we must break it."[2]

Literally, this letter helps illuminate the issue at hand: Maoism is without [*sans*] reality in France. And all its power of conviction stems from there. It is a lure capable of mobilizing the libido and inspiring the most brazen to fight tooth and nail against what Lacan calls the "impossible real."

It is manifest that revolution is impossible in France. Every serious person thinks so; from the bewildered judge who tried Le Dantec and Le Bris to the learned cretins in the Communist League ("The bulk of workers are not inclined to organize mass movements together…" says Weber, an expert in masses, who made the exact same diagnosis before May 1968!)

What is *manifest* is the impossible revolution. How can a *latent* reality, a social unconscious of revolution be deciphered from this evidence? There are two ways to proceed: either stand with 600 million Chinese people and make a great leap forward through imaginary fog and historical dreams…or side with this "impossible reality" and build the revolutionary machine piece-by-piece with a clear head. Without fooling oneself, without harboring illusions about being the bearer of some historic mission, justly serving the people and all that tasteless catholicity.

Granted, only the first path has been effective since May 1968. Only the craziest French Maoists have had the nerve and the guts to keep trying to leave the student ghetto, to join with young workers in a shared struggle, and to start opening a path to revolution in 1970. All of this in the midst of disorder, an unbelievable war of words, which these comrades surely could not have done without, one would believe, if we compare them with the paralysis and inhibitions that plague the anarchists, the unorganized and the enlightened intellectuals. This is how it is! The dumber it is, the better it works! People are digging up the decaying myth of the Resistance in France! And why not the united National Front while we are at it?

People are recycling entire phrases spoken by President Mao Zedong more than 30 years ago in a despotic China; France is being described as a plain littered with dry wood on the verge of bursting into flames: "A spark will soon set the plain on fire." There is talk of "young people going on little Long Marches to the factories"; the uprising in the Argenteuil slums has become "the French Naxalbari."

In short, these are mad times, and yet it is still working! Doesn't the efficiency of this movement stem precisely from its artificial character? With Freudianism, the artificiality of "literal" interpretation remained within the limits of psychopathology; with Surrealism it remained within the confines of literature; but with the Proletarian Left's pseudo-Maoists it is as if we were witnessing mass Freudian-Surrealism. This could be what makes movements like the Zengakuren, the Black Panthers, the Weathermen, and others so fascinating. In its exiomatic, revolution in capitalist countries will require a good deal of paradox, black humor, spectacle, provocation, and desperate violence.

The great merit of the Proletarian Left in France is the audacity of its public approval of sabotage, issuing the order word that "It's right to kidnap bosses," calling for them to be painted with mercurochrome while waiting to be hung, and launching detachments to attack their own fearfulness. Then there are their expeditions, less murderous than Che Guevara's, but no less respectable.

It is as if the Cultural Revolution had put a certain model of spontaneous struggle into circulation, struggle which more or less escaped the Chinese Communist Party apparatus for a while.

Now, in several capitalist countries now, these new forms of struggle are developing under the banner of Maoism in a de facto return to the sources of violent revolution, long kept in ideological shackles by the major theorists of Marxism-Leninism.

Basically, it's the Cultural Revolution without Mao, even against Mao! If this is what is really developing, there will surely be lots of fans! Never mind the grimacing return to Stalinism, the taste for the military side of things, the directives, the boy-scoutism, the "disdain for fatigue," the "courageous labor" style, "simple life and hard struggle"…

If the struggle started by the Proletarian Left grows, its future objective contradictions will liquidate this whole mania for centralism, a mania caused more by anxiety than by any disgusting bureaucracy. Aside from the customary perverted priests, all these comrades, in their hesitant attempts to build a new instrument for revolutionary struggle, will be led to question these cookie-cutter formulas, as well as the rigid, bureaucratic attitudes that are objectively against the rise of mass struggle.

Up to the present, the labor movement has subsisted on theories that have refused to take desire into consideration. By upholding the ideology of the dominant class in terms of moral and sexual repression, labor organizations have created their own forms of bureaucratic perversion. The evolution of productive forces, the bankruptcy of bourgeois institutions from the conjugal family to the state, it all contributes to exploding this superego.

Neo-Stalinist Maoism (not the Proletarian Left's version) and the various forms of revisionism are the last ramparts of a certain image of the person injected into the worker movement, underpinned by a Manichaean methodology and an unconscious introjection of bourgeois policing under the imperatives of good behavior: "These militants must be the best workers, good children, agitating for the good and the happiness of the people."

In truth, desire, the desire of the revolutionary masses, does not really care about good and evil! First and foremost, it calls for smashing the relations of production, including their elements of imaginary alienation.

In May, the last barriers of Stalinism and bourgeois morality cracked. They are still in place but no one still believes in them.

No matter how the simulacra of militant traditionalism try to come back like a bunch of old whores, it doesn't work anymore! "Never again the party of Maurice Thorez!" No more theories about unions as transmission belts between the party and the masses. Something else must be found: if possible, something else altogether different! Something that combines revolutionary efficiency and desire.

23

We Are All Groupuscules

To agitate is to act. We could care less about words; we want actions. It's easy to say, especially in countries where the material forces are increasingly dependent on the technology of machines and the development of science.

Overthrowing tsarism required bringing tens of millions of the exploited masses together and mobilizing them against the brutal repressive machine of society and the Russian state. It meant making the masses aware of their irresistible force against the weakness of the class enemy, a weakness that was revealed and proven in the struggle for power.

For those of us in wealthy countries, things are different; we may have to face more than just a *paper tiger*. The enemy has infiltrated everywhere; it has spread out a vast petit bourgeois inter-zone to attenuate class contours as much as possible. The working class itself has been deeply infiltrated, and not only through company unions, treasonous parties, social-democrats and revisionists... It is also infiltrated by *participating materially and unconsciously* in the dominant systems of state monopoly capitalism and bureaucratic socialism. First, material participation on a global scale: the working classes of economically developed countries are objectively involved, be it only by the growing gap in the relative standard of living and the international exploitation of former colonies. Then, there is unconscious participation in many different ways: workers more or less passively endorsing the dominant social models, attitudes and mystifying value systems of the bourgeoisie—scourges of theft, sloth, disease, etc.—reproducing on their own alienating institutional objects like the conjugal family and the intra-familial repression between the sexes and ages that it implies, or becoming attached to their nation with its inevitable after-taste of racism (without mentioning regionalism and idiosyncrasies of all kinds: professional, syndical, sports-related, etc. and all of the other imaginary barriers that are artificially raised between workers, such as the ones that are particularly visible in the large-scale organization of the market of sports competitions, etc.).

From a very young age, and if only because they learn to read on the faces of their parents, the victims of capitalism and bureaucratic "socialism" are consumed by unconscious anxiety and guilt, which represent one of the essential parts that keep the system of individual self-subjection to production in working order. Internal cops and judges are even more effective than those of the Ministry of the Interior and Justice. Achieving this result depends on developing a heightened antagonism between an *imaginary ideal*, which is taught to individuals by means of collective suggestion, and a completely *different reality* that is waiting for them around the corner. Audio-visual suggestion and the mass media work like a charm! It leads to a deranged promotion of a maternal and familial imaginary world crisscrossed by so-called masculine values, which tend to repudiate and demean the female gender, with another layer promoting an ideal of mythical love, magic comfort and health to mask the negation of finitude and death. Ultimately, it is a system of demands that perpetuates the unconscious dependence on a system of production, the technique of "incentives."

The result of this work is the serial production of individuals who are as poorly prepared as possible to face life's most important trials. Helpless, they face reality alone, without options, mired in a stupid morality and imposed ideals that they cannot escape. They are made fragile, vulnerable, ready to grab hold of any institutional garbage prepared to accommodate them: school, hierarchy, army, learning fidelity, submission, modesty, the taste for work, family, nation, union, and many more... Their entire life is now poisoned to one degree or another by the uncertainty of their conditions with regard to the processes of production, distribution and consumption, by the concern over their place in society and the place of their companions. Everything becomes a problem: a new birth, or "it's not working out well at school," or "the older ones are bored and playing around," illness, marriage, housing, vacations, everything is a pain...

A minimum amount of climbing up the pyramid of relationships of production then becomes inevitable. No need to draw a picture or give a lesson. Unlike young workers, activists from a student background who go to work in a factory are guaranteed to "find something else" if they get fired. Whether they want to or not, they cannot escape the potential that marks them with a hierarchical place "that could be much better." The truth for workers is a de facto and almost absolute dependence on the machine of production. Desire is crushed, except in its residual or "standardized" forms, well-intentioned or activist desire; or drugs become a refuge, if not madness or suicide! Who will show the percentage of "work-related accidents" that were really unconscious suicides?

Capitalism can always arrange things and smooth them over locally, but for the most part and essentially, everything has become increasingly worse. In twenty years, some of us will just be twenty years older, but humanity will have almost doubled in size. (If the calculations by experts are correct, the Earth will reach at least 5 billion inhabitants in 1990.) This may cause a few more problems along the way! Since no one and nothing is capable of preparing or organizing anything for these new arrivals—except for a few dreamers in international organizations that have not resolved a sin-gle important political problem in the twenty-five years of their existence—it seems clear that many things are going to happen in the coming years. Things of all kinds, covering the whole spectrum: revolutions, but also horrors like fascism and its ilk. What should we do? Wait and see? Start acting? OK, but where, what, how? Pick one thing at random. It is not that simple. The response to many actions has been predicted, organized and calculated by the machines of state power. I am convinced that all of the possible variants of another May 1968 have already been programmed on an IBM. Maybe not in France because they are too poor and, at the same time, too well paid to know that this kind of foolishness is not a guarantee and that nothing serious has been found to replace the armies of cops and bureaucrats. In any case, it is time for revolu-tionaries to reexamine their programs; some of them are really starting to show their age! It is time to abandon all triumphalism—which should be written with a double "l"—and notice that not only are we up to our necks in shit, but the shit has penetrated each one of us, and each one of our "organizations."

Class struggle no longer occurs along a clear boundary between proletariat and bourgeoisie that can easily be seen in cities and towns. It is also written in the countless scars on the skin and in the lives of the exploited by marks of authority, rank and standards of living. It has to be deciphered from the different vocabularies they use, their manners of speaking, car brands, fashions, etc. It is end-less! Class struggle has contaminated the attitudes of teachers with *their* students, parents with *their* children, doctors with *their* patients. It has reached inside each of us with *our* ego, with the ideal "standing" that we think we have to attribute to ourselves. It is time to organize at every level to confront this generalized class struggle. It is time to develop a strategy for each of these levels, because they affect each other. What would be gained, for example, by offering the masses a program of anti-authoritarian revolution against the little bosses and the like, if the militants themselves still carry the overactivated bureaucratic viruses, if they still act like utter bastards or perfect Catholics with the militants of other groups, within their own group, with their friends or on their own? What good is it to confirm the legitimacy of the aspirations of the masses if we deny desire wherever it rears its head in daily life? Shrewd politicians are out of touch with reality. They think that we can, that we must do away with all of our concerns in this domain to mobilize its energy for general political objectives. Wrong! In the absence of desire, energy eats away at itself in the form of symptoms, inhibitions and anxiety. And yet, they have had enough time and opportunity to realize this themselves!

Investing the energy capable of modifying the relationships of force is not something that will drop out of the sky; it does not emerge spontaneously from the right program or the pure science of theories. It is determined by transforming biological energy— libido—onto the objectives of social struggle. It is too easy to reduce everything to the famous main contradictions. It is too abstract. It is even a defense mechanism, something that helps develop group fantasies, structures of misunderstanding, a bureaucratic trick; always taking cover behind something that is always behind, always somewhere else, always more important and never within reach of an immediate intervention by those involved. It is the principle of the "just cause" that makes people swallow all of the little dirty tricks, the small-scale bureaucratic perversion, the petty pleasure they take in imposing on you—"for a good cause"—people that piss you off, forcing you to take purely sacrificial and symbolic actions that no one cares about, starting with the masses themselves. It is a form of sexual satisfaction diverted from its normal objectives. This type of perversion would have no importance if it was aimed at something other than revolution—there are plenty of other objects!

The trouble is that these monomaniacs of revolutionary leadership, with the unconscious complicity of "the base," succeed in miring militant investment in particularist impasses. It's *my* group, *my* belief, *my* newspaper; we are right, we follow our own line, we exist against the other line, we are a small collective identity embodied in a local leader… We didn't go through this in May '68! Everything was going more or less well until the "spokesperson" of this or that began to reemerge on the scene. As if words needed spokespeople to carry them. They carry themselves to the masses very well and with incredible speed, when they are true. The work of revolutionaries is not to carry words, to have things said, to transport or transmit models and pictures. Their work is to tell the truth where they are, no more and no less, without exaggeration and without tricks. How is this work of truth recognized? It's very simple, there is a way that works every time: revolutionary truth is something that doesn't piss you off, something you want to be involved in, that takes away your fear, that gives you strength, that makes you ready to go full tilt, no matter what, even if it kills you. We saw the truth at work in May '68; everyone understood it right away. The truth is not theory or organization. Theory and organization only get involved after the truth appears. They always find their way in and take things over, even by deforming them or lying. Self-critique is always for theory and organization, not desire.

The question now is the work of truth and desire everywhere where things collide, inhibit each other, get bogged down. De facto and de jure groupuscules, communes, gangs, and everything else on the left have as much analytical work to do on themselves as they do political work to do outside themselves. If they don't do it, they always risk falling into the madness of hegemony, the obsession with greatness that makes some dream of rebuilding the "party of Maurice Thorez" or Lenin, Stalin or Trotsky, each one as boring and irrelevant as Jesus Christ or de Gaulle, or any of the others who never stop dying.

Each one has its own little annual congress, its little CC [Central Committee], its big PB [Politburo], its secretariat and its secretary-general, and its career militants with seniority, and in the Trotskyist version, everything doubled on an international scale (world congress, international executive committee, IS [International Secretariat], etc.).

Why don't groupuscules multiply infinitely instead of eating each other? A groupuscule for everyone! In each factory, each street, each school. Finally, the reign of the core committees! These groupuscules, however, would accept to be what they are where they are. And, if possible, a multiplicity of groupuscules would replace the institutions of the bourgeoisie: family, school, union, sports club, etc. Groupuscules that would not be afraid, along with their objectives for revolutionary struggle, to organize themselves to ensure the material and moral survival of each one of their members and of all of the lost souls around them...

Then, anarchy! No coordination, no centralization, no headquarters... Just the opposite! Take the Weathermen in the USA. They are organized in tribes, gangs, etc., but it doesn't prevent them from coordinating and doing it very well.

What changes if the question of coordination is not between individuals but between basic committees, artificial families, communes... The model of the individual by the dominant social machine is too fragile, too open to any type of suggestion: drugs, fear, family, etc. In a basic group, a minimum of collective identity can be retained without megalomania, with a system of control at hand. Then the desire in question may be in a better position to speak or to fulfill its militant commitments. First, respect for private life must be abandoned: it is the beginning and end of social alienation. An analytical group, a *unit of desiring subversion*, has no private life; it is turned both inside and out, towards its contingency, its finitude, and towards the objectives for which it is fighting. The revolutionary movement must therefore build a new form of subjectivity that no longer relies on the individual and the conjugal family. Subversion of the abstract models exuded by capitalism, which continue to be supported by most theorists, is the absolute precondition for reengaging the masses in revolutionary struggle.

For the moment, it is of little use to draw up plans for what the society of tomorrow should be—production, state or no state, party or no party, family or no family—when in truth there is no one to serve as a support for utterances about them. Utterances will continue to float in the void, undecidable, as long as *collective agents of enunciation* are not ready to explore things in reality, as long as we have no means to step back from the dominant ideology that sticks to our skin, which speaks of itself within us, which leads us to commit the most stupid acts and repetitions despite ourselves, and tends to make it so that we are always beaten on the same beaten paths.

Bibliography

Preface. "Three Group-Related Problems." Preface by Gilles Deleuze to Félix Guattari, *Psychanalyse et transversalité* (Paris: François Maspero, 1972), i-xi. Deleuze and Guattari met in the summer of 1969, in Limousin, and very quickly decided to work together. In 1972, *L'Anti-Oedipe* signaled the beginning of their collective efforts, which would continue for twenty years, producing *Kafka—pour une littérature mineure* (1975), *Mille plateaux* (1980), and *Qu'est-ce que la philosophie* (1991). For a statement on their collaboration, see Deleuze's "Letter to Uno: How Félix and I Worked Together," in *Two Regimes of Madness*, trans. Ames Hodges and Mike Taormina (Los Angeles: Semiotext(e), 2007), 237–240.

1. "On Nurse-Doctor Relationships." Transcript of a discussion at La Borde with Jean Oury, September 1955.

2. "Monograph on R.A." Psychotherapy report for a medical review, 1958.

4. "Ladies and Gentlemen, the SCAJ." "La S.C.A.J. Messieurs-Dames," *Bulletin du personnel soignant des cliniques du Loir-et-Cher* [Bulletin of healthcare personnel in the clinics of the Loir-et-Cher region] 1, 1957.

6. "The Transference." This short presentation to the GTPSI (Groupe de travail de psychotherapie institutionnelle; Working Group of Institutional Psychotherapy), also referred to as the Groupe de travail de psychologie et sociologie institutionnelle (Working Group of Institutional Psychology and Sociology), dates from 1964. The GTPSI was founded in 1960; upon expansion in 1965, it became known as the SPI (Société de psychotherapie institutionnelle).

7. "Reflections on Institutional Therapeutics." "Réflexions sur la thérapeutique institutionnelle et les problèmes d'hygiène mentale en milieu étudiant," *Recherches universitaires* 3, no. 2 (1964). A report presented to the MNEF (Mutuelle nationale des étudiants de France; National Students' Mutual of France) as a technical consultation.

8. "Transversality." "La transversalité," *Revue de psychothérapie institutionelle* 1 (1964). A report presented to the first International Psychodrama Congress, held in Paris in September 1964.

9. "Reflections on Institutional Psychotherapy for Philosophers." "Réflexions pour des philosophes à propos de la psychothérapie institutionnelle," *Cahiers de philosophie* 1 (1966; repr. *Recherches* 1 [1966]). *Cahiers de philosophie* was the review of the Philosophy Group of the Sorbonne.

10. "Nine Theses of the Left Opposition." These theses were first developed in very condensed form—a few pages—by a group of militants of the Opposition de gauche (Left Opposition) during its formation, to be presented by Jean Claude Polack in the name of the non-Trotskyist left at the VIII Congress of the UEC (Union of Communist Students), which was held in Montreuil in 1965. They were later expanded by Guattari to be presented and discussed at a Left Opposition course organized in Poissy in October 1965. The passages presented here were selected from a version supplemented and expanded by François Fourquet, prefaced by Gérard Spitzer and published as a brochure in 1966: *Neuf thèses de l'opposition de gauche* (Paris: Editions librairie de l'Etoile, 1966).

11. "From One Sign to the Other (excerpts)." "D'un signe à l'autre," *Recherches* 2 (1966). This text was composed from a wide variety of reflections inspired by the seminar of Jacques Lacan. Guattari conveyed the main part of this argument directly to Lacan, in a letter dated December 8, 1961. Guattari's letter focused primarily on Lacan's April 26, 1955 seminar, published in *La Psychanalyse* 2 (1957) as "La Lettre volée" [The Purloined Letter], and later reprinted in *Écrits*.

12. "The Group and the Person." A talk presented to a working group at La Borde in 1966, and put into writing in April 1968.

13. "Causality, Subjectivity, and History." The first three sections summarize lectures, along with the discussion that followed each one. The first two were given to the "Theory Committee" of the FGERI (Federation of Institutional Study and Research Groups). In October 1965, some dozen groups, working along the lines of institutional analysis, federated within the FGERI: they consisted of about three hundred psychiatrists, psychoanalysts, psychologists, nurses, academics, teachers, urban-studies researchers, architects, economists, members of cooperatives, filmmakers, and so on.

The CERFI (Center for Institutional Study, Research, and Training), a member of the FGERI, publishes the journal *Recherches*, and a series of *Cahiers de recherches*; the CERFI also commissions various public and private bodies to produce specialized studies (on plant, cooperation, health, education and so on).

14. "Counter-Revolution is a Science You Can Learn." "La contre-revolution est une science qui s'apprend," *Tribune du 22 mars* (June 5, 1968; repr. in *Le Journal de la Commune étudiante*, Paris: Éditions du Seuil, 1969).

15. "Self-Management and Narcissim." *Tribune du 22 mars* (June 5, 1968; repr. in *Le Journal de la Commune étudiante*, Paris: Éditions du Seuil, 1969).

16. "Excerpts from Discussions: Late June 1968." The people participating in this discussion, most likely, were: Félix Guattari (F); François Fourquet (FF); Jean-Claude Polack (P); Michel Rostain (MR); Jean-Pierre Muyard (J-P M); Jean-Jaques Lebel (L); and Jo Panaget (J).—Trans.

17. "Students, the Mad, and 'Delinquents.'" "L'étudiant, le fou et le katangais," *Partisans* 46 (February–March 1969). A paper given at the Third International Congress of Psychodrama, Sociodrama, and Institutional Therapy, held in Baden in September 1968.

18. "Machine and Structure." "Machine et Structure," *Change* 12 (1972). Initially intended as a lecture for the Freudian School in Paris in 1969.

19. "Reflections on Teaching as the Reverse of Analysis." *Lettres de l'Ecole freudienne de Paris* 8 (January 1971). A talk given for the Masochist Maoists or the Impossible May Presentation to the Congress of the Freudian School of Paris, for which the theme was the teaching of psychoanalysis, on April 17, 1970.

20. "Where does Group Psychotherapy Begin?." From the *La Borde Personnel Bulletin*.

21. "Raymond and the Hispano Group." "Raymond et le grouper Hispano," a letter published as an appendix to *Ouvriers face aux appareils* [*Workers against Apparatuses*] (Paris: Éditions Maspero, 1970), an anthology relating to an experiment in activism at the Hispano-Suiza factory. Guattari's letter was also an homage to Raymond Petit, who instigated the experiment and coedited the book; he died just before it was published.

22. "The Masochist Maoists or the Impossible May." *L'Idiot international* 8–9 (July–August 1970).

23. "We are All Groupuscules." "Nous sommes tous des groupuscules," *L'Idiot Liberté* 1 (December 1970).

Notes

Preface by Gilles Deleuze: Three Group-Related Problems

1. Guattari was initially a militant connected with Trotskyism (which would get him thrown out of the French Communist Party), and then later agitated in several different groups (viz., la Voie communiste, l'Opposition de Gauche, and le mouvement du 22 mars); at the same time, he joined the team of experts at the now famous La Borde clinic, when Dr. Jean Oury first opened it in 1953. It is in this clinic that the foundations of institutional psychotherapy (in which the psychotherapeutic cure is thought of as inseparable from the analysis of institutions) would be defined in both practical and theoretical terms, following the pioneering work of Dr. Tosquelles. Guattari, as a member of the CERFI (Center for Research and Institutional Formation), was a student of Lacan's from the very beginnings of the seminar and a member of the French Freudian school in Paris. The texts from *Psychoanalysis and Transversality* retrace the steps of his entire development from a theoretical and practical standpoint.

2. Marcel Jaeger, "L'Underground de la folie," in "Folie pour folie," special issue, *Partisans* 62–63 (Nov.–Feb. 1972).

3. *Cahiers de Vérité*, "Sciences humaines et Lutte des classes" series, 1 (1968).

4. Deleuze has here added a note on a personal copy: "for example, political economy is decided at least decided at a European-wide level, whereas social politics remains the concern of the State."

5. See Michel Foucault, *History of Madness*, trans. Jonathan Murphey (London: Routledge, 2006).

1. On Nurse-Doctor Relationships

1. The P.Psy.F. was a comedic project to start a "French Psychiatric Party."

2. Monograph on R.A.

1. In English in the original.—Trans.

2. Jacques Lacan, "The Mirror Stage as Formative of the *I* Function as Revealed in Psychoanalytic Experience," in *Écrits: The First Complete Edition in English*, trans. Bruce Fink (New York: W. W. Norton & Company, 2006), 75–81.

3. Collapse of a Life Not Lived. Loss of the "I"

1. R.A.'s name in capital letters.

4. Ladies and Gentlemen, the SCAJ

1. Sous-Commission d'animation pour la journée [Sub-Committee for Daily Activities].

2. In the text, Guattari refers to *le SCAJ* (masculine), while it comes from *la Sous-Commission* (feminine) .—Trans.

5. Introduction to Institutional Psychotherapy

1. Connected to the Fédération des Croix-Marines [National Federation of Assistance to Mental Health, Croix Marine].

2. Significant work in training psychiatric nurses was carried out in the context of the Centre d'entraînement aux méthodes actives [Center for Training in Active Methods]. See the journal *Vie sociale et traitement* [Social life and treatment].

3. A reference to a presentation by J. Schotte: "Le Transfert, dit fundamental de Freud pour poser le problem: psychanalyse et institution" [Transference, called fundamental by Freud for posing the problem: psychoanalysis and institution], *Revue de psychotérapie institutionnelle* [Review of institutional psychotherapy] 1 (1965).

4. Wilhelm Reich, *Mass Psychology of Fascism*, trans. Theodore P. Wolfe (New York: Orgone Institute Press, 1946).

6. The Transference

1. See Schotte, "Transfert."

2. See Gaston Bachelard, *The Philosophy of No*, trans. G. C. Waterston (New York: Orion Press, 1968).

3. Lacan, *Écrits*, 78.

7. Reflections on Institutional Therapeutics

1. G. Couchner, "Les Psychopathies industrielles" [Industrial psychopathy], in "La Psychopathologie des temps modernes" [The psychopathology of modern times],

special issue, *Revue des sciences médicales* [Review of medical science] 154 (Jan. 1964): 42.

2. See Fernand Oury and Aïda Vasquez, *Vers une pédagogie institutionnelle* [Towards an institutional pedagogy] (Paris: Maspero, 1968).

3. Mutuelle nationale des étudiants de France [National Students' Mutual of France].

4. Bureau d'aide psychologique universitaire [University Psychological Counseling Center].

5. Groupe de travail universitaire [University working groups]

8. Transversality

1. Sigmund Freud, *New Introductory Lectures on Psychoanalysis*, trans. James Strachey, vol. 2 of *The Pelican Freud Library* (London: Penguin Books, 1973), 120–1212.

2. Ibid., 188.

3. Ibid., 141.

4. Schotte, "Transfert."

5. Arthur Schopenhauer, *Parerga and Paralipomena*, trans. E. F. J. Payne, vol. 2 (Oxford: Oxford University Press, 1974), 651–652.

6. I use this term in a more general sense than it is given by Winnicott.

9. Reflections on Institutional Psychotherapy for Philosophers

1. A psychosociological technique, studied, for example, in the framework of a "social laboratory," loses its meaning, its updated laws lose their value, as soon as one attempts to reconstitute them in an institutional context.

2. Note that this notion is complementary to the notions of the "partial object" in Freudian theory and the "transitional object" defined by D. W. Winnicott. On the latter, see Winnicott's "Transitional Objects and Transitional Phenomena," *International Journal of Psycho-Analysis* 34 (1953): 89–97.

3. An expression used by Lacan in his seminar, and used here in a different context.

4. I will not address here the very important questions of how these groups are formed, how they function, and how they are controlled.

5. To borrow Jean Oury's expression.

10. Nine Theses of the Left Opposition

1. The notion of the "subjective," which we prefer to use here instead of "class consciousness" for various reasons, should not be understood in the sense of *subjectivism*, but in its original meaning—that is, as opposed to "objective," or in opposition, for example, to *passivity of the base*, etc.

2. Union des femmes françaises [Union of French Women].

11. From One Sign to the Other (excerpts)

1. This "bord joli" is only a friendly caricature of Serge Leclaire's "Pôor(d)j'e-li." See *Psychoanalyzing: On the Order of the Unconscious and the Practice of the Letter*, trans. Peggy Kamuf (Stanford: Stanford University Press, 1998), 81.

2. The PRETTY BANK of the river. Senator BORGEAUD READS in his bed.—Trans.

12. The Group and the Person

1. Fédération des Groupes d'Étude et de Recherche Institutional [Federation of Institutional Study and Research Groups]; producers of the journal *Recherches*, published in Paris.

2. Louis Althusser, "Philosophy as a Revolutionary Weapon," interview by Maria Antoniette Macciocchi, in *Lenin and Philosophy and Other Essays*, trans. Ben Brewster (New York: Monthly Review Press, 2001), 3–7.

3. *Cahiers de la Vérité*, "Sciences humaines et lutte de classes" series, 1 (1968): 6. "Indeed the theories of M. Guattari and his friends are themselves an alienation…"

4. Sigmund Freud, "Group Psychology and the Analysis of the Ego," trans. James Starchey, in vol. 18 of *The Standard Edition of the Complete Psychological Works of Sigmund Freud* (London: Hogarth Press, 1955), 67–143

5. Karl Marx, introduction to *Grundrisse*, trans. Martin Nicholaus (London: Penguin Books, 1993), 86. Emphasis added.

6. Union des Jeuncsses Républicaines de France (the youth movement of the French Communist Party).

7. Union Nationale des Étudiants de France [National Union of French Students].

8. Freud, "Group Psychology," 42.

9. It would be particularly interesting to apply this idea to popular religious heresies.

10. This would be a way out of Russell's paradox, a way of avoiding reifying it as a totalizing whole.

11. This is the difference between my idea of group phantasy and Bion's idea of the phantasy of *the* group.

12. And, conversely, is not the individual phantasy the individuated small change of collective phantasy production?

13. The notion of an "institutional object" is complementary to the "part object" of Freudian theory and the "transitional object" as originally defined by D. W. Winnicott; see Winnicott, "Transitional Objects."

14. "Groupuscules" refer to members of the ensemble of little groups found on the left of the French Communist Party in the period leading up to 1968. This was originally a pejorative term of the Party establishment, but was later adopted by the groups themselves.

13. Causality, Subjectivity, and History

1. The "Old Man" could apply equally to Lenin, Stalin, or Trotsky; 44 rue Le Peletier in Paris is the headquarters of the Communist Party Central Committee.

2. Lacan, *Écrits*, 743.

3. A condensation chamber that makes the movements of ionizing particles visible.—Trans.

4. The French is "il," which means both *he* and *it*. The nearest approximation to this in English seems to be "it," but readers will find this section clearer if they bear in mind that "it" can be used to mean *he*, or *it* as a subject, or the indefinite it of "it's raining," "it is true," etc.—Trans.

5. This implies an idea of the sign closer to Louis Hjelmslev's "glossématique" than to syntagmatics; see *Prolégomènes à une théorie du langage* [Prolegomena to a theory of language] (Paris: Minuits, 1984).

6. Refer to the notion of the "situème," introduced by Claude Poncin in a thesis presented in Nantes in 1962; see "Essai d'analyse structurale appliquée à la psychothérapie institutionnelle" [Structural analysis test applied to institutional psychotherarpy] (s.l.: s.n., 1962; s.l.: Association culturelle du personnel, 1995).

7. Summary of a commentary on Isaac Deutscher's life of Trotsky, published in the review *Critique*, June 97.

8. "For *pace* the philosophers, reality is not united with the possible in necessity, but necessity is united with the possible in reality."—Soren Kierkegaard.

9. Isaac Deutscher, *The Prophet Armed* (Oxford: Oxford University Press, 1954), 501.

10. See the translation of the fourteen issues of *Isvestia* from Kronstadt in *La commune de cronstadt* (Paris: Bélibaste, 1969); also Daniel Guérin, *Ni Dieu ni maître* [No gods no masters] (Lausanne: Éditions de Delphes La Cité, s.d.), 556.

11. Deutscher, *Prophet Armed*, 83. See also Trotsky's report written immediately after the Congress: *Report of the Siberian Delegation*, trans. Brian Pearce (London: New Park Publications, 1979). Additionally, see Trotsky's *Our Political Tasks* (London: New Park Publications, 1979).

12. Isaac Deutscher, adopting Trosky's analysis of Nazism, talks of the "political neurosis of impoverished millions [that] gave National Socialism its force and impetus." *The Prophet Outcast* (Oxford: Oxford University Press, 1963), 133.

13. Louis Fischer, *The Life of Lenin* (New York: Harper and Row, 1964).

14. Deutscher, *Prophet Armed*, 56.

15. Deutscher, *Prophet Armed*, 35, 66, 87. The Stalinists, always ready to abuse, spoke of his refusal as an insult to Lenin.

16. One might apply here what Lacan says of the subjective drama of the philosopher who has to contain a major crisis in his thinking: that drama "has its victims, and nothing allows us to say that their destiny can be inscribed in the Oedipal myth," except, as he says later on, that the whole myth is itself brought into question. *Écrits*, 738.

17. Deutscher, *Prophet Armed*, 80n.

18. From a talk given at a Left Opposition training course at Bièvres, Easter 1966.

19. "Transversatity," after all, is no more than an attempt to analyze democratic centralism!

20. Cahiers Libres Collectif, *Ouvriers face aux appareils* (Paris: Éditions Maspero, 1970), 266ff.

21. Nor in any other, but that is not our concern here. As Lacan has written: "An economic science inspired by Capital does not necessarily lead to its utilization as a revolutionary power, and history seems to require help from something other than a predictive dialectic." *Écrits*, 738.

22. "Almost" is perhaps putting it strongly: Max Nordau was to be murdered by a supporter of Theodore Herzl's.

23. Extracts from a piece that was to have appeared as an introduction to an important special issue of *Recherches*, on the consequences of American aggression in Vietnam or the countries of Southeast Asia as a whole. This voluminous set of documents, compiled by working groups of specialists and militants, failed to appear because of the

events of May 1968: the delay in publishing meant that the most important articles were out of date, and its compilers could no longer be brought together.

24. This text was written just before the upheavals of May 1968.

16. Excerpts from Discussions: Late June 1968

1. National Pedagogy Institute of the Rue d'Ulm and Scolastic Radio-Television in Ivry. The decision to occupy the IPN was made by the instructors of the FGERI (Federation of Groups for Institutional Study and Research) after meeting in a general assembly. The Situationists of the "Committee to Maintain the Occupations" joined this occupation later, along with the teachers of the Paris region and part of the staff of the Institute.

2. Union of Republican Youth in France: a youth organization set up after the Liberation by the FCP to break up the unified youth movement that existed at the time.

3. In English in the original.—Trans.

4. In English in the original.—Trans.

5. Jean Medam, "A propos de la circulation monétaire" [On currency circulation], *Recherches* 1 (1966): 17–26.

17. Students, the Mad and "Delinquents"

1. Regional bodies, some of which have brought together nurses, psychiatrists, psychologists, and others, are questioning official teaching.

2. By psychiatric district, I mean the French system of institutions and projects outside hospitals, arranged by districts, each supposed to respond to the mental-health requirements of some 70,000 people (providing day hospitals, dispensaries, homes, special workshops, family placements, home visits, etc.).

3. See *Recherches universitaires* 3, no. 2 (1964), devoted to these problems; it contains an article of mine, "Réflexions sur la thérapeutique institutionnelle et les problèmes d'hygiènc mentale en milieu étudiant" [Reflections on institutional therapy and problems of mental hygiene in student life].

4. Fédération Nationale dcs Étudiants de France: a minority, right-wing, student group.

18. Machine and Structure

1. To adopt the categories suggested by Gilles Deleuze, *structure*, in the sense in which I am using it here, would relate to the generality characterized by a position of exchange or substitution of particularities, whereas the *machine* would relate to the

order of repetition "as a conduct and as a point of view [concerning] non-exchangeable and non-substitutable singularities." *Difference and Repetition*, trans. Paul Patton (New York: Columbia University Press, 1994), 1. Of Deleuze's three minimum conditions determining structure in general, I shall retain only the first two:

(1) There must be at least two heterogeneous series, one of which is defined as the signifier and the other as the signified.

(2) Each of these series is made up of terms that exist only through their relationship with one another.

Deleuze's third condition, "two heterogenous series [converging] toward a paradoxical element, which is their 'differentiator,'" relates, on the contrary, exclusively to the order of the machine. *Logic of Sense*, trans. Mark Lester (New York: Columbia University Press, 1990), 50–51.

19. Reflections on Teaching as the Reverse of Analysis

1. See the function of the "One Extra" [*Un En Plus*], "Just a One" [*Un Sans Plus*], "One More" [*Un Encore*], and "One Too Many" [*Un De Trop*]. Lacan, Écrits, 401.

2. Working groups within the EFP [French School of Psychoanalysis], that Lacan indicated in the founding charter of the Freudian School of Paris (June 1964) would be composed of "at least three people and at most five, four being the right balance. *Plus one* person responsible for the selection, discussion and the outcome to be reserved for each person's work." Jacques Lacan, "Founding Act," in *Television: A Challenge to the Psychoanalytic Establishment*, trans. Denis Hollier, Rosalind Krauss, and Annette Michelson (New York: W. W. Norton & Company, 1990), tk. In fact, the existing "cartels" are far from the count and the formula!

3. Lacan's first weekly seminar was held at Sainte-Anne Hospital.

4. "*Scilicet*: you can know, is the meaning of this title. You can know now that I have failed in teaching that has only been addressed to psychoanalysts for twelve years…" These are the first three lines of the first issue of *Scilicet*, the EFP review. Jacques Lacan, "Introduction de Scilicet au titre de la revue de l'EFP," *Scilicet* 1 (1968), 3.

5. Still in the *Letters*, on the subject of Nassif's text, Lacan states: "… What is called an analytical dialog depends in fact on a foundation that is perfectly reducible to a few essential articulations that can be formalized." "Intervention sur l'exposé de J. Nassif," *Lettres de l'école freudienne* 7 (Mar. 1970): 42.

6. Term proposed by Lacan to designate the patient in psychoanalytical treatment.

20. Where Does Group Psychotherapy Begin?

1. At the time, the entire clinic was divided into four groups.

2. The BTUs are composed on average of 8 residents (+ or - 2) and 2 or 2+1 monitors that maximize common ground. Furthermore, the La Borde Clinic is managed by functional committees split evenly between "cared for" and "caregivers." What makes BTU's committees original is that they abolish, as much as possible, the difference between "cared for" and "caregivers": whatever the question, outside entities don't address "normal or sane" *people* alone, but the entire BTU as a group-subject. Clearly, the consistency of the BTU does not depend on its numbers. It depends above all on the fantasies that its members bring to the table.

21. Raymond and the Hispano Group

1. Centre laïque des auberges de jeunesse et de plein air [Secular Center for Youth and Outdoor Hostels].—Trans.

2. See "Nine Theses of the Left Opposition," in the present volume.

22. The Masochist Maoists or the Impossible May

1. *Cahiers de la Gauche prolétarienne* 2 (May 1970), 108.

2. Comrades from the Proletarian Left (GP) could reflect on this phrase from Kierkegaard: "It is (to describe it figuratively) as if an author were to make a slip of the pen, and that this clerical error become conscious of being such—perhaps it was no error but in a far higher sense was an essential constituent in the whole exposition—it is then as if this clerical error would revolt against the author, out of hatred for him were to forbid him to correct it, and were to say, 'No, I will not be erased, I will stand as a witness against thee, that thou art a very poor writer.'" *The Sickness Unto Death*, trans. Walter Lowrie (Princeton: Princeton University Press, 1941), 118–19.